Approaching the World's Religions

Approaching the World's Religions

Volume 2

An Evangelical Theology
of Religions

Robert Boyd

CASCADE *Books* • Eugene, Oregon

APPROACHING THE WORLD'S RELIGIONS
Volume 2: An Evangelical Theology of Religions

Copyright © 2017 Robert Boyd. All rights reserved. Except for brief quotations in critical publications or reviews, no part of this book may be reproduced in any manner without prior written permission from the publisher. Write: Permissions, Wipf and Stock Publishers, 199 W. 8th Ave., Suite 3, Eugene, OR 97401.

Cascade Books
An Imprint of Wipf and Stock Publishers
199 W. 8th Ave., Suite 3
Eugene, OR 97401

www.wipfandstock.com

PAPERBACK ISBN: 978-1-4982-9595-6
HARDCOVER ISBN: 978-1-4982-9597-0
EBOOK ISBN: 978-1-4982-9596-3

Cataloguing-in-Publication data:

Names: Boyd, Robert, author.

Title: Approaching the world's religions : vol. 2, an evangelical theology of religions / Robert Boyd.

Description: Eugene, OR: Cascade Books, 2017 | Includes bibliographical references.

Identifiers: ISBN 978-1-4982-9595-6 (paperback) | ISBN 978-1-4982-9597-0 (hardcover) | ISBN 978-1-4982-9596-3 (ebook)

Subjects: LCSH: Religions | Religion—Methodology.

Classification: BL41 B68 2017 (print) | BL41 (ebook)

Manufactured in the U.S.A.   06/19/17

©Cranfield, C. E. B. (2004) *Critical and Exegetical Commentary on the Epistle to the Romans, II.* New York: T. & T. Clark, an imprint of Bloomsbury Plc. Used by permission.

All quotes from the Christian scriptures will be from the Revised Standard Version (RSV), unless otherwise indicated or the scriptures are being quoted by a secondary source. Revised Standard Version of the Bible, copyright 1952 [2nd edition, 1971] by the Division of Christian Education of the National Council of the Churches of Christ in the United States of America. Used by permission. All rights reserved.

Erickson, Millard J. *How Shall They be Saved? The Destiny of Those Who Do Not Hear of Jesus.* Grand Rapids: Baker Academic, a division of Baker Publishing Group, 1996. Used by permission.

The Holy Bible, English Standard Version® (ESV®) Copyright © 2001 by Crossway, a publishing ministry of Good News Publishers. Used by permission. All rights reserved.

Scripture quotations marked (NIV) come from the Holy Bible, NEW INTERNATIONAL VERSION®, NIV® Copyright © 1973, 1978, 1984, 2011 by Biblica, Inc.® Used by permission. All rights reserved worldwide.

Scripture quotations marked (NRSV) come from the New Revised Standard Version Bible, copyright © 1989 National Council of the Churches of Christ in the United States of America. Used by permission. All rights reserved worldwide.

Contents

Preface | vii
Acknowledgments | ix

Introduction to Volume 2 | 1

Part 1: Preliminary

1. Christian Relationship with the World | 7
2. Religious Diversity, Evangelical Theology, and Methodological Issues | 17
3. Religious Diversity and Evangelical Thought: Agency of Salvation | 36
4. Religious Diversity and Evangelical Thought: Recipients of Salvation | 58

Part 2: Reconstruction Proposal

5. Biblical Materials: An Evangelical Perspective | 101
6. An Interim Outline of Theology of Religions: A Proposed Evangelical Perspective | 136
7. Basic Notion of General Revelation and Evangelical Theology | 152
8. General Revelation and an Evangelical Theology | 170
9. General Revelation and an Evangelical Theology of Religions | 196

Part 3: Application

10. The Great Commission and the Law of Love | 219

Bibliography | 235
Name Index | 247

Preface

There are many different reasons for an author to write a book. Sometimes they may want to report a body of information to their audience. Other authors may believe they have answers that their audience should think about. Still others write in hopes that their audience may seriously respond to the written materials, not by embracing what is said, but by raising their own questions and seeking answers. This project is not written because I believe I have the right answers or the best answers; I know better. Rather, it is hoped that this project challenges a group of individuals to ask questions and seek better answers than I have offered. Within the Christian religion, we find a fascinating story of Paul and Silas visiting Beroea. We are told "these Jews were more noble than those in Thessalonica, for they received the word [from Paul and Silas] with all eagerness, examining the scriptures daily to see if these things were so" (Acts 17:11). The Beroeans' immediate response was not to reject the message because it was something new to them, nor did they simply embrace the message. Rather the Beroeans were open to the message and then examined the scriptures—testing the message of Paul and Silas. Because of their response to the new message, the Beroeans are called noble. I do not ask my readers to accept my interpretations of the various world religions, or my evaluations of the various philosophical positions discussed in the following pages, or my proposals for the development of an evangelical theology of religions. Rather I hope my readers will respond by asking their own questions, making their own critical study in a way such that they too will be called noble. This involves philosophically thinking about the world religions and the theology of religions.

While some philosophers may see their written work as an attempt to advocate a particular approach, this writer sees philosophy as a tentative work. The job is never complete: there is always more to do, and any one individual will not do it. Philosophical inquiries should stimulate discussion and dialogue. This writer does write from a particular philosophical/theological stance. Philosophically I am influenced by analytical philosophy, especially the work of P. F. Strawson, who emphasized looking for connections. The pragmatic philosophy of Charles Peirce drives me to make sure I am not engaged in discussions regarding the number of angels that can dance on the head of a pin. Religiously, I am committed to the Christian tradition, and theologically to a form of evangelical thought. Do these positions influence my work? Of course! But hopefully not to the point that I am intellectually unfair with positions contrary to these positions. This project is offered not with the idea of having the final answers, but rather with the hope that it will stimulate discussion and dialogue, both among those who share common interests with me and with those who have different positions than I. The study of world religions is an exciting enterprise, especially if we understand it as an ongoing engagement with the world and those that make up the world.

Finally, this project is seen as foundational for a study and development of a theology of religions. The theology of religions, roughly, is concerned with how members of one religious tradition view members of another tradition. Today we live in a secular global society. Only after we have seriously considered the world religions can we hope to make progress with one of the most exciting new fields of theology. In the second volume of this project, we explore how evangelical Christians can affirm the particularities of their theological perspective and develop a positive approach that promotes dialogue and interaction with members of other faith traditions. For those readers who do not share my religious beliefs, this volume should provide an example for you to work on a theology of religions for your tradition. However, it should be noted that many readers might prefer to start with the second volume and then work through the first. This project is not presented as a linear work, but one looking for connections and desiring to promote dialogue.

Acknowledgments

Any project like this comes to fruition because of the work of many individuals and because of many opportunities. It is impossible to name all; however, some individuals or groups of individuals must be acknowledged. For the past twenty years I have had the wonderful opportunity to teach philosophy and world religions at Fresno City College. The demographics of Fresno, California, reflect the diversity of religious traditions found in our secular global society today. For many years I had the opportunity to work with members of various religious traditions, as I was involved in the Fresno Multifaith Exchange. They taught me much. This required me to think through some of my presuppositions regarding other religious traditions while maintaining my evangelical stance. Several of these essays were initiated as I wrote my dissertation for the University of Wales, Lampeter. I had the fortunate opportunity to have Dr. Alan Race as my supervisor. Although theologically we were very different, it was a great experience from which I benefited much. I wish to also thank Dr. K. C. Hanson, my editor at Cascade Books (an imprint of Wipf and Stock Publishers), and his staff for their support and direction. Finally, I must thank my wife, Kathy, for her patience and support as I have worked on this project. Not only has she read every essay and commented, but also she was a great traveling partner as we visited religious sites in the UK, India, Russia, and China. She continues to be a great travelling partner through life. Thank you! In spite of all the great advice I have received over the years, I am solely responsible for the content of this project, since I have not always heeded that advice.

Introduction to Volume 2

Evangelical theology strives to be evangelical, conservative, and contemporary. In a world in which everyone is "Christian," evangelical theology provides a balanced position between fundamentalism and liberalism. While theological debates within the family will occur, to be evangelical is a breath of fresh air for many. However, we do not live in such a world. We do find ourselves living in a secular global society. It is secular because no religious organization dictates how we live our lives. It is global for at least two reasons. First, our technology brings us immediately in contact with faraway places. Second, and of more importance, we can simply step outside our front doors and visit neighborhoods that reflect a global pluralism. This raises the question, how shall we then live?

For some this secular global society is a call for retreat and sequestering in their own little encampment. This response may allow one to be conservative, but it is not evangelical, nor is it contemporary. The purpose of this project, *Approaching the World's Religions*, is to challenge us to think about and become educated regarding a global society that is religious and secular. In the first volume, *Philosophically Thinking about World Religions*, my intent was to challenge some of the presuppositions we find regarding the world's religions. On the one hand, we discover that the great religious traditions do not all say the same thing. On the other hand, there are many common denominators among the traditions. These common denominators can give us common ground to work on as we then examine our differences. Furthermore, the variants within a given tradition can be great; hence, to pigeonhole a particular member of a tradition may result in a stereotype. The intent of this volume, *An Evangelical Theology of Religions*, is to suggest a direction for evangelicals to think about the secular global society in which they live in a way that is not only conservative but also evangelical and contemporary.

This volume is not intended to offer *the* evangelical stance; evangelical thought is much too broad for a single voice to dictate what evangelical thought is as a whole. Rather, it offers an example of how the tradition might approach religious diversity in an evangelical way, with the purpose of encouraging individuals and, as a result, the tradition to explore ways of being evangelical, conservative, and contemporary. It assumes four key points: (1) God is a God of developing relationships with the created. (2) An evangelical theology of religions will focus upon individuals who practice non-Christian religions and not on the institutions of religion. (3) The challenge to develop a theology should not drive us to reject the fundamental beliefs of evangelicalism, but should encourage a move beyond our typical dualistic thinking. (4) Theology should always be about God, be from God, and lead to God.

An Evangelical Theology of Religions is divided into three distinct sections. The "Preliminary" section attempts to present the problem and some solutions that have been offered by evangelicals since Carl Henry's call to distinguish evangelicalism from fundamentalism but before the mid-1980s. We begin with an essay that introduces many of the problems facing an evangelical in the twenty-first century. It introduces a number of thought projects that will be revisited as additional information is provided. (Readers should expect to find examples and ideas repeated through this volume. As a teacher, I have discovered that repetition is critical.)

The second essay considers how evangelicals responded to religious diversity prior to the 1980s. (While the study of the theology of religions had been explored as early as the 1960s, evangelicals did not begin a systematic consideration until the mid-'80s.) The second essay, also, addresses some methodological issues, such as definitions, that are foundational for the study. After entering the field of theology of religions, evangelicals focused on three distinct issues over the next twenty or so years: the nature of religious truth, the agency of salvation, and the recipients of salvation. (Since the nature of religious truth is more of a philosophical issue, it was addressed in the first volume of this project.)

The third and fourth essays examine and evaluate the work of evangelicals during that period prior to 2005 regarding the agency and recipients of salvation. It will be shown that evangelicals stand in firm commitment that Jesus Christ and only Jesus Christ is the agency of salvation. On this foundational point, evangelicals are exclusivists. However, it will be shown that evangelicals are not exclusivists regarding the recipients of salvation, but rather they are inclusivists. While there is complete unity on the agency issues, there is no consensus regarding how evangelicals understand their inclusivism. (It should be noted that this project does not attempt to consider evangelical theology as reflected in the church universal. My focus is primarily limited to North American evangelicalism. This is not because only that segment of evangelicalism has anything to offer. Quite to the contrary; however, as an evangelical living in North American, I must work out a theology that is conservative, evangelical, and contemporary to the culture in which I live. Evangelicals living elsewhere must work out their own conservative, evangelical, and contemporary theology.)

The second section, "Reconstruction Proposal," is a proposed direction for the development of an evangelical theology of religions. It begins with an essay that looks at some selective biblical materials. Then an interim outline for an evangelical theology is proposed in the sixth essay of this volume. The next three essays focus on the notion of general revelation and its possible use to develop an evangelical theology of religions that is conservative and contemporary.

The third section, "Application," consists of a single essay that strives to address the evangelical aspect of our tradition. We consider how the Great Commission (Matthew 28) and the Law of Love (1 Corinthians 13) might be implemented as we consider how we shall then live in light of the above proposal. It brings back to the table three motifs seen throughout this project: dialogue, cooperation, and trust building. Therefore, this essay brings us back to God and ends at a similar point as the first volume: divine action and human replication.

Part 1

Preliminary

1

Christian Relationship with the World

Evangelicalism and World Religions[1]

The theology of relationships is vital, not only for those who wish to be relevant in their theology today, but for those who seek to understand the mind of God. For, if our theology does not speak of relationships in a contemporary setting, it may become irrelevant for individuals today and fail our contemporary and often impersonal society. Furthermore, we must not ignore that the God portrayed in the Scriptures is self-revealing and seeking relationships with the created. Establishing relationship and community seems to be a vital desire and activity of the Christian God. In this essay I wish to focus on the Christian relationship as it pertains to the world. As one who identifies himself as an evangelical Christian, I will address this focal point from an evangelical perspective. While there is much misunderstanding regarding evangelical theology, there seem to be three crucial aspects of the tradition. First, it is committed to the Christian Scriptures. Second, it is committed to evangelism and discipleship. And third, it exhibits a level of theological tolerance absent in other forms of conservative Protestant Christianity. Whereas in some cases evangelicalism has exhibited tolerance of other parts of the Christian tradition, it has lacked such tolerance of non-Christian faith traditions. It is this relationship, i.e., between evangelical Christians and members of other religions that I wish to direct our attention. This essay will not address those exhortations to be "in the world, but not of the world." That aspect of the relationship between Christians and the world, which calls for some level of separation, is outside the scope of this project. Furthermore, evangelicals continue, and rightly so, to emphasize evangelism and sharing the gospel. This too is outside the scope of this paper. My purpose is to address an aspect of the Christian's relationship to the world that is often overlooked. I will claim that evangelical

1. First published in *Direction Journal: A Mennonite Brethren Forum*, 244–54. Used with permission.

Christians should embrace a position that is both agnostic and optimistic as they seek relationships with members of other faith traditions. In order to accomplish this task I will begin by briefly laying out foundational information. Then in the second section, I present five general observations pertinent to constructing an evangelical theology of Christian relationship with the world, i.e., with those outside of the Christian faith. This essay will introduce issues that will be further explored in later essays.

Foundational Information

It has been suggested that Romans 12 provides a model for Christian relationships with the world. However, this Pauline literature must be seen in its context. If we are to understand Romans 12 as a model, it must be viewed in the context of the entire book of Romans. Chapters 1 through 8 are often seen as a doctrinal dissertation, which ends with a confidence that God is able to accomplish that which God desires. This confidence in God's ability poses an interesting dilemma for our writer. God had established a covenant with the Jewish people. This promise included that the Christ would come through that group of people (Gal 3:15–18), but the Old Testament suggests that God's covenant also intended to bring that group of people into a final community with God.[2] Yet, Paul faces the apparent reality that as a people, the Jews had rejected the Christ. He addresses this dilemma in chapters 9 through 11. Two things are significant from these three chapters for our current purpose. First, Paul is optimistic that Israel, the Jewish people, has a future in God's plan. God will accomplish what God had promised. Notice the Christ had come and was rejected, yet Paul expects a future for his people; he expects them to experience a relationship with God. God has not replaced Israel with the church. Second, Paul does not seem to understand how God will accomplish this. Hence, Paul is both hopeful and agnostic regarding the future of Israel and its relationship with God. As a result, this concrete example connects the doctrinal chapters of Romans to its practical applications in chapters 12 through 15. It is Paul's stance of agnosticism and optimism that lays the foundation for chapter 12 of Romans as a model for the Christian relationship in the world.

The relationship between Christians and members of other faith traditions is a critical issue within the theology of religions. Discussions in this field of theology frequently identify three basic categories: pluralism,

---

2. Some forms of evangelical theology do claim that the promise of community was passed on to the church with the rejection by Jews. However, not all evangelical theologies would agree that the promises given to Israel were inherited by the church.

inclusivism, and exclusivism or particularism.³ For evangelicals concerned about their relationship to the world and specifically to members of other faith traditions, these three categories are obstacles, for they oversimplify the complexity of evangelical theology and its understanding of other traditions. Regarding the agency by which God brings individuals into community, evangelicals are exclusivists. Jesus Christ is the only means by which community is possible with God. Atonement is possible only because of the Christ-event. However, regarding the recipients of salvation or those to whom God gives community, evangelical theology acknowledges that there are individuals outside of the church who are saved. (A quick glance at the "great cloud of witnesses" is provided in Hebrews 11, and the list consists of many who never knew Jesus Christ or knew of him.) The Christ of Colossians is a cosmic Christ whose impact goes far beyond the church. So in this sense, evangelicals are inclusivists. Yet when we ask, "Who may possess religious truth?" evangelicals cast the net even wider. While Christians claim a superior revelation in both the written and living Words, evangelicals must not deny that God reveals through general revelation, e.g. conscience and nature. Given the Noahic covenant and the scope of general revelation, evangelicals are pluralists regarding religious truth. As a result, any attempt to categorize evangelical theology in terms of the typical typology is doomed to fail. Having sketched the foundational position of this discussion, I will now present five general observations, as well as two critical elements, if an evangelical stance is to be developed regarding Christian relationships with the world.

General Observations

The development of an evangelical theology of religions provides a fascinating challenge. It must be faithful to those elements that may be seen as key characteristics of evangelicalism, and it must present a story of how evangelicals should understand and relate to individuals who belong to non-Christian faith traditions. These two points can create tension. The tension may exist because evangelicals, like most human beings, tend to think in terms of either/or, black/white, Christian/non-Christian, us/them, and so forth. The challenge facing evangelicals is to develop a theology that does not reject the foundational beliefs of evangelicalism but that does encourage a move beyond dualistic thinking. This is my first observation. Krister Stendahl offers sound advice, which if heeded by evangelicals may be very

---

3. These categories were set forth by Race, *Christians and Religious Pluralism*.

helpful.[4] He proposes stepping back and looking at a wider panorama than is normal when developing a theology. For understandable reasons, evangelical theologians have focused on Jesus Christ and the Christian church. However, Jesus Christ and the Christian church are only part of a larger drama. Stendahl suggests that we can best see this larger drama as we look at the message and mission of Jesus Christ, which was the kingdom. Stendahl says, "my guess is that this very term expressed the continuity with the old and eternal dream of God's for a mended creation, for a redeemed world. Kingdom is more than a King and a Lordship, and Reign. The kingdom of God, the kingdom of heaven, stands for a mended creation, with people and things, a social, economic, ecological reality."[5] It is the kingdom that captures "the sweeping vision of God's total work."[6] The kingdom speaks to God's drawing the entire creation back into community with its Creator. From this reference point, the dualism frequently encountered within evangelical theology can be transcended but its distinctive features can be maintained. The Christian church, while crucial within God's drama, is not the only act within the epic. The Christian story does contain essential elements of the epic, but God's drama is a call to the entire cosmos. The Christian Scriptures speak to this wider scope.[7] If an evangelical theology of religions is to be embraced, the evangelical community must see itself as not only part of the Christian act, but as part of the larger drama. The evangelical community must understand that while the good news they proclaim is essential in God's work of reestablishing community with the cosmos, the reestablishment is broader than the Christian church. This movement of seeing one's group as part of a greater drama is enhanced by two important elements:

4. Stendahl, "Notes," 7–18.

5. Ibid., 9.

6. Ibid., 8. It should be noted that a major topic of discussion that led to the development of progressive dispensationalism was a reassessment of the concept of kingdom. "The theme of the kingdom of God is much more unified and more central to progressive dispensationalism than it is to revised dispensationalism. Instead of dividing up the different features of redemption into self-contained 'kingdoms,' progressive dispensationalists see one promised eschatological kingdom which has both spiritual and political dimensions . . . Progressive dispensationalists put primary emphasis on the eternal kingdom for understanding all previous forms of the kingdom including the Millennium. They make no substantive distinction between the terms kingdom of heaven and kingdom of God" (Blaising and Bock, *Progressive Dispensationalists* 54). "If one wants to see how God accomplishes his kingdom, one must see how that program and the promises tied to it are linked together through the Scripture's description of the career of Jesus Christ" (Bock, "Reign of the Lord Christ," 37). Also see Saucy, *Case for Progressive Dispensationalism*, 81–110.

7. For examples see Gen 12:3; Ps 67:2–3; Isa 2:2–4; 60:2–3; Matt 28:19; Luke 2:32; Acts 11:18; Col 3:11; and Rev 7:9.

broadening one's understanding of general revelation and participating in interreligious dialogue.

A second general observation is that for evangelicals the other world religions are non-Christian. To suggest that adherents of other religions are anonymous Christians or that other traditions house individuals who will become Christians is an injustice to both those other traditions and Christianity. Religions, including Christianity, are culturally connected attempts to make sense of ultimate concerns. Evangelicals, as they attempt to understand religions, have three basic options available to them. First, they can assume all religions are fundamentally the same. The differences among the various traditions can be explained as cultural variances. Second, evangelicals can assume that all other faith traditions are false and contain no hope or truth. Christianity is an anomaly among the world religions for it has the truth. Finally, they can assume that while the various non-Christian religions may contain some religious truths and spiritual benefits, they fail to provide the foundational component that makes it possible for persons to reestablish community with God. Once again, in this option, Christianity as a religion is an anomaly for it claims that the foundational component for reestablished community is Jesus Christ. This third option is the stance most consistent with the evangelical theology.[8]

Furthermore, an evangelical theology of religions must maintain a level of agnosticism. An evangelical theology must acknowledge its limited nature when addressing areas in which we do not have complete, or clear, revelation. An evangelical theology of religions must be agnostic in the sense that it cannot declare the mind of God beyond what God has chosen to reveal in a clear fashion. However, because evangelicals understand God to be a God of justice and mercy and because the Scriptures do clearly declare that some outside of the Christian church are saved, an evangelical theology of religions must be optimistic. We have cited examples of individuals such as

---

8. Evangelicals have rejected the first stance for three basic reasons. First, the various faith systems do portray radically different pictures on issues that are crucial to given faith traditions. Second, this position may lead to an adoption of positions that have been considered heretical by mainstream Christianity. Third, this position may lead to a less than respectful position of other faith systems by denying essential characteristics that make them distinct faith traditions. This is a problem of any reductionistic approach to religion. While we did see those who are identified with evangelicalism holding the second stance, it was claimed that if evangelicals are to develop a theology of religions, this second stance must be rejected as being inconsistent with their basic theology. While there is a long history of Christians taking this route, it does not fit with an evangelical worldview. Furthermore, this position fails to acknowledge the common ground found among the various traditions. Typical of a fundamentalist approach to Christianity, this route tends to put God into a box and claims that those who hold the "truth" know God better. Truth is defined by what they hold to be true.

Abraham and Moses, who are outside the church; but the Scriptures speak about their being saved. (We will say more on this point in the following observation.) This optimism cannot be converted into a form of universalism because the Scriptures do indicate that some will not be saved. However, God's goodness and mercy are not limited to members of the church; they extend to all. Therefore, an evangelical theology of religions must be both agnostic and optimistic. This is my third general observation.

The fourth general observation is more specific than the preceding three, and builds upon them. An evangelical theology of religions begins with an understanding of Christianity as based in Jesus Christ. As Harold Lindsell claims, "The deity of Christ is the foundation of the Christian faith. The denial of it invalidates the entire structure of Christian theology."[9] To claim members of other faith-traditions as being anonymous Christians is to deny the very foundation of evangelical thought and to deny these other traditions their own voice. Since they deny the deity of Christ, they must be non-Christian if an evangelical understanding of Christianity is embraced.[10] The Manila Manifesto proclaimed this uniqueness of Jesus Christ. "We affirm that the Jesus of history and the Christ of glory are the same person, that this Jesus Christ is absolutely unique, for he alone is God incarnate, our sin-bearer, the conqueror of death and the coming judge . . . We affirm that other religions and ideologies are not alternative paths to God, and that human spirituality, if unredeemed by Christ, leads not to God but to judgment, for Christ is the only way."[11] While an evangelical theology of religions will embrace these affirmations, it will point out that some of the conclusions drawn within the manifesto must be challenged. The manifesto explains, "because men and women are made in God's image and see in creation traces of its Creator, the religions which have arisen do sometimes contain elements of truth and beauty. They are not, however, alternative gospels. Because human beings are sinful, and because 'the whole world is under the control of the evil one,' even religious people are in need of Christ's redemption."[12] An evangelical theology will embrace this assessment. However, this assessment continues, "We, therefore, have no warrant for saying that salvation can be found outside Christ

---

9. *Harper Study Bible*, 1621 (footnote for John 20:28).

10. This claim statement is not beyond controversy. Within the Christian church there are individuals who do deny the deity of Jesus Christ. That dialogue is outside the scope of our present discussion. An evangelical theology of religions must stay focused upon coming to grips and interacting with positions proposed by those outside of the church, i.e., other faith traditions.

11. Stott, *Making Christ Known*, 231.

12. Ibid., 235.

or apart from an explicit acceptance of his work through faith." An evangelical theology of religions will embrace this conclusion, but only up to the disjunctive. While evangelical theology does claim that salvation for all is based upon the work of Christ, it acknowledges that some, presumably Abraham and Moses, for example, are saved without explicit knowledge of his work. In this sense, an evangelical theology of religions must go beyond the Lausanne Movement of 1974–1989. While the deity of Jesus Christ and the atonement, made possible because of his death and resurrection, are foundational, and while explicit acceptance of his work may be required to be a Christian, salvation is not limited to Christians. God is at work in the entire cosmos, not just the Christian church.

Let us consider a hypothetical scenario that focuses upon an individual in Janakpur, Nepal, during the nineteenth century. In this scenario, the individual had no knowledge of Jesus Christ, nor was he familiar with Abraham and the faith traditions that derive from Abraham. According to evangelical theology, this individual is not a Christian. However, in this scenario, this individual concluded that God does exist and has specific moral expectations of God's followers. Furthermore, he realized that his right standing before God is not the result of his performing ritual offerings, but is based upon the mercy and grace of God. The individual believed that God is holy, just, all-powerful, and so forth. According to the scenario, the individual realized that he was not worthy to stand in the presence of God, yet God desired a relationship with him. In this scenario, his knowledge of God was not based on the teaching of the local priests, but upon his contemplation of the cosmos and carefully attending to his own conscience. While his culture and religious background fostered an attitude of seeking God, his answers were primarily found as he considered what evangelicals have referred to as general revelation. Part of this revelation may have been latent revelation, which had been preserved by oral tradition before it became part of the teachings of his own religion. We might ask, is it possible that he may appropriately respond to the revelation he has at hand such that God might assign salvation based upon the work of the cross of Jesus Christ? Is it possible that this individual possessed an appropriate faith?[13] Evangelical theology must acknowledge that it is possible, given the scenario and the biblical evidence of salvation given to individuals between Noah and Abraham and beyond. God may accept his faith as appropriate even though he has no knowledge of Jesus Christ. As a result, the evangelical response is not necessarily bleak, for while evangelical theology is

---

13. "For by [faith] the men of old received divine approval" (Heb 11:2). All quotes from the Christian Scriptures will be from the Revised Standard Version (RSV), unless otherwise indicated, or unless the Scriptures are being quoted by a secondary source.

Christocentric, it also is Trinitarian. The work of God is not limited to the atoning work of Jesus Christ, but includes the work of the Spirit by which God draws individuals into community. It is possible that the individual from Janakpur arrived at his understanding of God and himself via the cosmos and self-examination because of the moving of the Spirit of God, much like Abraham or Moses arrived at appropriate faith.

Let us consider another scenario. In this case, our individual has the last name of Singh. While he was born in India, as a young man he traveled to the United States and is now a faithful, devout member of the Nanak Sar Gurdwara in Fresno, California. Even though he has lived in North America for many years, his knowledge of Christianity is filtered through his Sikh worldview. He is ignorant of the atoning work of Jesus Christ. However, like our individual from Janakpur, he has come to understand God as holy, just, all-powerful, and merciful. He understands that God desires to have a special relationship with him and that relationship is based in God's mercy and grace, not his membership in the Khalsa.[14] Mr. Singh came to an understanding similar to the one reached by our individual from Janakpur. While all thought project scenarios are hypothetical, they are still real possibilities. It is conceivable that this individual, while in North America, might embrace a worldview closer to one held by his counterpart in Janakpur rather than a worldview held by someone attending Riverpark Bible Church, also in Fresno. Rather than dealing with this individual as if he had a strong knowledge of God may interact with this individual in ways more consistent with the ways God dealt with those after Noah but before Abraham. Those who have knowledge of the work of Jesus Christ, even though they may be neighbors. The same Spirit who illuminates individuals to understand their sinfulness before God and how the atoning work of Christ is applied to them by God such that they appropriately respond to the New Testament message also illuminates those whose current available revelation is limited to general revelation.

Our fifth and final general observation regarding evangelicals and their relationship to the world draws attention to the pragmatic nature of evangelical theology. Evangelical theology is church oriented and seeks to be practical. Therefore, an evangelical theology of religions must be able to address not only a theoretical assessment and response to faith-traditions as religions, but to faith traditions as practiced by individuals. According to evangelical theology, God seeks individuals, not institutions, such

---

14. Those of the Sikh tradition who desire membership in the Khalsa undergo a special baptism and are required to wear five specific items: *kachh* (a pair of underwear), *kanghā* (a wooden comb), *karā* (a steel bracelet), *kes* (uncut hair), and the *kirpān* (dagger) (McLeod, *Sikhs*, 45).

as religions. As a result, an evangelical theology of religions will focus on individuals and their relationship or community with God. As human institutions, religions themselves are not the focus of an evangelical theology of religions. The focus is upon individuals who practice other religions. While the Christian Scriptures clearly indicate, "Believe in the Lord Jesus, and you will be saved" (Acts 16:31) and "for all have sinned and fallen short of the glory of God" (Rom 3:23), the Bible also presents a merciful, just God who knows the intent of the heart, the inner being, and judges based on that. An evangelical theology of religions seeks to understand God's potential interactions with individuals of non-Christian religions, and describes how evangelicals ought to interact with those individuals. It must strive to understand the intent of a worshiper and be capable of asking practical questions such as, is it possible that the God worshiped by an individual member of another religion is the same God who reached out and provided the means of reestablished community through Jesus Christ? Or, what can the evangelical church learn about spirituality or practices of spirituality from an individual outside of the Christian church? Questions such as these do not solicit easy answers.

In order for evangelicals to develop a theology of religions that is consistent with their fundamental beliefs and the above general observations, two elements are critical. Because of their complexity, they can only be introduced here. First, a broader understanding of the value of general revelation is necessary. General revelation, including latent revelation, provides an explanation of how non-Christian traditions or individuals within those traditions can possibly possess knowledge of God and other spiritual insights. Second, evangelicals must increase their participation in interreligious dialogue if they are to gain any understanding of individuals from other faith traditions. While some may claim that interreligious dialogue is not part of a theology of religions, given their emphasis on individuals, dialogue is crucial for evangelicals. Dialogue provides the opportunity to gain an understanding of others. Hence, participation in interreligious dialogue seems to be a necessary condition in order to make appropriate assessments of those who belong to other traditions. These elements must be explored at another time.

In conclusion, Christian relationships with the world require the development of a theology of religions. In this essay, the focus has been on particular observations for an evangelical theology of religions; however, it is the belief of this writer that they are pertinent to other Christian traditions as well. While Christians are exhorted not to conform to the ways of the world, they are to be in the world and develop relationships with individuals in the world (Romans 12–14). These relationships require

Christians to be both agnostic and optimistic regarding individuals of the world, i.e., outside of the church. It is possible that some members of other faith traditions possess knowledge of the same God evangelicals worship. However, an evangelical theology of religions must acknowledge itself agnostic regarding the details of how God will accomplish the reestablishment of community with the created. In developing an evangelical theology of religions, evangelicals should not feel compelled to tie together all the loose ends. At times, the preservation of tension is preferred. Like other areas of theology, this particular field must be approached with a sense of awe, a sense of reverence, a sense of excitement as we watch God doing God stuff. For the evangelical, theology is always about God and should lead to God.

2

Religious Diversity, Evangelical Theology, and Methodological Issues

The previous essay raises many questions for those who consider themselves evangelical Christians. We may question the implications of the scenarios presented or the claim that evangelical theology has a pragmatic nature. However, its challenge is one that we cannot afford to overlook. The challenge facing evangelicals is to develop a theology that does not reject the foundational beliefs of evangelicalism while encouraging a move beyond dualistic thinking. The remainder of this project is an attempt to work toward that end. In this particular essay, we have the goal of laying the foundation. Evangelicals began to systematically consider the theology of religions in the mid-1980s, so we must consider how evangelical theology dealt with religious diversity prior to that time. This will be the focus of the first section. In the second section of this essay, we will address methodological issues that will help us in the following essays. During the twenty-year period following the mid-1980s, evangelicals focused their work in the theology of religions in three areas: religious truth, agency of salvation, and recipients of salvation. Essays 3 and 4 below will examine their contribution in the latter two areas. The area of religious truth has been examined elsewhere.[1]

Pre-1980s

Well into the 1960s, most North Americans had little if any contact with individuals whose religious tradition was not Christianity. However, as immigration policies changed, so did their neighborhoods. No longer could they view those of other faith traditions simply as "heathens" in far distant lands. Those of alien faiths became their coworkers, their neighbors, their friends. The Sunday school question regarding "those who have never heard" took

---

1. Boyd, "Nature of Religious Truth," 31–48. Reprinted in volume 1, *Philosophically Thinking about World Religions*, 47–66.

on new meaning. Other Christian traditions such as Roman Catholicism had already been seriously engaged with this issue as they grappled with the phrase "outside the church there is no salvation" and with the reforms of Vatican II. Paul Tillich raised the issue in his Bampton Lectures, which he delivered at Columbia University in 1961.[2] However, North American evangelicalism was slow to respond. As a result, foundational issues for the theology of religions were established without their input. The purpose of this essay is to lay the groundwork by introducing some of the foundational issues of the theology of religions and of evangelicalism.

Some of those foundational issues, developed before evangelicals became involved with the field, were consistent with evangelical theology, while others were inconsistent. The emphasis placed on interreligious dialogue is a valuable and necessary condition for the development of a theology of religions.[3] This issue calls for a wide spectrum of religious and theological perspectives to engage in dialogue—listening and talking with one another. While there are different reasons for individuals to participate in this dialogue, all that come to the table for dialogue agree upon two basic facts. First, all acknowledge that the world in which we live is religiously diverse. Second, if we are to celebrate this diversity, we must show respect for all who come to the table of dialogue—as well as those who choose not to participate. Only when we embrace diversity and allow for variances can we properly celebrate the pluralist societies of the modern world. A position of tolerance, in its most positive form, is not one that demands everyone else to look and talk alike. A position of tolerance embraces individuals who are different. It celebrates the humanity of all, the common issues that confront us, while accepting our dissimilarities.

Evangelicals and others, as they have engaged in the theology of religions, have challenged some of the foundational issues formulated by evangelicals in the 1960s and '70s. Some have challenged the definitions given to

2. Tillich, *Christianity and the Encounter of World Religions*.

3. Various terms have been used to refer to what I am calling interreligious dialogue. It is often referred to as "multifaith" or "interfaith" dialogue. Each term elicits a connotation that is useful. "Multifaith" captures a dialogue among the involved religious traditions. "Interfaith" points to the dialogue between. It could be suggested that "multifaith," while foundational, may focus upon sharing ones history and understanding of a given tradition. However, "interfaith" may focus on the region between the various faiths. Given this, at one level in religious dialogue the sharing of histories and understandings is essential. In order to clarify and demystify, dialogue among the religions must occur. However, some of the most interesting aspects of religious dialogue are found in that space between the religions. Hence, my preference for "inter-" In some traditions, the concept of "faith" does not easily fit for some practitioners, e.g., Buddhism and Judaism—hence, the term "interreligious" is used. (I want to thank Alan Race for suggesting the various implications of these terms.)

key concepts used within the theology of religions, words like "exclusivism," "inclusivism," and "pluralism." Others have simply proposed some modifications to the definitions. More problematic, not only for evangelicals but also for other faith groups, is the presupposition of some forms of pluralism and how those doing the theology of religions frequently address diversity.

A common presupposition shared by many practicing interreligious dialogues is based upon a distinction made by Immanuel Kant. Kant distinguished between "historical faith" and "pure religious faith." For Kant, the particulars of a faith tradition are not critical. What is critical is the pure religious faith that is common to all faith traditions.[4] Many contributions by evangelicals, as well as others, to the field of theology of religions have focused on this reductionist presupposition. The details of these contributions must wait and will be presented in subsequent essays. However, for now it is sufficient to suggest that Kant's presupposition, and its contemporary forms, presents a possible problem; it is possibly inconsistent with the emphasis upon dialogue. There are two aspects to this problem.

First, to trivialize the particulars of a faith, any faith, is to rip the distinctiveness of the faith away. Imagine Judaism without the notion of covenant. While some members of the faith tradition are willing to give up and let go, many of that tradition cannot give up the notion of a covenant relationship with the Master of the Universe. As a result, the demand of "sameness" will exclude many who need to be at the table of religious

---

4. Kant's metaphysical dualism carries over to his dichotomy between historical faith and pure faith. For example, "There is therefore no norm of ecclesiastical faith other than Scripture, and no expositor thereof other than pure *religion of reason* and *Scriptural scholarship* (which deals with the historical aspects of that religion). Of these, the first alone is *authentic* and valid for the whole world; the second is merely *doctrinal*, having as its end the transformation of ecclesiastical faith for a given people at a given time into a definite and enduring system. Under this system, historical faith must finally become mere faith in Scriptural scholars and their insights . . . Thus historical faith can become an ecclesiastical faith (of which there can be several), whereas only pure religious faith, which bases itself wholly upon reason, can be accepted as necessary and therefore as the only one which signalizes the *true* church" (Kant, *Religion within the Limits of Reason Alone*, 105–6). Wilfred Cantwell Smith proposes a new conceptual apparatus that distinguishes between "an historical 'cumulative tradition,' and the personal faith of men and women" (*Meaning and the End of Religion*, 175). When "religion" focuses on the latter, "God is the end of religion also in the sense that once He appears vividly before us, in His depth and love and unrelenting truth all else dissolves; or at the least religious paraphernalia drop back into their due and mundane place, and the concept of 'religion' is brought to an end" (ibid., 181). John Hick also has a similar reductionism. In a most un-Kantian move, he proposes that religion is really about "the transformation of human existence from self-centredness to Reality-centredness" (Hick, *Interpretation of Religion*, 240).

dialogue. The reductionary assumption, as a result, may limit those who participate in dialogue.

Second, this presupposition itself may be inconsistent with the very notion of dialogue. Imagine a dialogue between members of the Christian tradition and members of the Islamic tradition. In our fractured world today, these two faith traditions have much in common to talk about. Not only are both interested in healing the fracturedness and promoting peace, but for both faith traditions the pursuit of true worship is vital. However, as traditions they have distinct differences. In the past, we have addressed these differences by means other than dialogue, but surely we can, and must, learn from history. In a positive, healthy dialogue, differences can be addressed. Dialogue can promote correction as long as dialogue is not limited. In some cases, solutions may be worked out. In other cases, we may not arrive at a solution, but may gain respect for and better understanding of all who are at the table. If dialogue is to be taken seriously, it must not assume that all at the table really hold the same position, are pursuing the same goals, or even worshiping the same God. Dialogue should promote trust.

A final important note regarding dialogue must be offered. When we are seated in dialogue with those of different faith traditions, it is very difficult for us to hold on to a straw man. Recently I read an article on fundamentalism. While I agreed with much of what the authors said about fundamentalism, I found myself rejecting the article as a whole because of the straw men they constructed in order to show why fundamentalism is problematic. Each of the charges they made against fundamentalism, they, the authors, committed. They were very selective, they made the situation much more simplistic than it is, and they illustrated an arrogance that rejects all who disagree. When members of different faith traditions are in dialogue, we can celebrate diversity and avoid creating straw men. Gotthold Lessing taught us a valuable lesson, which must not be forgotten by those engaging in interreligious dialogue.[5] Each of us believes that we have the truth, but, in humility, we must acknowledge that we might be wrong.

While North American evangelicals have been very involved in missionary activities and therefore involved with individuals of other faith traditions, their academic involvement in the field of theology of religions did not begin to blossom until the 1980s. As North American evangelicals began seriously considering their attitude toward and relationship with those faith traditions other than Christianity, they began wrestling with issues such as these: the nature and fairness of God, the person and work of Jesus Christ,

---

5. Gotthold Lessing, *Nathan the Wise* (1779).

the nature and activity of the Holy Spirit, the nature of revelation and truth, and the status of those who have never heard the gospel message.

In order to appreciate the delicacy exhibited by those evangelicals working within the field of theology of religions, we should review the basic elements of evangelical theology and its methodology. Its methodology reflects the three dogmas of evangelicalism, which were outlined by Clark Pinnock in a brief article in *Christianity Today*.[6] Pinnock claims that a theology that reflects evangelicalism must be evangelical, conservative, and contemporary. It must be faithful to the gospel message. It must exhibit "an essential *fidelity* to the doctrinal structure of the biblical and Christian tradition."[7] Furthermore, it must demonstrate a *"responsibility* to the contemporary hearers of the Gospel whereby we seek to communicate the message meaningfully to them and apply it creatively to the modern situation."[8] Given these three elements, Pinnock suggests that the theological methodology adopted by evangelicals should be bipolar. "We should strive to be faithful to historical Christian beliefs taught in Scripture, and *at the same time* to be authentic and responsible to the contemporary hearers."[9] Evangelical theology should strive for balance, maintaining traditional theology while addressing issues of contemporary concern.

North American evangelicalism was slow to respond to the contemporary issue of religious diversity. Nevertheless, as early as 1964, Bernard Ramm began raising the issue of other faith traditions for evangelicals. After a discussion in which he rejects universalism,[10] Ramm asks whether this means that the door is "slammed shut upon every person who has not heard the name of Christ?"[11] Ramm maintains "that the only basis for redemption of any man in any period of human history, before Christ or after Christ, is the death and resurrection of Jesus Christ."[12] However, he suggests that God's grace may be wider than a typical understanding of the gospel might lead one to believe.[13] He closes his article as follows, and, in so doing, he opened the door for evangelicals to begin their own discussion of this contemporary theological issue:

---

6. Pinnock, "Evangelical Theology," 23–29.
7. Ibid., 23 (italics original).
8. Ibid.
9. Ibid.
10. Ramm, "Will All Men," 22–25, 33.
11. Ibid., 24.
12. Ibid.
13. Ibid., 25.

We do not slam the door shut on all those millions who have not heard the name of Christ any more than we can restrict a saving knowledge of God only to Israelites in the Old Testament. We do pronounce that only the cross and resurrection of Christ saves. We equally pronounce that the non-Christian religions are devoid of saving truth. But there may be many hearts outside the sound of the gospel who have felt after God, who did seek for honor and immortality, who do have the true circumcision of the Spirit, and to these hearts God applies the salvation of Jesus Christ.

We only know that the wideness of God's mercy as testified in Scripture does not narrow the horizon of God's grace down to just those placed where his grace is clearly pronounced whether in Israel or the Christian church. Only in the final day of judgment, when the secret of men's hearts is made known, can we speak a final word as to who is saved and as to who is lost.[14]

Millard Erickson, then at Bethel Theological Seminary, was the next evangelical to enter into the discussion.[15] Like Ramm, Erickson begins by affirming that the Scriptures teach Jesus Christ as the only way of salvation. "Yet, [he acknowledges] our knowledge of the goodness, justice, and fairness of God leads us to ask how he could condemn those who have never heard of Christ and thus scarcely have had a chance to believe."[16] From here, Erickson turns to two theologians whom conservative Christians have respected for many years, Charles Hodge and Augustus H. Strong. Hodge takes the position that there is no hope of salvation for individuals who have never heard, but Strong suggests there might be hope.[17] With a split decision, Erickson turns to the first two chapters of Romans, looking at what we understand as general revelation. "What can be known apart from the specially revealed law, then, seems to be two major tenets of faith: (1) God exists and is powerful and creative (ch. 1); (2) God is a holy, moral God, who

14. Ibid., 33.

15. Erickson, "Hope for Those," 122–26.

16. Ibid., 122–23.

17. "Since Christ is the Word of God and the Truth of God, he may be received even by those who have not heard of his manifestation in the flesh. A proud and self-righteous morality is inconsistent with saving faith; but a humble and penitent reliance upon God, as a Savior from sin and a guide of conduct, is an implicit faith in Christ; for such reliance casts itself upon God, so far as God has revealed himself,—and the only Revealer of God is Christ. We have, therefore, the hope that even among the heathen there may be some, like Socrates, who, under the guidance of the Holy Spirit working through the truth of nature and conscience, have found the way of life and salvation" (Strong, *Systematic Theology*, 843).

requires certain actions of men (ch. 2)."[18] However, how can one who has never heard of Jesus Christ respond appropriately to God? Erickson sees a possible answer as Paul, in 10:18, quotes Psalms 19:4. "Their voice has gone out to all the earth, and their words to the ends of the world." Erickson believes that Paul is claiming that all have heard the basic gospel message via general revelation without knowing the specifics, which are available only through special revelation. The basic elements of the gospel message, Erickson suggests are (1) The belief in one good powerful God. (2) The belief that he (man) owes this God perfect obedience to his law. (3) The consciousness that he does not meet this standard, and therefore is guilty and condemned. (4) The realization that nothing he can offer God can compensate him (or atone) for this sin and guilt. (5) The belief that God is merciful, and will forgive and accept those who cast themselves upon his mercy.[19] If it is possible that an individual can believe and act upon these elements, then it also is possible, according to Erickson, that the individual "is redemptively related to God and receives the benefits of Christ's death."[20] Erickson, like Ramm, does not attempt to integrate the traditional position of salvation as possible only through the Christ-event with the contemporary issue of those who have never heard, but suggests there is a possible integration.

Before looking at a third major contribution by a North American evangelical during the 1970s, one additional contribution, supported by North American evangelicals, must be acknowledged: The International Congress on World Evangelization at Lausanne of 1974. This congress produced the Lausanne Covenant.[21] Three points of the covenant have specific implications for the development of a theology of religions for evangelicals. From points 1 and 4, I cite only the relevant segments, but cite the entire third point.

> 1. The Purpose of God
>
> ... He has been calling out from the world a people for himself, and sending his people back into the world to be his servants and his witnesses, for the extension of his kingdom, the building up of Christ's body, and the glory of his name ...
>
> 3. The Uniqueness and Universality of Christ
>
> We affirm that there is only one Saviour and only one gospel, although there is a wide diversity of evangelistic approaches. We

---

18. Erickson, "Hope for Those," 123.
19. Ibid., 125.
20. Ibid.
21. "Lausanne Covenant," 313–20.

recognize that all men have some knowledge of God through his general revelation in nature. But we deny that this can save, for men suppress the truth by their unrighteousness. We also reject as derogatory to Christ and the gospel every kind of syncretism and dialogue which implies that Christ speaks equally through all religions and ideologies. Jesus Christ, being himself the only God-man, who gave himself as the only ransom for sinners, is the only mediator between God and man. There is no other name by which we must be saved. All men are perishing because of sin, but God loves all men, not wishing that any should perish but that all should repent. Yet those who reject Christ repudiate the joy of salvation and condemn themselves to eternal separation from God. To proclaim Jesus as "the Saviour of the world" is not to affirm that all men are either automatically or ultimately saved, still less to affirm that all religions offer salvation in Christ. Rather it is to proclaim God's love for the world of sinners and to invite all men to respond to him as Saviour and Lord in the wholehearted personal commitment of repentance and faith. Jesus Christ has been exalted above every other name; we long for the day when every knee shall bow to him and every tongue shall confess him Lord.

4. The Nature of Evangelism

. . . Our Christian presence in the world is indispensable to evangelism, and so is that kind of dialogue whose purpose is to listen sensitively in order to understand . . .

This covenant is significant because it does represent the biblical and Christian tradition, which Pinnock suggested as one aspect of his bipolar approach to doing evangelical theology. It, also, contains elements of contemporary concern. Part of evangelism requires believers to be in dialogue, a "dialogue whose purpose is to listen sensitively in order to understand."[22] However, unlike the explorations of Ramm and Erickson, the covenant clearly denies that general revelation provides adequate content for salvation. In addition, it denies any approach that maintains that "Christ speaks equally through all religions and ideologies."[23] This covenant must be addressed if evangelicals are to develop an adequate theology of religions.

The final pre-1980s contribution by an evangelical addressing issues relevant to the theology of religions comes from Clark Pinnock.[24] At issue

22. Ibid., 315.
23. Ibid., 314.
24. Pinnock, "Why Is Jesus," 12–15, 32, 34.

in this article are religious pluralism and the evangelical's stance for the uniqueness and finality of Jesus Christ. While acknowledging that the traditional Christian understanding of the person of Jesus Christ is deeply offensive to those of other faiths, Pinnock maintains that this issue cannot be compromised. However, the uniqueness of Jesus Christ does not mean evangelicals should ignore the contemporary reality, in which we find religious diversity. Conservative Christians have often made this mistake. Rather, "we certainly can learn to proclaim the truth in a loving style which is fully aware of the existence of other convictions."[25] Pinnock's bipolar approach to theology is illustrated as he lays the foundation for an evangelical confronting religious pluralism.

> The essence of this style is humility. We are not personally or corporately superior because we are Christians ... We are aware of how much more God needs to teach us and are not closed to hearing Him speak to us even through the members of other faiths ... The challenge of religious pluralism is not to abandon the finality of Christ, but to grow in the ability to enter into dialogue with those of other faiths, sharing a winsome and winning testimony of His saving power.[26]

While Pinnock has expanded the evangelical response beyond his predecessors, he still finds it necessary to confront the question regarding those who have lived and died without knowing anything about the Christian gospel. Pinnock points out that one tradition simply claims there is no hope for them. However, he does not view this tradition as satisfactory. He cites C. S. Lewis's agnostic position in which Lewis says that "God has not told us what His arrangements with the unevangelized are."[27] Possibly God has not closed the door on those who through no fault of their own have not responded to the gospel message, and neither should we. Another position, cited by Pinnock, is rooted in some of the early church fathers and popular today, claims, "that people encounter God in the context of their own local religion. Christ is thought to be present 'incognito.'"[28] Pinnock points out that this position is problematic because the Scriptures do not present "alien" traditions in a favorable way. Furthermore, Pinnock points out "when the religions are actually studied, it is apparent that almost none of them say anything about the grace and mercy of God, so that a person under their influence would proceed to that conviction more despite his

25. Ibid., 14.
26. Ibid., 14–15.
27. Ibid., 15.
28. Ibid.

religious system than because of it."[29] Another option that Pinnock suggests is exegetically possible, based on 1 Peter, is the so-called second-chance theory. He points to Cranfield and Pannenberg for this position.[30]

Pinnock closes this article with an appeal to the nature of God and a challenge for evangelicals. Because of the goodness of God, God will not simply abandon those who have not heard. Furthermore, "we must become more sensitive to the religious pluralism that pervades the world, and learn how to testify to our Lord in a humble, loving and open manner. And more work needs to be done in theology to show that belief in the finality of Jesus does not preclude belief in His true universality as well."[31] Whether Pinnock or other North American evangelicals have successfully developed a theology of religions that exhibits the delicate balancing act that Pinnock's bipolar approach calls for, several points are clear. First, some evangelicals were starting to grapple with the issues related to the theology of religions prior to the 1980s. Second, the primary issues that evangelicals must deal with were laid out in this early period. Finally, an adequate bipolar approach to evangelical theology regarding the theology of religions was not developed in this formative period. The extent to which evangelicals made progress between 1980 and 2005 will be surveyed in essays 3 and 4. However, because basic definitions are so critical to this area of theology and there is an inconsistency in the usage of basic terminology, the next section of this essay presents the basic terminology to be used in the remainder of this project. It also presents the criteria to be used for evaluating the work of evangelicals in this field.

---

29. Ibid., 32.

30. "The idea in 1 Peter which describes Jesus' victory over hell as a preaching of repentance, takes the image of the early Christian missionary proclamation; and this notion brings out the universal scope of Jesus' act of representation or substitution in his cross and the universality of salvation mediated through it . . . What . . . is to happen to the people who have certainly heard the message of Christ but who—perhaps through the fault of those very Christians who have been charged with its proclamation—have never come face to face with its truth? . . . Do they remain shut out for ever from the presence of God which has been made accessible to mankind through Jesus? The Christian faith can say 'no' to this urgent question . . . [W]hat took place for mankind in Jesus also applies to the people who either never came into contact with Jesus and the message about him, or who have never really caught sight of the truth of his person and his story. In a way that is hidden from us—and in a way hidden even from themselves—the lives of these people may yet be related to the revelation of God which appeared in Jesus . . . The meaning of the Christian acknowledgement of the conquest of the kingdom of death and Jesus Christ's descent into hell lies in the universal scope of salvation" (Pannenberg, *Apostles' Creed*, 94–95).

31. Pinnock, "Why Is Jesus," 34.

Methodological Issues

In order to analyze and evaluate the work done by evangelicals in the field of theology of religions, we must be clear regarding the general criteria by which their work will be examined. Theological positions are philosophical positions in several ways. First, one can make the case that theological problems reduce to problems of philosophy. Paul Tillich tells the story of the fundamentalist minister who asked, "Why do we need philosophy when we possess all the truth through revelation?"[32] The moment religion begins to talk of *truth* it is connecting with philosophical thought. In fact, as Tillich points out, "we cannot avoid philosophy, because the ways we take to avoid it are carved out and paved by philosophy."[33] Second, theological positions present a conceptual system by which we make sense and order the world around us. Such a conceptual system is a philosophical system. Therefore theological stances can be evaluated as philosophical positions, and this includes the work done by evangelicals in the theology of religions. Not only must we be clear regarding the general criteria to be used for evaluation purposes, but also we must be clear on the meaning of the various key terms used in this field of theology. While Alan Race laid the groundwork by defining key concepts used in the theology of religions,[34] two developments make clarification of terms essential. First, the research in the theology of religions has expanded beyond the issue on which Race was focused. Second, some researchers in this field use terms other than those proposed by Race.[35] While other theologians use the same terms, some assign them different meanings.[36] Our evaluation of North American evangelicals' contribution requires clarity of general criteria and basic terms, but it also requires an understanding of why this field of theology is crucial for an adequate evangelical theology. The evangelical response must be evaluated in light of whether it lays an adequate foundation for fulfilling the purpose of evangelical theology. Given these three components, we will be positioned to evaluate, in the following chapters, the contribution by North American theologians to the field of the theology of religions.

---

32. Tillich, *Biblical Religion*, 10.

33. Ibid.

34. Race, *Christians and Religious Pluralism*.

35. For example, McGrath uses the term "particularist" instead of "exclusivist" (*Christian Theology*, 545–46).

36. Pinnock claims to be an inclusivist, but he maintains that salvation is possible only through Jesus Christ. According to Race's understanding, Pinnock's limitation of salvation only through Jesus Christ would make Pinnock an exclusivist.

The history of philosophy presents ample examples of philosophical debate regarding how the evaluation of conceptual positions takes place.[37] While different schools of philosophy may embrace particular criteria, four basic criteria are identifiable: (1) internal consistency, (2) viability, (3) harmony between empirical knowledge and implications or presuppositions of position, and (4) relation to other alternative positions.

Internal consistency: A position has internal consistency when it is possible to maintain that all of its constituent components are true at the same time. A philosophical position that is self-contradictory should be avoided because from inconsistent premises anything can be proved. As a result, preference is given to theological positions that are internally consistent.

Viability: Is the position even plausible? Viability may encompass more than whether the position is plausible. It may encompass ramifications or implications of the position. A preferred theological position will be plausible, as will its implications. The criterion of viability raises two crucial questions. First, is the position useful? Does it do any work? Second, does the position fit in with other accepted beliefs?

Harmony between empirical knowledge and implications or presuppositions of the position: While we may recognize potential flaws in our

---

37. For example, Lawhead suggests six criteria: conceptual clarity, consistency, coherence, comprehensiveness, compatibility with established facts, and support by compelling arguments (*Philosophical Questions*, 33–34). Or Keith E. Yandell's twelve criteria for assessing conceptual systems. "(R1) An incoherent conceptual system, because of its incoherence, cannot provide an adequate account of the truth of the matter in question; ... (R2) A system that essentially contains a contradiction is false for that reason, and cannot be true until the contradiction is removed ... (R3) If it is essential to the truth of conceptual system T that a kind K_1 of propositions be translatable or reducible without remainder into propositions of kind K_2, and they cannot be so translated, then T is false ... (R4) If it is essential to the truth of a conceptual system T that propositions of kind K_1 cannot be translated or reduced without remainder to propositions of kind K_2, but they can be so translated or reduced, then T is false ... (R5) If conceptual system T is such that belief that T is true is epistemically self-defeating, then T is false ... (R6) If a conceptual system T entails that there is no moral knowledge, then T is false ... (R7) If a conceptual system T is such that "T is true" and "T's truth conditions obtain" are incompatible, then T is false ... (R8) If the only rationale for T is that T solves problem P, and, given T, P remains, T should be rejected. (R9) If T entails that sensory experience is never veridical, or that there is no external world, there is excellent reason for rejecting T ... (R10) Any theory T which cannot explain or illumine data within T's reference range is (in any form of T in which this is so) to be rejected ... (R11) If a conceptual system T contradicts well-confirmed data D, then if T cannot justify so doing, T is (probably) false ... (R12) If T requires one or more ad hoc hypotheses, T is epistemically defective in ways perhaps not yet plain" (Yandell, *Christianity and Philosophy*, 272–86).

empirical knowledge of the world, such knowledge does seem crucial when developing a conceptual position. A preferred theological position will be in harmony with what we know about the empirical world; it should provide an explanation of empirical events, and it should predict events that will occur in the empirical realm.

Relation a given position has with other alternative positions: The preferred position will be at least as likely or viable as any alternative position, it should harmonize as well as any alternative position, and it should have at least as much predictive power as any alternative position.

Much of the debate, but not all, within the field of theology of religions stems from miscommunication due to an inconsistent usage of basic terminology. While a good definition should be concise, it must also be accurate. Some of the debate in the field arises because of a preference of conciseness to the detriment of accuracy. The theology of religions is too complex for simple, concise definitions that are overarching and fail to account for the diverse issues found in this field of theology. While some of the following definitions may appear obvious, it is important to specify how the key terms will be used in the following chapters. As we have already noted, there is a great amount of inconsistency in how these terms are used in the literature. As a result, it may be questioned whether the following definitions are the correct lens by which to classify evangelical thought. If by "correct" we mean the "only proper" lens, then I would suggest we are demanding more than language can render. However, if by "correct" we mean appropriate and useful, I believe the definitions will be vindicated in the following essays. Another result of the inconsistent usage of basic terms in the literature itself will be that we may find times, as the literature is evaluated, when we assign a given term to a theological position held by a given evangelical and that term is not what the evangelical has used to describe his/her own position. For example, a particular evangelical may claim his/her position to be an exclusivist position, but given the definitions and how this evangelical describes his/her own position, we may claim their position is that of an inclusivist. When this discrepancy occurs, it will be noted and an explanation will be provided.

Evangelical theology: Evangelical theology is a systematic contemplation of orthodox Christian beliefs in light of Scripture, tradition, and the mission of the church and in which Scripture is understood as the norm.[38]

---

38. "For evangelical theology Scripture is both the primary source and the highest

Evangelical theology of religions: The theology of religions is that field of theology that deals with how the home tradition views and interacts with other traditions. Therefore, an evangelical theology of religions is concerned with a Christian perspective consistent with the basic elements of evangelicalism on other faith traditions. This perspective on other religions has frequently evolved around three distinct issues: truth, recipients of salvation, and agency of salvation. As evangelicals continue to work within this field, other areas of research should emerge.

Truth/Falsehood: A sentence/claim is true if the sentence/claim accurately presents reality given the context of the sentence/claim. It is false if it does not accurately present reality given the context of the sentence/claim. Truth and falsehood are properties of some sentences/claims.

Recipients of Salvation: In the broadest sense, salvation occurs when a person has obtained their proper end or purpose. Hence, depending on how a faith tradition understands the proper end or purpose of a person, what constitutes salvation will vary from one tradition to another. For the Christian tradition, salvation involves redemption, reconciliation, satisfaction, and justification, and results in an everlasting personal relationship with God the Creator. For evangelicals, salvation has both a here-and-now aspect as well as an eschatological aspect. Persons obtain or receive salvation.[39] There are two basic views of salvation.

> *Restrictivist view of Salvation*: Claims that not all persons are saved.[40]

---

norm. However, the primacy of Scripture does not exclude tradition as a secondary source and norm for theology . . . Evangelical theology is also reflection on the sources of the faith and mission of the church in mutual relation. Theology should never be a merely academic enterprise, but rather the search for biblical understanding in the context of the ministry and mission of the church . . . Evangelical theology is properly 'task theology,' i.e., theology hammered out in response to the challenges posed by the Great Commission" (Davis, *Foundations of Evangelical Theology*, 44–45).

39. There is evidence that "recipients of salvation" is broader than persons, e.g., the Christian Scriptures speak of a new heaven and new earth; however, within the current literature the focus has been on persons.

40. Frequently evangelicals hold a very narrow understanding of this restrictivist view of salvation. Pinnock says, "A majority of evangelicals today are hardline restrictivists in my estimation. The only possibility for encountering God and receiving salvation in this view is to exercise explicit faith in Jesus Christ in this earthly life" (*Wideness in God's Mercy*, 12).

Universalist view of salvation: Claims that all persons are saved.

Agency of Salvation: The means or vehicle by which salvation is potentially obtained or made possible.

Before we can continue with our presentation of definitions, we need to address a current development within the field. As we indicated earlier in this chapter, Alan Race helped establish a taxonomy of terms that have been used in this area of theology. The taxonomy has been challenged in recent literature.[41] Someone who has challenged Race's taxonomy is Harold Netland of Trinity Evangelical Divinity School. Even though Netland used the basic threefold taxonomy (i.e., pluralism, inclusivism, and exclusivism) in his earlier writings in this area,[42] in an unpublished paper,[43] he rejects it. Netland offers four reasons for his current position. First, he notes "adoption of the three categories is fairly recent."[44] Netland points out, earlier theologians discussed other faith traditions in other ways and were not limited to these three categories. Second, Netland points to the inconsistency present in the literature regarding the usage of these terms. While many use the terms, it is apparent that the terms mean different things to different writers. Third, Netland cites Paul Griffiths, who calls for an enlarging of the categories; such an enlargement of the categories makes it "more difficult to classify particular thinkers without qualification."[45] Finally, Netland maintains that the threefold taxonomy "tends to be reductionistic in its emphasis upon belief or doctrine over other aspects of religion."[46] "The simple categories of exclusivism, inclusivism and pluralism are hardly adequate for

---

41. Veli-Matti Kärkkäinen offers his own typology: ecclesiocentrism, Christocentrism, theocentrism, and realitycentrism. "The most serious theological problem [with the older threefold typology] is its one-sided focus on the question of who is going to be saved: Exclusivism holds that only those in the church, with the exception of a few others related to the church, such as unbaptized infants, will be saved. Inclusivism adds to these the faithful followers of other religions, but only because of Christ's saving work. Pluralism says all will be saved. Salvation, of course, is a key issue, but it is not the only one. *Theology* of religions inquires first into the *theological* meaning and significance of religion, religiosity and particular religions—Christianity included—and into how Christianity *theologically* relates to other religions. The older terminology, as will become evident, also tends to be pejorative, especially with regard to exclusivism" (*Introduction to the Theology of Religions*, 165–66).

42. Netland, *Dissonant Voices*; Netland, *Encountering Religious Pluralism*; Netland, "Professor Hick on Religious Pluralism," 249–261; and Netland, "Exclusivism, Tolerance, and Truth," 77–95.

43. Netland, "Thinking Christianly about Religious Diversity."

44. Ibid., 4.

45. Ibid., 5.

46. Ibid.

capturing the range of issues demanding attention as well as the many possible responses to them."[47]

While Netland's insights are accurate, they are not sufficient to reject the basic taxonomy. A taxonomy provides a language and conceptual framework by which we can handle complex concepts. Race's taxonomy is still valuable so long as it is capable of dealing with the complexity of the discussion within the field and so long as we understand that any taxonomy has its limits. Following Griffiths's lead, we can identify subcategories under each of the basic categories. In presenting it in what follows, we are not suggesting the threefold taxonomy (i.e., pluralism, inclusivism, and exclusivism) is adequate for dealing with all issues that will arise in the field of the theology of religions. However, the taxonomy, along with the suggested subcategories, is helpful for understanding much of the discussion in the discipline to date. As theologians venture beyond the beliefs or doctrine of faith traditions and explore other aspects of the theology of religions, such as spirituality or social issues, the taxonomy will need to be either modified or replaced with another model.[48]

The following definitions are given in reference to pluralism, inclusivism, and exclusivism as related to the three issues cited above: truth, recipients of salvation, and agency of salvation.[49]

Pluralism:

> *With respect to truth*: All religious claims are equally true. As a result, interreligious dialogue is valued.
>
> *With respect to recipients of salvation*: Individuals of all religions may obtain salvation.

---

47. Ibid., 6. In a personal correspondence (October 31, 2005), Netland lists some of the issues, which he believes go far beyond the three categories. The list includes "questions about continuity/discontinuity between a particular non-Christian religion and the Christian faith; the degree to which we might be able to accept or build upon aspects of a non-Christian religion in communicating the gospel or 'indigenizing' Christian identity and witness locally; how we ought to live as human beings as citizens among "religious others," and the implications of this for public policy, etc."

48. For example, upon preliminary reflection, it seems that the threefold taxonomy could be easily modified regarding the issue of spirituality; however, the threefold taxonomy will likely be a hindrance when examining social issues within the theology of religions.

49. This taxonomy has been strongly influenced by Paul Griffiths's *Problems of Religious Diversity*. The issue of religious truth is not dealt with in this work, but see Boyd, "Nature of Religious Truth," which is listed in the bibliography and reprinted in volume 1 of this project.

With respect to agency of salvation: All religions are vehicles to salvation, and no religion is more effective than another.

Inclusivism:

With respect to truth: It is possible that religious claims, which are true, will be found in multiple religions. Two forms:

Closed inclusivism with respect to truth: The form of inclusivism with respect to truth that maintains that nothing of significant religious value can be learned from other religious traditions. All significant religious truths are found in one's own tradition. As a result, interreligious dialogue is not valued.

Open inclusivism with respect to truth: The form of inclusivism with respect to truth that maintains that truth of significant religious value can be learned from other religious traditions. While one's own tradition is somehow privileged, new truths or insights may be gained from those of other faith traditions. As a result, interreligious dialogue is valued.

With respect to recipients of salvation: While individuals who belong to a particular religion may obtain salvation, some individuals who do not belong to that religion may also obtain salvation.

With respect to agency of salvation: While not all roads lead to salvation, there are several different vehicles by which salvation is provided.

Exclusivism:

With respect to truth: Religious claims, which are true, are found only among the claims of one's own religion. Interreligious dialogue is not valued except for evangelistic purposes.

With respect to recipients of salvation: Only individuals who belong to a particular religion will obtain salvation. Those who have never heard the gospel message cannot be saved.

With respect to agency of salvation: There is only one vehicle or source of salvation.

By recognizing the various subcategories of pluralism, inclusivism, and exclusivism, it is possible to develop a theology of religions that is more vibrant and flexible. For instance, as we shall see in the following sections of this essay, some evangelicals will develop a theology that is exclusivist in respect to both recipients of salvation and agency of salvation, but are inclusivist in respect to truth. Others could maintain an exclusivist position in respect to agency of salvation, embrace pluralism in regards to recipients of salvation, and be an inclusivist regarding truth. While the expansion of pluralism, inclusivism, and exclusivism makes for more complexity, it does allow the evangelical theologian greater diversity in grappling with the complexity of the discipline.

The final issue to be established in this chapter and by which we must decide whether evangelicals have been successful in their contributions to this field of theology is why this branch of theology is crucial to the evangelical enterprise. If evangelicalism is to be consistent with its core understanding, then it must develop a vibrant theology of religionsconsistent with its core beliefs. In the pluralistic world in which we find ourselves, evangelicals have two basic options. They can hide and pretend that we do not live in a world of religious diversity, or they can learn to engage in meaningful interreligious dialogue.

Bernard Ramm understood that the distinction for his day between fundamentalism and evangelicalism was how the two camps of conservative orthodox Christianity responded to the Enlightenment. "Fundamentalism attempts to shield itself from the Enlightenment. It attempts to do its theological and biblical tasks as if the Enlightenment had never happened. On the other hand, the evangelical believes that the Enlightenment cannot be undone. He must use the valuable tools of research developed during the Enlightenment, and he cannot ignore the entire change of the intellectual climate of Europe and America that the Enlightenment produced."[50] For the evangelical today, the point of demarcation may be our response to the religious diversity of the present world. We can do our theology as if ours is the only religion in town, or we can grapple with those issues of the theology of religions. The former response is not viable if evangelical theology is to be contemporary and significant in the present pluralistic world. The latter response is not without its difficulties.

> The task of retooling theology for our generation is important, serious, and imperative, but dangerous. If we do not retool, we risk becoming obsolete and failing to reach our own generation. If we retool the wrong way, we retool the biblical faith out of existence. The great theological giants of the first part of the twentieth century had one great conviction in common: to restate the Christian faith so as to make it credible to men of the twentieth century. The worry of the evangelical is that men like Bultmann and Tillich retranslated the Christian faith out of existence. This is the danger of restating the Christian faith. In our zeal to be

---

50. Ramm, *Evangelical Heritage*, 70.

contemporary we may lose our biblical foundation and present a modernized unbiblical version of Christianity.[51]

As we examine the North American evangelical's contribution to the theology of religions, we must evaluate positions in light of the criteria used to evaluate any conceptual system. However, we also must ask whether their contribution is consistent with their vision, which distinguishes them from other forms of conservative orthodox Christianity. We must ask how successful they have been in "retooling" their theology for the beginning of the twenty-first century.

51. Ibid., 73.

3

Religious Diversity and Evangelical Thought

Agency of Salvation

As we view the work of evangelicals in the field of the theology of religions, it is evident that evangelical theology faces a major challenge because of the complexity of the issues and the temptation to simplify these issues. To embrace a particular characterization as representing the evangelical response to problems posed by the theology of religions will only undercut the very fabric of evangelicalism and relegate this field of study to a trivial status. As a result, it was suggested in the previous essay that we identify subcategories under the major categories of Alan Race's threefold taxonomy. In this essay, our concern is with the evangelical position regarding the agency of salvation, the means or vehicle by which salvation is potentially obtained or made possible. We start with this subcategory for two reasons. First, the response to this issue is the heart and soul of evangelical theology. Second, as we shall see in the following essays, this subcategory is the only one on which evangelicals speak in unison.

At issue in this essay is the means or agency by which God has chosen to provide salvation to persons. Those working in this field have given three basic responses. On one end of the spectrum is the claim that all religions are vehicles to salvation, and no religion is more effective than any other. Ultimately, all paths lead to the same God. The form of pluralism that sees all religions traversing up the same mountain only taking different paths may illustrate this approach. On the other end of the spectrum is the claim that there is only one vehicle or source of salvation. The form of exclusivism that maintains that Jesus Christ is the only way to God the Father illustrates this position. It is this position that evangelicals in unison proclaim. A third response to the issue of agency is a middle ground position. It maintains that while salvation can be obtained via a number of different vehicles, not all religions provide an acceptable vehicle. This position is that of an inclusivist approach to agency. For example, an inclusivist might maintain that

Jesus Christ provides a means for Christians, the Four Noble Truths work for Buddhists, but the vehicle of suicide advocated by Heaven's Gate does not provide salvation.

Evangelicals working in the field of the theology of religion have unanimously embraced an exclusivist position regarding the agency of salvation. For evangelical Christians, Jesus Christ is the agency or vehicle God has chosen to provide salvation. Because evangelicals have spoken in unison on this issue, we need not cite all possible examples of the evangelical stance of exclusivism in regards to the agency of salvation. However, as we shall see, while they have spoken in unison, they have done so as a symphony, and we need to see some of the various voices.

As we saw in the previous essay, evangelicals prior to the 1980s maintained that Jesus Christ was the only means of salvation. While they may not have used the term "exclusivism" to describe their position, the term accurately portrays their position. In 1981 Stephen Davis, a colleague of John Hick at Claremont, published "Evangelicals and the Religions of the World."[1] While Davis, a professor of philosophy, does address the epistemological problems of John Hick's and Wilfred Cantwell Smith's positions, his driving claim is that Christianity is an exclusivist religion.[2] As one moves through his argument, it becomes clear that when he refers to Christianity, what he is referring to is evangelical Christianity. As was typical during this period, Davis tends to blend the issues that have emerged within the field. J. Ronald Blue also blended the issues of agency of salvation and recipients of salvation.[3] However, it is clear that Blue does embrace an exclusivist position regarding agency. "Only the God-man, Jesus Christ, can reach across the gulf between a perfect God and a perverse human race."[4] Some evangelicals have continued to confuse the various issues within the field of the theology

1. Davis, "Evangelicals," 8–11.

2. "Let us define an exclusivist religion as one whose adherents regard it as the one and only true way . . . By this definition, some of the religions of the world are clearly exclusivist. In my opinion, Christianity is one such religion" (ibid., 8).

3. Blue, "Untold Billions," 338–50. Blue does show the complexity of the issue as he points out how the question "Are they really lost?" touches the "very foundation of theology." "The character of God is questioned: 'Is God just?' This is a challenge to theology proper. The sufficiency of Christ is questioned: 'Is Christ the only way?' This is a challenge to Christology. The necessity of the Cross is questioned: 'Did Christ have to die?' This is a challenge to soteriology. The depravity of man is questioned: 'Is man inherently sinful?' This is a challenge to biblical anthropology. The judgment of sin is questioned: 'Is not evil relative?' This is a challenge to hamartiology. The role of the church is questioned: 'Is the church God's unique witness?' This is a challenge to ecclesiology. The culmination of history is questioned: 'Is there a future reckoning?' This is a challenge to eschatology" (ibid., 341).

4. Ibid., 348.

of religions, and, as a result, they have failed to illustrate the complexity of the subject. O. S. Hawkins in an article for the *Southwestern News* said, "When church leaders begin to question the validity of the exclusivity of the gospel and begin to believe that religious truth is not all important—as some have done—it is only a matter of time until long held religious confessions and doctrines lose their relevance, resulting in a theological wandering."[5] However, many evangelicals have carefully proclaimed their exclusivity in a fashion that does reflect the complexity of the subject.[6]

For Clark Pinnock, Lausanne II (1989) was the turning point for evangelicals regarding the theology of religions. In an article published in 1990, Pinnock said,

> Though one cannot be dogmatic, it seems reasonable to hope that this event will mark a turning point in our thinking and have wide repercussions in the evangelical camp worldwide. My hope would be that, just as Lausanne I in 1974 placed social action on its own agenda and subsequently onto the agenda of other evangelicals, so Lausanne II will become our Vatican II, opening people's minds up to a more globally inclusive vision. In any case, the time has come for evangelicals to begin to address the issues surrounding dialogue and a Christian theology of religions.[7]

In this article, Pinnock outlines a proposal, consisting of two inseparable axioms and three recommendations for an evangelical theology of religions. Pinnock maintains the universality of God's salvation, and his "first axiom insists that the promises of God are not tribal or restrictive . . . The gospel has an emphatically global reach."[8] His second axiom maintains that salvation is provided only through Jesus Christ. "Salvation has been provided for all humanity through the person and work of Jesus Christ his only Son. Because he gave his life as expiation for sin and rose again there is a basis of a salvation to offer and the knowledge of the gracious God. Apart from Jesus we would not have sufficient reason to believe that there is a generous God with a saving global reach or think to approach him as our merciful Savior . . . God saves the many through the One."[9] This exclusivity, Pinnock

---

5. Hawkins, "Question for Our Time," 12.

6. As we shall see in the next essay, some evangelicals have extended their exclusivity of Jesus Christ to an exclusivity of recipients of salvation. Other evangelicals have taken an inclusivist approach.

7. Pinnock, "Toward an Evangelical," 359–60.

8. Ibid., 361.

9. Ibid., 362.

points out, is in opposition to the theocentric approaches of some religious pluralists such as John Hick and Paul Knitter. He stresses that "the high Christology of traditional theology does not entail a narrow conception of God's grace."[10] For Clark Pinnock, Jesus Christ is the exclusive agent by which God provides salvation to the whole world.[11]

In a very polemic article, Donald G. Bloesch, Professor of Theology at the University of Dubuque Theological Seminary, is primarily responding to the new theological model "with its emphasis on individuality, pluralism, and relativism."[12] However, he echoes the exclusivity of Jesus Christ while affirming the universal nature of God's mercy, which we saw in Pinnock.[13]

10. Ibid., 363. "Leaving aside their [Hick and Knitter's] momentous decision to regard belief in the incarnation as a myth, one must also question the idea that Christians can be God-centered in a meaningful way without also being Christ-centered . . . The "God" of religious pluralism tends to be completely unknowable like Kant's noumenon, something beyond good and evil, beyond personhood, undefinable and an inconceivable mystery" (ibid.).

11. While they are outside the scope of this present essay, it is interesting to note the three recommendations given by Pinnock in this article. (1) "We ought to view other religions in the framework in which we view everything else as Christians—namely, in the context of the kingdom of God, which has come proleptically into world history in advance of its final consummation. God is moving in to reign, and his power is challenging the powers of darkness and entering into conflict with them" (ibid., 364). 2) "We need to recognize that the situation with religions is analogous to the human cultures they are part of. If cultures can change and if Christ can transform them, then why not religions? If we grant the possibility of Christ transforming culture, we should grant the possibility of Christ transforming religions as well" (ibid., 366). (3) "Finally, there is a fresh thinking to be done in the area of the last things. As mentioned above, we need to entertain the larger Biblical hope. The gospel does not let us remain complacent with the scenario that consigns the majority to hell and expects the salvation of only a pitiful few. (Make no mistake, this harsh expectation is precisely what the traditional view entails.) The God and Father of our Lord Jesus is far more generous than that, and his promises are much larger than that" (ibid., 367; parenthetical remark is Pinnock's.) This exclusivist position, while being restrictive regarding the agency of salvation, does not entail a restrictivism regarding religious knowledge.

12. Bloesch, "Finality of Christ," 5.

13. "Against the new theologies Christians faithful to the biblical revelation must again affirm what Emil Brunner aptly called the scandal of *particularity*—the inexplicable fact that God revealed himself among one particular people in history, the Jews, that God became man at one point in history, and that his revelation in this people and in this person is definitive and final. God revealed himself once for all in this particular event or events. In the catholic evangelical theology I uphold, the superiority of Christianity lies in its willingness to be continually purified and reformed in light of the one great revelation of God in Jesus Christ, which cannot be duplicated by only heralded and obeyed. As biblical Christians we must also affirm the scandal of *universality*, viz., that this one revelation is intended for all, that Christ's salvation goes out to all, including the outsider and the sinner. The kingdom of God seeks to embrace not only the people of Israel, not only people of faith, but the whole world, including

This tension of universality/particularity has implications for the relationship between Christians and the major religions of the world.

> Biblical Christianity affirms that the Christian religion is founded on a unique revelation of God to humankind in the person of Jesus Christ and that this religion is a sign and witness to God's self-revelation. Christianity as a revelation must be distinguished from Christianity as an empirical religion, but the former can be perceived only through the eyes of faith . . . Thus the world religions should be treated not as ways to salvation but perhaps as pointers to salvation. Then they would not be categorically or uniformly repudiated as agencies of damnation, but regarded as signs of contradiction, for their conceptions of God unfailingly conflict with God's disclosure of himself in Jesus Christ.[14]

Continuing his polemic tone Bloesch claims, "The battle today is between the historical Christian faith with its confession of the reality of a supernatural God and the uniqueness of Jesus Christ, and the new spirituality, which embraces most of the recent theological and religious movements."[15]

Not all evangelicals see the battle lines so neatly drawn. "In Jesus Christ God acted decisively for human salvation: to do something which needed to be done, which had never been done before, and which would never be done again,"[16] claims Robert Culpepper, while calling for an open-ended exclusivism, a position to be explored in the next essay. Nor have all evangelicals embraced the term "exclusivism" when speaking of their own position, even though their position exemplifies what is called exclusivism. Stanley Grenz, after surveying the contemporary options in which he discusses exclusivism, inclusivism, and pluralism, turns his attention to the "Biblical Foundations of a Theology of the Religions."[17] He notes the biblical themes of creation, fall, and new creation, and maintains that an evangelical

---

the enemies of faith, though the pathway into the kingdom is only through faith and repentance. Christ died not for the righteous but for sinners; he justifies not the godly but the ungodly" (ibid., 6).

14. Ibid., 7. Bloesch's position is similar to Emil Brunner's. "All this the world of religions knows in a fragmentary and distorted form, as almost unrecognizable 'relics' of an 'original' revelation. From the standpoint of Jesus Christ, the non-Christian religions seem like stammering words from some half-forgotten saying. None of them is without a breath of the Holy, and yet none of them is the Holy. None is without its impressive truth, and yet none of them is the Truth; for their Truth is Jesus Christ" (Brunner, *Revelation and Reason*, 270).

15. Bloesch, "Finality of Christ," 9.
16. Culpepper, "Lordship of Christ," 318.
17. Grenz, "Toward an Evangelical," 55.

theology of religions should be developed within these motifs. His rejection of the contemporary options opens the door for several significant insights. "Evangelicals often conclude that Christianity is the only legitimate expression of special revelation, understood as the sole saving self-disclosure of God, and then deny any saving significance in all other religions. As we have seen, however, the Bible allows no such unequivocal rejection of the possibility of either faith or true worship beyond the central salvation-historical trajectory of Israel and the church."[18] Furthermore, Grenz shows an appreciation of other religious traditions and acknowledges their contribution to promoting community, which he understands as "God's overarching intent."[19] However, Grenz maintains an exclusivism regarding the agency of salvation. "Christians must maintain the finality of Christ. We may find insight in the religions, even affirm them as embodiments of aspects of God's intention for humankind. But, in the end, we humbly conclude that no other religious vision encapsulates the final purpose of God as we have come to understand it. Both the divine diagnosis of the human predicament and the ultimate answer are given in Christ."[20]

While evangelicals have expressed their exclusivism regarding the agency of salvation in various ways and with varying degrees of humility, Harold Netland provides a careful presentation of this position. In the context of setting forth six general foundational themes for an evangelical theology of religions, he provides a clear yet concise statement of the evangelical position.

> 5. *In his mercy God has provided a way, through the atoning work of Jesus Christ on the cross, for sinful persons to be reconciled to God.* Here we confront one of the great mysteries in Scripture—the Creator is gracious and merciful, a God of love who

---

18. Ibid., 60.
19. Ibid., 61.
20. Ibid., 63. Grenz vividly illustrates why the subcategories are needed to capture the evangelical stances within the theology of religions. While maintaining an exclusivist approach regarding agency, he embraces, at least, an inclusivist attitude toward truth. "Our claim does not intend to deny the presence of divine knowledge beyond the boundaries of the church, however. Just as in the biblical era, so also today, wherever people are drawn—even through other religions—to worship the Most High God, there the true God is known. For all the exclusivism it implies, the confession of the finality of Christ nevertheless remains an inclusivist—perhaps even a pluralist—declaration. It means that wherever God is truly known, the God who is known is none other than the One who is revealed through Jesus Christ . . . This confession means that Jesus is the vehicle through whom we come to the fullest understanding of what God is like . . . [T]he finality of Christ means that through the incarnate life of Jesus we discover the truest vision of the nature of God" (ibid., 64).

deeply cares for all people (Jn 3:16; 1 Jn 4:8). God's terrible wrath against sin and unfathomable love for all persons come together in a marvelous way in the life, death and resurrection of Jesus of Nazareth. In the incarnation—an utterly unique, one-time event in which the eternal Creator became man and took upon himself the sins of the world (2 Cor 5:21)—God himself took the initiative, proving a way for sinful persons to be forgiven and reconciled with him (Jn 3:16-18; Eph 2:4-5; 1 Pet 3:18). God's love for all people is manifest most clearly in the cross, when he gave his own Son to suffer and die as our substitute to pay the penalty for our sin (1 Jn 4:9-10). Salvation is rooted in the sinless person and atoning work of Jesus Christ (Rom 3:25; 2 Cor 5:18-19, 21; Heb 2:17; 1 Jn 2:2; 4:10), and it is because of this that Jesus is the only Savior for all of humankind, including followers of other religions. No one is reconciled to God except through the cross of Jesus Christ.[21]

The evangelical exclusivistic position is clearly a Christocentric view.[22] Evangelical exclusivists find support for their position of the centrality of Jesus Christ in the New Testament writings.[23] Furthermore, they maintain that the traditional orthodox understanding of Jesus Christ within Christianity has been that Jesus Christ is the only way to God.[24] Jesus Christ

---

21. Netland, *Encountering Religious Pluralism*, 319 (italics original). His other five foundational themes are 1. One eternal God, 2. God as sovereign, 3. God as gracious, 4. God's creation, and 6. The community of the redeemed.

22. Referring to the evangelical stance as being Christocentric is made in the context of discussing the agency of salvation. We shall see in the next essay that while some evangelicals will maintain a Christocentric position regarding the recipients of salvation, some evangelicals will take an ecclesiocentric position.

23. Cf. Matt 11:27; Luke 12:8-9; John 14:6; Acts 4:12; Rom 3:21-26; 5:12-21; 1 Tim 2:5-6.

24. This claim is difficult to support based upon the early church fathers. "In the conception of the Fathers there is less clarity concerning the saving work of Christ than there is concerning the person of Christ . . . [A]ll the Fathers speak of the vicarious suffering of Christ. There is no reflection upon the question why and how Christ's work has redeeming power . . . While there are no errors in the[ir] views, a unified and systematic teaching is lacking" (Heick, *History of Christian Thought*, 48–49). Also, see Kelly, *Early Christian Doctrines*, 375). However, it would be incorrect to assume that the early church fathers ignored the issue of atonement. Irenaeus (125–202) developed the recapitulation theory; Origen (185–254) proposed the ransom theory; and Pelagius suggested a moral-example theory. The first systematic treatment of the substitutionary atonement comes from the eleventh century with Anselm's *Cur deus homo*, which may be viewed as the satisfaction theory. While the early church did not develop a statement regarding why Jesus Christ is considered the only way to God, the position has been developed within what is perceived as traditional orthodox Christianity. For example, the "vicarious atonement in the Christian system is made by the *offended* party. God is

being the sole agency for salvation captures the heart and soul of evangelical thought. Donald Bloesch claims that the core of evangelical theology is Jesus Christ and evangelism. "Of the various meanings associated with the term *evangelical*, the theological meaning is primary. *Evangelical* is derived from the Greek word *evangelion*, meaning message of salvation through the atoning sacrifice of Christ. It contains a missionary thrust because it is centered in the proclamation to the world of the good news of salvation. It also entails an appeal to conversion and decision on the basis of the free grace of God."[25] An exclusivist position regarding the agency of salvation promotes both a high Christology and evangelism. We have seen that while evangelicals have spoken in unison, they have expressed their exclusivism in symphonic fashion. However, how are we to evaluate their position? This evaluation will consider four issues that I outlined in the previous essay: internal consistency, viability, harmony between empirical knowledge and implications or presuppositions of position, and its relation to other alternative positions.

Internal Consistency

As a conceptual system, is evangelical thought regarding the vehicle or means of salvation internally consistent? Is it logically possible to embrace as true the basic beliefs of evangelical theology and at the same time embrace their exclusivity regarding agency? Furthermore, is the evangelical stance of exclusivity consistent with the basic conceptual system of Christianity?

Whether the evangelical stance is internally consistent with its own conceptual system is not the most interesting issue; however, we must start with this question before addressing issues that are more interesting. Given the basic characteristics of evangelicalism as set forth in the preface and the first essay, the exclusivist stance regarding agency of salvation is consistent, although a potential problem is readily raised. The exclusivist stance clearly is consistent with its commitment and understanding of the Christian Scriptures. Furthermore, evangelicals must be evangelistic for two reasons. First, the Scriptures command believers to go and make disciples, to proclaim the good news. Second, if Jesus Christ is in fact the only way, then out of love for God and for their fellow humans, they must be evangelistic. However, the third thread or aspect of evangelicalism suggested in the preface is that

---

the party against whom sin is committed, and he is the party who atones for its commission. Vicarious atonement, consequently, is the highest conceivable exhibition of the attribute of mercy" (Shedd, *Dogmatic Theology* 2:384).

25. Bloesch, *Essentials of Evangelical Theology*, 1:7.

evangelicalism exhibits a level of theological tolerance absent in other forms of conservative Protestant Christianity. If evangelicals maintain that Jesus Christ is the only means of salvation, then it may be questioned how they can be considered theologically tolerant. At the center of this critique lies an assumption that one could not maintain an exclusivistic stance regarding agency and at the same time be theologically tolerant. However, it is unclear why this assumption should be considered true. To be theologically tolerant does not entail or even imply that one accepts as true theological positions with which one disagrees. To be theologically tolerant means to have an attitude that allows others to hold positions contrary to one's own even if you believe them to be wrong.[26] What is critical here is the attitude with which evangelicals hold their exclusivist stance. From Ramm through Pinnock to Grenz, evangelical leaders have maintained the need to hold their position with an attitude of humility.[27] Unfortunately, human nature, as well as uninformed comments, has prevailed, and the attitude of humility has been missing at times. While this situation does misrepresent the evangelical position, it does not support a claim that within the evangelical stance an internal inconsistency exists. It does suggest that at times evangelicals have practiced a bad theology.

A much more interesting and problematic issue emerges when one asks whether the exclusivism of evangelicals regarding agency is consistent with basic Christian thought. In other words, some might claim that this exclusivism is inconsistent with the basic Christian worldview. How might this claim be constructed?

One starting point might be the basic assumption of God's nature and from this develop an argument that shadows what is frequently referred to as the problem of evil. It is assumed that God is omniscient, omnipotent,

---

26. "We must not, however, confuse the problem of tolerance with this solution of the question of truth. Tolerance is a humane attitude, which respects the personality of the other, but it has nothing to do with the truth or falsity of the "other's" opinions and ideas. In this sense the genuine Christian missionary in particular will be "tolerant," yet at the same time he may not believe that there is any truth in the religion of those among whom he lives" (Brunner, *Revelation and Reason*, 219).

27. While humility entails tolerance, the converse is not true. This humility is not due to a preferencing of pluralism, but rather due to two basic presuppositions. First, if a truth-claim is discovered to be true, evangelicals believe their holding that truth-claim is only by the grace of God. God is the self-revealer. The second presupposition is regarding the very nature of any theological stance. Theological truth claims "should be regarded as human constructions rather than universal absolutes embodying divine truth" (Cohn-Sherbok, "Jewish Religious Pluralism," 326–327). All theological stances should be held with humility for they are theoretical frameworks, which may be wrong. Evangelicals, as should all theologians, should exhibit an attitude of humility. This attitude, however, should not preclude the taking of a stance.

and omnibenevolent. Added to this assumption is the empirical evidence that most individuals, in the history of time, never hear the gospel message regarding Jesus Christ; hence, most individuals lack the opportunity to respond favorably to Jesus Christ. This conclusion leads to two distinct issues: one issue dealing with recipients of salvation and the other with agency. The former issue lies outside the scope of this essay, but the second clearly is pertinent. If Jesus Christ is the exclusive agency of salvation, then most individuals in human history were born without even having an opportunity for salvation. However, this scenario is contradictory to a God who is omniscient, omnipotent, and omnibenevolent. Hence, exclusivism is false and God must provide all individuals equal opportunity to salvation.[28] If this charge cannot be answered, then it is possible that the evangelical stance is inconsistent with basic Christian thought.

Within evangelical thought, there are at least three different approaches for responding to the charge. (These approaches are not mutually exclusive.) One approach has been to focus on the type of knowledge, which some claim that God has, known as "middle" knowledge. A second approach is to focus on the work of Jesus Christ and its ramifications. Evangelicals, like other Christians, will point out that the dilemma created above is a false dilemma. While it is true that God is omniscient, omnipotent, and omnibenevolent, God is more than what these three terms capture. We will briefly survey each response.

William Lane Craig offers an excellent discussion of Luis Molina's doctrine of middle knowledge.[29]

> God possesses knowledge of all true counterfactual propositions, including counterfactuals of creaturely freedom . . . , He knows what contingent states of affairs would obtain if certain

---

28. Exclusivism is not the only position open to this charge. Both pluralism and inclusivism are also proven to be false if this accusation is misapplied. Since all religions are historical, that is they develop in time, there are individuals who existed prior to the development of religion; hence some individuals fall outside of the agency of salvation advocated by any religion. The exception to this problem would be a theology that advocates a universalism in which all individuals are saved based upon the essential nature of individuals, or more precisely things. However, it is unclear how this move ultimately avoids the charge. What becomes critical, when we understand the depth of this charge, is how the faith tradition provides for an explanation of or solution to the problem, or both. Whether one embraces a pluralist approach to agency or an exclusivist approach, the foundational reply must give an explanation that is consistent with the other beliefs of the tradition. The solution to the charge appears, in some cases, only as we consider the issue of recipients of salvation. Hence, the charge does not necessarily prove any particular approach to agency as false; the charge merely highlights a problem that the approach must be capable of handling within its own system of thought.

29. Craig, "No Other Name," 172. Molina (1535–1600) was a Spanish Jesuit.

antecedent states of affairs were to obtain; . . . God knows what any free creature *would* do in any set of circumstances. This is not because the circumstances causally determine the creature's choice, but simply because this is how the creature would freely choose. God thus knows that were He to actualize certain states of affairs, then certain other contingent states of affairs would obtain.[30]

Based on middle knowledge, Craig shows that the propositions "God is omniscient, omnipotent, and omnibenevolent," and "Some individuals do not have the apparent opportunity to accept the gospel message" are consistent. According to the middle knowledge defense, God knew that some individuals would freely choose not to accept the message even if they were given the opportunity.

> For God in His providence has so arranged the world that anyone who would receive Christ has the opportunity to do so. Since God loves all persons and desires the salvation of all, He supplies sufficient grace for salvation to every individual, and nobody who would receive Christ if he were to hear the gospel will be denied that opportunity. As Molina puts it, our salvation is in our own hands.[31]

While Craig does not offer an argument for middle knowledge, he does show that if counterfactual discussions are brought into the discussion and if one assumes that God does have middle knowledge, then the exclusivism regarding agency is not inconsistent with basic Christian notions of God.[32]

A second type of response to the charge of inconsistency is to focus on the work of Jesus Christ and its ramifications. Evangelical theology understands the work of Christ regarding atonement to have cosmic effects. While different theological persuasions within the evangelical camp may apply the atoning work differently, there is a consensus that more than the "church" benefit from the work of Jesus Christ.[33] Bloesch says, "The

---

30. Ibid., 177–78.
31. Ibid., 186.
32. Craig closes his article with a statement that reflects the humility that other evangelicals have expressed. "No orthodox Christian *likes* the doctrine of hell or delights in anyone's condemnation. I truly wish that universalism were true, but it is not. My compassion toward those in other world religions is therefore expressed, not in pretending that they are not lost and dying without Christ, but by my supporting and making every effort myself to communicate to them the life-giving message of salvation through Christ" (ibid., 186–87).
33. Millard Erickson claims that our understanding of the order of God's decrees influences our understanding of the possible benefits the work of Christ has for the

atonement of Jesus Christ signifies a transformation of the human situation, and not simply the possibility of a future salvation."[34] He favorably refers to both Luther and P. T. Forsyth as they remind "us of the cosmic dimensions of the atonement, . . . His [Jesus Christ's] victory is the basis for every man's reconciliation."[35] Norman Geisler, who holds the position that salvation only comes through the gospel of Jesus Christ (so that general revelation is insufficient for salvation)[36] supports an unlimited atonement view.[37] Stuart Hackett expresses very nicely the evangelical position that the exclusivity of agency is not inconsistent with basic Christianity because of the scope of the work of Jesus Christ.

> Nor is the unique and unparalleled mediatorship of Jesus universal merely in taking in the whole scope of humanity since

---

world outside the church. He lists the three basic positions and the logical order within each position. "Supralapsarianism: 1. The decree to save (elect) some and reprobate others. 2. The decree to create both the elect and the reprobate. 3. The decree to permit the fall of both the elect and the reprobate. 4. The decree to provide salvation only for the elect. Infralapsarianism: 1. the decree to create human beings. 2. The decree to permit the fall. 3. The decree to elect some and reprobate others. 4. The decree to provide salvation only for the elect. Sublapsarianism: 1. The decree to create human beings. 2. The decree to permit the fall. 3. The decree to provide salvation sufficient for all. 4. The decree to save some and reprobate others." Both supralapsarianism and infralapsarianism limit the salvific effects of atonement to the elect, whereas sublapsarianism understands the atonement to be unlimited or universal in its intent. (Erickson, *Christian Theology*, 842–43).

34. Bloesch, *Essentials of Evangelical Theology*, 1:162.

35. Ibid., 162. Bloesch himself is of the Reformed tradition, but rejects A. A. Hodge's understanding of limited atonement. Rather, Bloesch claims, "the truth in the doctrine of limited or definite atonement is that its efficacy does not extend to all persons. It is universal in its outreach and intention but particular in its efficacy. Perhaps we can say that all mankind is reconciled and justified in principle (de jure) but not in fact (de facto) insofar as not all have apprehended and appropriated their justification and redemption" (ibid., 165).

36. Geisler, *Systematic Theology*, 458–63.

37. "The biblical, theological, and historical basis for the universal (unlimited) extent of the Atonement are solid. With one notable and explainable exception (the later Augustine), there is no significant voice in the whole history of the church up to the Reformers that defended limited atonement. Indeed, the Bible is emphatic that God loved the whole fallen world and that Christ died for the same. The theological arguments spring from God's omnibenevolence are powerfully in favor of unlimited atonement—that Christ died for the sins of all human beings. Any denial of this truth arbitrarily limits God's love to only some and is based on an indefensible form of voluntarism" (ibid., 387). Erickson also embraces the unlimited atonement position. "We conclude that the hypothesis of universal atonement is able to account for a larger segment of the biblical witness with less distortion than is the hypothesis of limited atonement" (*Christian Theology*, 851).

Jesus' historical appearance. It is also universal in time by including that entire segment of humanity that preceded Jesus in the humanly historical sense, so that all those who were truly committed to God before the historical appearance of Jesus were nevertheless encompassed by divine grace and forgiveness through the vicarious redemption in Jesus—even though that redemptive vocation had not yet been historically fulfilled, and even though these previously admitted members of the divine spiritual community were totally ignorant (or, in some cases, no more than vaguely and imprecisely aware through prophecy that they did not clearly understand) of the historical form that God's redemptive provision would assume in Jesus (Rom 3:25; Heb 2:9; 9:14, 15). In a sense, then, there is a sort of exclusivism here, since it is being claimed that salvation in Jesus is God's only objective redemptive provision for all the times and ages of man, for all the cultures and civilizations of the human species. But it is not a morally or logically objectionable exclusivism, since it is thus exclusive only by its total inclusiveness of all humanity within the scope of Jesus' redemptive satisfaction to the unconditional claim of divine moral law on all of the same humanity (1 John 2:2). Just because Jesus is the *one* Redeemer, it is the case that absolutely *no* human being is excluded from Jesus' totally unlimited saving provision.[38]

Finally, evangelicals, like other Christians, will point out that the dilemma created above is a false dilemma. While evangelicals claim that God is omniscient, omnipotent, and omnibenevolent, they believe these characteristics only capture part of the picture regarding God. God is more than these three terms portray. Basic Christian thought has also embraced the position that God is holy, just, merciful, and so forth. Thus, the objection is based on a partial understanding of who God is. Hence, the exclusivity regarding agency, which is held by evangelicals, does satisfy internal consistency.

Viability

Is the evangelical stance of exclusivism regarding agency of salvation a viable position? This criterion brings two aspects into the discussion. First, is this stance useful? Does it do any work within the theology of religions for

---

38. Hackett, *Reconstruction of the Christian Revelation Claim*, 244. Some of the implications of Hackett's statement will be seen in the following essay where it will be suggested that many evangelicals have taken an inclusivist stance regarding the recipients of salvation.

evangelicals? This aspect is pragmatic in nature, but an important aspect of viability. Second, does this stance fit in with evangelical ideas? This second aspect is different from internal consistency discussed above. Instead of focusing on whether the stance and basic evangelical ideas can be held to be true at the same time, here the focus is how well this stance harmonizes with basic evangelical ideas.

Is this stance useful for evangelicals working within the field of the theology of religions? We can identify at least three ways the exclusivity of agency is (potentially) useful for evangelicals. First, it provides the foundation for evangelicals to work in this area of theology. As I indicated above, evangelicals hold a high Christology. Jesus Christ is the foundation of all their theology. Second, it promotes humility. If Jesus Christ is the only way to God and an evangelical believes he or she has a relationship with God, then that relationship did not come about because of the superiority of the individual, but by the grace of God for providing the way and then making it known to that individual. Finally, the stance of exclusivity should be a stimulus for engaging in dialogue with those who are God-seekers within other faith traditions. If Jesus Christ is the unique savior of all peoples, then evangelicals must be compelled to bring this unique message to the roundtable of interreligious dialogue. While the evangelical's stance on agency is useful, there is little question whether they have appropriated this usefulness and placed themselves at the roundtables of dialogue. While the stance is viable in this aspect, North American evangelicals have been negligent in applying this important stance.

The second aspect of viability inquires whether the stance harmonizes with basic evangelical ideas. This question forces us back to the bipolar theological method suggested by Clark Pinnock and presented in the first section of this essay. For this position of exclusivism to be viable, it must be faithful to the historical Christian faith and, at the same time, it must be authentic and responsible to the contemporary situation. The former situation presents little problem for the evangelical. The latter may be problematic, and it is best considered as we address the third criterion for assessing conceptual systems.

The evangelical stance that Jesus Christ is the only way to God does represent the historical Christian faith, but is the historical position even viable? Is historical Christianity useful in the contemporary situation? It is viable if we understand that salvation begins with the fall. If the fall did not occur, then salvation would not be needed; there would not be alienation, condemnation, or enslavement, which persons currently experience.[39] Fur-

---

39. Grenz, *Created for Community*, 99.

thermore, the historical Christian faith has acknowledged the holiness of God. It has maintained that the doctrine of salvation is based on the nature of God and the nature of persons. As a result of the fall, God and humanity, the Creator and the creature, fell out of community, and the creation has been judged and enslaved. Because of this state of affairs, drastic measures were required if there was to be a restoration of fellowship. As Bloesch points out, "one cannot begin to fathom the mystery of the cross unless one perceives both God's anguish over sin and his inviolable holiness that refuses to tolerate sin."[40] Salvation, the process of restoring the fellowship between Creator and creature, restoring community among persons, obtaining forgiveness, and obtaining freedom, requires a mediator, one who brings the Creator and creature back together. Within traditional Christianity this mediator is Jesus Christ; hence, the evangelical stance is faithful to the historical faith,[41] and the historical faith is useful in the contemporary situation for it offers humankind hope.[42]

Harmony between Empirical Knowledge and Presuppositions of Position

While the evangelical stance that Jesus Christ is the only way to God is viable, it may be problematic given the contemporary pluralist world today. At issue is a presupposition held by some evangelicals that seems out of harmony with the empirical knowledge we have regarding the religious diversity of our contemporary world. Before discussing this presupposition, it may be beneficial to justify using empirical knowledge in critiquing theology.

While Bruce Nicholls is not a North American evangelical, his opening paragraph of an article he wrote for *Stimulus* provides a compelling backdrop to the problem we must address at this point.

> A vital and coherent Christian theology emerges from the dynamic dialogue between the true and authoritative text—the Word of God—and the ever-changing pluralities of our human

---

40. Bloesch, *Essentials of Evangelical Theology*, 1:152.

41. Shedd, *Dogmatic Theology*, 353–77.

42. "The Fall of man in God's creation is both inconceivable and unalterably inexcusable, and therefore the word 'disobedience' does not exhaust the facts of the case. It is revolt, it is the creature's departure from the attitude which is the only possible attitude for him, it is the creature's becoming Creator, it is the destruction of creatureliness. It is defection; it is the fall from being held in creatureliness . . . The theological question does not arise about the origin of evil but about the real overcoming of evil on the Cross; it asks for the forgiveness of guilt, for the reconciliation of the fallen world" (Bonhoeffer, *Creation and Fall; Temptation*, 76).

and social context. Therefore we approach the question of the witness to the uniqueness and finality of Jesus Christ not as observers of an objective analysis of scientifically verifiable facts but as participants in the drama between God's self revelation and the created world of which we are part. We are players, not spectators. The context of doing good theology is in both the quietness of the study and the noise of the marketplace.[43]

In a very cogent fashion, Nicholls captures the tension that Pinnock calls for in his bipolar approach. The Christian theologian must struggle with the tension between the Scriptures and the world in which we are participants. While evangelicals do not want society or culture to dictate their understanding of the Scriptures, two important points must be acknowledged. First, evangelicals must understand that to some extent their society, their culture, has already influenced their understanding of the Scripture, if only in how they communicate it. Evangelical leaders are typically conscious of this issue and their hermeneutics attempt to handle this problem.[44] Second, they must be sensitive to the ever-changing social changes and reconstruct their theology in relation to those changes if necessary. Since theology is an attempt to formulate beliefs in a systematic fashion, it goes beyond the clear teachings of the Scripture, the dogma. The evangelical theologian attempts to construct a theology that is consistent with the Scriptures. While the Scriptures have not changed, their understanding of those sacred writings and the social conditions in which they apply the Scriptures is in constant change.

Due to the contemporary social conditions, evangelicals are more aware of religious pluralism and the religious beliefs of those outside the church than previous generations of evangelicals. Evangelicals today are compelled to acknowledge that in other faith traditions there are individuals

---

43. Nicholls, "Compelling Witness," 19.

44. A. Berkeley Mickelsen illustrates this as he discusses subjectivity in the interpretation process. "The interpreter, like the historian, must become involved. Hence, he cannot be a neutral spectator. It is true that this involvement may bring a wrong kind of subjectivity—that is, the interpreter may pretend to be clarifying the idea of Paul or John when in reality he is setting forth his own idea. No procedure could be more erroneous. Yet we cannot escape subjectivity in our interpretation of the Bible. An interpreter brings to bear upon the text all that he is, all that he knows, and even all that he wants to become. It will help us just to be aware that this is so. Knowing this, we must try to be so molded by God that the distortion brought about by our subjectivity will be at a minimum . . . Interpretation is more than intellectual procedures, attitudes, and assumptions, but these do enter into a man's subjectivity and consequently must always be open to correction. Failing to be open to self-correction is like a man's having 20/200 vision and steadfastly refusing to wear glasses" (Mickelsen, *Interpreting the Bible*, 65–66).

who are sincerely seeking God and whose lives are above reproach, at least from a human perspective. As a result, their theology is being challenged. Some of the presuppositions that have marked their understanding of the "heathen" do not harmonize well with the empirical evidence found in the other faith traditions.

Earlier in this essay as we were discussing whether the evangelical stance is internally consistent, we noted that the doctrine of atonement, as held by evangelicals, might provide one type of response to the charge of inconsistency with basic Christian thought. It was noted that some evangelicals hold a limited atonement position, and one form of limited atonement is supported by the position known as supralapsarianism.

> Some [Calvinists] are so zealous for particularism that they place discrimination at the root of all God's dealings with his creatures. That he has any creatures at all they suppose to be in the interest of discrimination, and all that he decrees concerning his creatures they suppose he decrees only that he may discriminate between them. They therefore place the decree of "election" by which men are made to differ, in the order of decrees, logically prior to the decree of creation itself, or at any rate prior to all that is decreed concerning man as man; that is to say, since man's history begins with the fall, prior to the decree of the fall itself. They are therefore called Supralapsarians, that is, those who place the decree of election in the order of thought prior to the decree of the fall.[45]

The presupposition of supralapsarianism is out of harmony with the contemporary pluralistic world in which some individuals who belong to other faith traditions are sincerely seeking God. However, it is not clear that this form of limited atonement is an actual objection to the evangelical stance for it is unclear that any major representative of evangelicalism today holds this position. A limited atonement position is often associated with Calvinism, and many evangelicals do have Calvinistic leanings; however, both Loraine Boettner and Louis Berkhof, representatives of the Calvinistic tradition, embrace infralapsarianism.[46] Furthermore, while this position and its sister form of limited atonement may be problematic for evangelicals regarding

---

45. Warfield, *Plan of Salvation*, 88.

46. Boettner, *Reformed Doctrine of Predestination*, 127; and Berkhof, *Systematic Theology*, 125. Strong and Thiessen, two other older theologians whom evangelicals have embraced, hold sublapsarianism, or an unlimited atonement. Strong, *Systematic Theology*, 777; and Thiessen, *Introductory Lectures in Systematic Theology*, 344. Thiessen points out that "in later life Calvin accepted the unlimited theory of atonement" (343).

their understanding of the recipients of salvation, it does not address their stance on the agency of salvation.

Relation to Other Alternative Positions

As we evaluate the evangelical's stance of exclusivism regarding the agency of salvation in relation to other alternative positions, we must take into consideration this stance in reference to other possible stances taken by other Christian theologies. We also must consider how this stance relates to other faith traditions.

As we outlined in the previous essay, there are two other basic positions regarding agency that Christian theologies have advocated. First, pluralism with respect to agency of salvation in its boldest form claims that all religions are vehicles to salvation, and no religion is more effective than another. Second, inclusivism with respect to agency of salvation claims that while not all roads lead to salvation, there are several different vehicles by which salvation is provided. Evangelicals, as well as nonevangelicals, have had much to say regarding pluralism, especially as presented by John Hick.[47] Since our purpose here is to provide an evaluation of the evangelicals' stance regarding the exclusive agency of Jesus Christ, we will not rehearse how evangelicals have critiqued Hick or pluralism itself. However, as we examine the exclusivistic stance in light of Hick's pluralism, two interesting points need to be presented. First, Hick's position is not a pluralistic stance that advocates all religions are vehicles of salvation, in spite of several claims that would support that position, such as the favorable quote with which he opens his essay on "The Pluralistic Hypothesis," from Jalau'l-Din Rumi: "The lamps are different, but the Light is the same."[48] Rather, he

> want[s] to explore the pluralistic hypothesis that the great world faiths embody different perceptions and conceptions of, and correspondingly different responses to, the Real from within the major variant ways of being human; and that within each

---

47. D'Costa, *John Hick's Theology of Religions*; Carruthers, *Uniqueness of Jesus Christ*; Griffiths and Lewis, "On Grading Religions, Seeking Truth, and Being Nice to People," 75–80; Netland, "Professor Hick on Religious Pluralism," 249–61; D'Costa, "Christian Theology and Other Religions," 161–78; McCready, "Disintegration of John Hick's Christology," 257–270; Alston, "Response of Hick," 287–88; Clark, "Perils of Pluralism," 303–20; Mavrodes, "Response of John Hick," 289–94; Plantinga, "Ad Hick," 295–98; Van Inwagen, "Reply to Professor Hick," 299–302; Meyer, "John Hick's Theology of Religions," 274–97; Kwan, "Is the Critical Trust Approach to Religious Experience," 152–69.

48. Hick, *Interpretation of Religion*, 233.

of them the transformation of human experience from self-centeredness to Reality-centredness is taking place.[49]

Hick's position regarding human transformation is not intended to include all religions; he is considering only the major faith traditions. Furthermore,

> each of the great traditions is oriented to what it regards as the Ultimate as the sole creator or source of the universe, or as that than which no greater can be conceived, or as the final ground or nature of everything. Further, the 'truthfulness' of each tradition is shown by its soteriological effectiveness. But what the traditions severally regard as ultimate are different and therefore cannot all be truly ultimate. They can however be different manifestations of the truly Ultimate within different streams of human thought-and-experience—hence the postulation of the Real *an sich* as the simplest way of accounting for the data . . . Since there cannot be a plurality of ultimates, we affirm the true ultimacy of the Real by referring to it in the singular.[50]

Those religions that do not promote transformation from self-centeredness to Reality-centeredness do not provide a means of salvation. Hick's modified or restricted pluralism is important because it appears to be more in line with the inclusivist stance regarding ultimate agency.

The second interesting point that we find as we consider the exclusivism of evangelicals in light of the pluralism of Hick stems from the postulate presented in the above quote. Hick continues,

> Without this postulate we should be left with a plurality of *personae* and *impersonae* each of which is claimed to be the Ultimate, but no one of which alone can be. We should have either to regard all the reported experiences as illusory or else return to the confessional position in which we affirm the authenticity of our own stream of religious experience whilst dismissing as illusory those occurring within other traditions.[51]

It is unclear why one should accept the disjunctive as Hick presents it. While some within the confessional position may believe that they have God, or their understanding of the Ultimate, in a box, most will acknowledge God to be more than they can say about God. Hick is correct that the creature cannot fully explain or describe the Creator. However, the evangelical theologian will be very uncomfortable with Hick when he claims that, "when we

---

49. Ibid., 240.
50. Ibid., 248–49.
51. Ibid., 249.

speak of a personal God, with moral attributes and purposes, or when we speak of the non-personal Absolute, Brahman, or of the Dharmakaya, we are speaking of the Real as humanly experienced: that is, as phenomenon."[52] For the evangelical as well as adherents of some other faith traditions, God is self-revealing. Thus to claim that God is personal, it is not merely a phenomenon, not merely the Real as humanly experienced, although we encounter the self-revealing within our own limited human experience. God is understood to be there and not silent.[53] Furthermore, why should evangelicals, who embrace the confessional position, necessarily assume that other faith traditions are illusory? Is it not possible to embrace a confessional position and still acknowledge value and truth in other faith traditions? An exclusivist stance regarding agency does not require evangelicals to view other traditions as illusory. Of course, this raises questions such as, how valuable are other traditions? And what do they say that is truth? The notion of general revelation, as historically understood by evangelicals, may be capable of making sense of the various religious languages and help the evangelical from assuming other traditions are illusory.

Finally, as we consider the evangelical stance regarding agency in relation to other alternative positions, we must consider how the position relates to positions taken by other faith traditions. Terry Muck claims that the exclusivism of evangelical thought is not unique among the world religions. "The religions of the world (at least the majority views in those religions) are as exclusivistic as Christianity. To be religious is to be committed to a single brand of religious truth."[54] Hence, the exclusivity of the evangelical stance is not an anomaly; it represents the typical response by individuals of faith.[55]

North American evangelicals, in a symphonic unison, embrace exclusivism in regards to the agency of salvation. Their claim is that Jesus Christ is the particularity through which God is drawing an alienated world back to community. Gabriel Fackre captures the evangelical position as he comments on John 4:42.

---

52. Ibid., 246.

53. "In historic Christianity a personal God creates man in His own image, and in such a case, there is nothing that would make it nonsense to consider that He would communicate to man in verbalized form. Why should He not communicate in verbalized form when He has made man a verbalized being in his thoughts as well as in communication with other men? Having created man in His own image, why should He fail to communicate to that verbalized being in such terms? The communication would then be three ways: God to man, and vice-versa; man to man; and man to himself" (Schaeffer, *God Who Is There*, 92).

54. Muck, "Evangelicals and Interreligious Dialogue," 519.

55. Some faith traditions clearly do not present an exclusivism. The Baha'i, as well as, Buddhism does not promote exclusivism.

Jesus Christ, "*the* Savior of *the* world"—for all, not the "for me" or "for us" of today's modernisms and postmodernisms. Here is a universal truth claim for Christ's scandalous particularity. But Jesus, the savior of the world from what? The answer can be found in another Johannine text, "I am the way, the truth, and the life. No one comes to the Father except through me" (John 14:6). This encompassing verse is the declaration that Jesus is the way/*hodos*/path that God makes into the world to save us from sin, thereby bringing *reconciliation* with God; to rescue us from error, bringing the *truth* of the knowledge of God, *revelation*; to deliver us from death, bringing *life* with God in all its aspects, *redemption*. Of such is the work of the Savior, the last two derivative from the first, following theologically the epexegetical role in the text of *aletheia* and *zoe* vis-à-vis the primary predicate, *hodos*.[56]

As evangelicals present their stance, they acknowledge that mistakes have been made in the name of exclusivism. For example, the lack of religious tolerance by those who embrace exclusivism has illustrated an attitude that lacks the humility, which evangelicals believe their theology demands. Evangelicals claim that those mistakes illustrate the practice of bad theology and do not count against their position.[57] When exclusivism regarding agency is portrayed by good theology, it will illustrate humility and love. It will illustrate a respect for other faith traditions.

Veli-Matti Kärkkäinen of Fuller Theological Seminary suggests that the evangelical's stance of exclusivism regarding agency of salvation may best be understood as reflecting their theology of religion and not part of their theology of religions.[58] While the theology of religions deals with how, in this case, evangelicals perceive other religions, Kärkkäinen defines the theology of religion as even more basic. It is part of the essence of their faith tradition. The issue of agency of salvation is foundational for evangelicals, hence part of their theology of religion. However, as Brunner saw, to embrace an exclusivist stance in which Jesus Christ is the only agent of salvation does have implications regarding their theology of religions.[59] As

56. Fackre, "Claiming Jesus as Savior in a Religiously Plural World," 3–4 (italics original).

57. Davis, "Evangelicals," 9.

58. Kärkkäinen, *Introduction to the Theology of Religions*, 21.

59. "The uncompromising, absolute attitude toward the world religions is the natural and inevitable consequence of the Christian faith itself. There is only one Jesus Christ, who was crucified for us, and has risen again for us; there is only one Mediator and one Saviour; hence 'there is none other name given under heaven whereby we must be saved'" (Brunner, *Revelation and Reason*, 220–21).

the following essays focus on the work of evangelicals in the theology of religions, we will note this work is based upon their foundational belief of Jesus Christ as the only way to God.

As we have surveyed the North American evangelical's theology of religion in regards to the issue of agency of salvation, we saw a clear stance of exclusivism. As we move forward in the next essay, we shall continue to look at the theology of religion as developed by evangelicals, but we will become increasingly interested in whether their theology of religion can produce an adequate theology of religions.

4

Religious Diversity and Evangelical Thought

Recipients of Salvation

In the previous essay, we saw that North American evangelicals proclaimed, in a symphonic unison, Jesus Christ as the exclusive means by which God provides salvation. At the end of that essay it was suggested that this position might best be viewed as part of their theology of religion. For evangelicals, it is the cornerstone of the Christian religion, the ontological foundation for the Christian faith and the salvation provided by this tradition. Given this cornerstone, what impact does it have as they begin to develop their theology of religions? Given their exclusivism regarding agency, how does this stance affect their response to the question, who are the recipients of salvation? With this question, the issue moves from the ontological issue to an epistemological one. What does the recipient of salvation have to *know* of Jesus Christ in order to appropriate salvation? Before I proceed on this excursion, I will present, very briefly, the normative evangelical understanding of the process of salvation, partly because evangelicals again speak in symphonic unison at this level, and partly because this understanding of the process of salvation provides a foundation for the symphonic response to the question of salvation's recipients—a response that lacks uniformity.

Evangelicalism, like other Christian theologies, understands salvation to be a process that includes justification, sanctification, and glorification. It is a process capturing at the same time both a here-and-now and a not-yet understanding. While the need for salvation is rooted in the fall, whereby sin entered the world, and while salvation influences the recipient's life in the world, salvation is not culminated until the eschaton, when God completes glorification and brings about a new heaven and a new earth. An individual, evangelicals hold, is justified when he/she accepts or appropriates the atoning work of Jesus Christ. Upon being justified, the believer becomes part of the bride of Christ, the church universal. Justification is understood to be immediate and does not necessarily involve external signs. The process of sanctification is that process of becoming more mature in his/her relationship with God, becoming more Christ-like. Typically, within evangelical thought, this process is nurtured in a local, visible church or community of believers. While different groups within evangelicalism may identify minor nuances in the above description, this is their normative understanding of the process of salvation. This creates a clear picture regarding who the recipients of salvation are: Christians who are living Christ-like lives. Millard Erickson presents the Protestant position in five clear points.

1. All persons have sinned. There is no such thing as a person who obeys God completely. All humans not only sin, but they are sinners by nature as well as by choice.

2. God is completely holy and as such expects his human creatures to be holy as he is holy.

3. As a violation of God's law and person, sin must be atoned for by payment of the penalty attached to it.

4. This provision of atonement for human sin has been made through Jesus Christ's sacrificial death.

5. The salvation accomplished through Christ's atoning death must be accepted by sinful humans. Its efficacy is not automatic.[1]

However, is the picture as clear as it may appear? Given the religious diversity of their modern communities and the work of individuals such as Clark Pinnock, John Sanders, and Stanley Grenz, North American evangelicals are reexamining their theology so that while it is faithful to the Scriptures and historical faith, it also communicates in a pluralistic society without negating the importance of evangelism and mission.

In the previous essay, we quoted Clark Pinnock as he saw hope that the Lausanne II conference might signal a change among evangelicals.[2] In June 1992, under the supervision of the Theological Commission of the World Evangelical Fellowship (now known as World Evangelical Alliance), eighty-five theologians from around the world convened in Manila. The theme of the conference was "The Unique Christ in Our Pluralistic World," and the participants produced the Manila Declaration, which was significant in

---

1. Erickson, *How Shall They Be Saved?*, 49–50.

2. "Lausanne II will become our Vatican II, opening people's minds up to a more globally inclusive vision. . . . [T]he time has come for evangelicals to begin to address the issues surrounding dialogue and a Christian theology of religions" (Pinnock, "Toward an Evangelical," 359–60).

several ways. Regarding the question, is it possible that there might be salvation in other religions? The participants claimed

> the question is misleading because it implies that religions have the power to save us. This is not true. Only God saves. All people have sinned, all people deserve condemnation, all salvation stems solely from the person and atoning work of Jesus Christ, and this salvation can be appropriated solely through trust in God's mercy.[3]

This claim is consistent with the findings of the previous essay: evangelicals maintain an exclusivism regarding agency of salvation. This stance and other points of agreement among evangelicals were also cited in the declaration.[4] However, the most significant point, relevant to the issue of recipients of salvation, was the acknowledgment that a consensus was not reached on a proper understanding of particularism. Up until the mid-twentieth century, particularism had been the traditional perspective of Christianity. Harold Netland says,

> This perspective can be described theologically in terms of the following three principles: (1) The Bible is God's distinctive written revelation; it is true and fully authoritative; and thus, where the claims of Scripture are incompatible with those of other faiths, the latter are to be rejected. (2) Jesus Christ is the unique incarnation of God, fully God and fully man, and only through the person and work of Jesus is there the possibility of salvation. (3) God's saving grace is not mediated through the teachings, practices or institutions of other religions.[5]

However, the participants of the Manila conference distinguished two kinds of particularism relevant to the theology of religions. Veli-Matti Kärkkäinen describes the two kinds in the following way:

> The more exclusive version, according to which only those who hear the gospel and respond to it in faith may be saved, is distinguished from a more generic particularism that, while not necessarily defining definitively the doctrine of salvation,

---

3. "WEF Manila Declaration," in Nicholls, ed., *Unique Christ*, 14.

4. "We did agree that salvation is to be found nowhere else than in Jesus Christ. The truth to be found in other religious teachings is not sufficient, in and of itself, to provide salvation. We further agreed that universalism (that all people without exception will be saved) is not biblical. Lastly, we agreed that our discussion of this issue must not in any way undercut the passion to proclaim, without wavering, faltering or tiring, the good news of salvation through trust in Jesus Christ" (ibid., 15).

5. Netland, *Encountering Religious Pluralism*, 48.

upholds the uniqueness of Christ among other savior figures of world religions. Those who hold the latter version of particularism may have differing views about the salvation of those who have never heard of Christ.[6]

On the one hand, particularism was understood in terms of an exclusivist stance regarding individual recipients of salvation. On the other hand, it was understood in terms of an inclusivist stance regarding recipients of salvation. Both positions maintain a high Christology; both positions view the Scripture as authoritative, but they differ regarding the potential salvation of those who have never heard of Jesus Christ. While the Manila Declaration documented the divide, Clark Pinnock's *Wideness in God's Mercy* was, and continues to be, the stimulus for heated theological debate among evangelicals.[7] As the twentieth century ended, North American evangelicals were divided on this issue, and those who embraced the exclusivist stance regarding recipients of salvation looked upon the inclusivists with suspicion as "selling out to pluralism." The remainder of this essay will provide illustrations of these two stances within evangelical thought. We begin with a brief review of Pinnock's *Wideness in God's Mercy*.

Departing from the Augustinian tradition, which holds that "God chooses a few who will be saved and has decided not to save the vast majority of humanity,"[8] and has been a benchmark for evangelical theology, Pinnock lays the foundation of his theology of religions in an "optimism of salvation" that is rooted in the universal love of God. He believes in the unbounded generosity of God and shows how this universal orientation is based on the Scriptures. This discussion, unfortunately, is marred by several glaring problems. Pinnock, in defending his inclusivist stance regarding recipients of salvation, assumes that exclusivism entails restrictivism in the strongest form, not merely particularism.[9] He does not defend this assumption and

---

6. Kärkkäinen, *Introduction to the Theology of Religions*, 147.

7. Pinnock, *Wideness in God's Mercy*. Pinnock has indicated that he wrote *Wideness in God's Mercy* in order to "stimulate restrictivists, who predominate in the leadership of evangelicalism, to explain their position better and to join the wider debate over religious pluralism" (Pinnock, "Response," 251.) John Sanders also, provided a source for further debate. ("Is Belief in Christ Necessary for Salvation?," 241–59; Sanders, "Perennial Debate," 20–21; Sanders, *No Other Name*; and Sanders, "Evangelical Responses to Salvation Outside the Church," 45–48).

8. Pinnock, *Wideness in God's Mercy*, 19. Whether Pinnock's description of the Augustinian tradition is accurate is open to discussion. The primary point of question is his phrase "has decided not to save the vast majority of humanity."

9. In the "Introduction" critical terms are defined. "By 'exclusivism' I mean the position that maintains Christ as the Savior of the world and other religions largely as zones of darkness. I will also speak of 'restrictivism,' which restricts hope to people who have

seems to ignore that evangelical thought is broader than the strict Reformed tradition, which claims that the salvific work of the cross-event is limited to the elect (i.e., the positions called limited atonement and supralapsarianism). Furthermore, his "hermeneutic of hopefulness" is flawed by his assumption that there is an inconsistency between exclusivism and the universal love of God. Historically, evangelicalism has embraced both points.[10]

More positively, Pinnock maintains that a biblical understanding of religions will acknowledge that some religions or aspects of a religion are false in that they promote activities that are contrary to the God of the Bible. However, he points out that we will also find aspects, such as moral conduct, of many religions that are consistent with Christian understanding. This is because of "common grace" or "prevenient grace". That is, evangelicals cannot simply dismiss other religious traditions as evil counterparts of the true religion, Christianity. Furthermore, he advocates that evangelicals, as truth-seekers, must engage in meaningful dialogue with those of other religious traditions and outlines some of the necessary conditions for such a dialogue.[11] Finally, Pinnock's concern turns to "hope for the unevangelized." After a discussion of universalism, which he refutes, Pinnock touches upon numerous eschatological topics ranging from annihilationism, postmortem encounter, and motivations for Christian missions. He concludes, "Hell is not the prison from which people are longing to be freed, but a sit-in where sinners have barricaded themselves in to keep God out."[12]

---

put their faith in Jesus Christ in this earthly life. By 'inclusivism' I refer to the view upholding Christ as the Savior of humanity but also affirming God's saving presence in the wider world and in other religions. By 'pluralism' I mean the position that denies the finality of Jesus Christ and maintains that other religions are equally salvific paths to God" (ibid., 14–15).

10. This notion of embracing both exclusivism and universal love is also seen in the biblical materials. In the Old Testament, we find God establishing an exclusive covenant with Abram and his descendent, yet all nations will benefit from the covenant. In the New Testament, Paul speaks of the "elect," yet in Colossians claims the Christ event to have cosmic benefits.

11. "Dialogue works when participants care for truth while respecting one another. Tolerance does not require relativism. Relativism actually threatens tolerance by assuming a dogmatic stance that frowns upon all nonrelativist positions" (Pinnock, *Wideness in God's Mercy*, 136). "Evangelical dialogue would be the kind that arises from caring about other people, the willingness to listen respectfully, a preparedness to step into their shoes and try to understand. It would mean clarifying differences where they exist, engaging in serious conversation, and seeking genuine communication. Proper dialogue means going beyond relativism and fideism to talk about the Gospel and the alternative truth claims together" (ibid., 138).

12. Ibid., 180. This is reminiscent of Jean-Paul Sartre's view of hell in *No Exit*. Of course, God is omnipresent, so sinners cannot keep God out and hell becomes the eternal presence of the one the sinner has tried to avoid (that is to say, God). "To be fully

In the second chapter of *A Wideness in God's Mercy*, Pinnock addresses a number of issues having to do with Christology, including his defense of a high Christology (i.e., the claim that Jesus Christ is God and Savior). Yet he maintains "that a high Christology does not entail a narrow outlook."[13] His position of a high Christology is not new for evangelical theology. What is novel is his claim that it does not entail a narrow outlook regarding other faith traditions.

It is important to understand just what he means by "a narrow outlook". Who is having this narrow outlook? Who is being viewed by this narrow outlook? What does a narrow outlook mean? It will be helpful to answer the second question first. "Those who worship God outside churches" are the ones being viewed by this narrow outlook.[14] The context clearly points to those who are not part of the Christian tradition but are worshiping God according to the religious tradition of their culture. Those he refers to as pagan saints.[15] Those who have this narrow outlook are members of the evangelical community. Pinnock claims the narrow outlook is not merely exclusivism but restrictivism, which he believes is entailed by exclusivism. Pinnock says, "A majority of evangelicals today are hardline restrictivists in my estimation. The only possibility for encountering God and receiving salvation in this view is to exercise explicit faith in Jesus Christ in this earthly life."[16] While it is clear how exclusivism entails restrictivism, which claims that not all persons are saved, it is not clear that exclusivism entails the hard-line restrictivism that Pinnock suggests that it does.[17]

---

conscious of the nearness of God and yet to be excluded from him is what the ancient dogmas saw as the tortures of hell" (Pannenberg, *Apostles' Creed*, 191).

13. Pinnock, *Wideness in God's Mercy*, 51.
14. Ibid., 50.
15. Ibid., 92–94.
16. Ibid., 12.
17. Pinnock's stance betrays his presupposition that Augustinianism is a major flaw of traditional evangelical thought. Can we identify examples of hard-line restrictivism within evangelical thought? Yes, some within the tradition maintain, "Christ's saving work was limited in that it was designed to save some and not others . . ." (Steele and Thomas, *Five Points of Calvinism*, 39). This form of Reformed theology is a hard-line restrictivism and unquestionably Augustinian. Pinnock seems to maintain that if the doctrine of limited atonement or restrictivism can be called into question, then Augustinian theology must be replaced by Arminianism. (This is the position of *The Grace of God, the Will of Man*, which Pinnock edited.) However, Charles Hodge points out that "Augustinians readily admit that the death of Christ had a relation to man, to the whole human family, . . . It is the ground on which salvation is offered to every creature under heaven who hears the gospel" (Hodge, *Systematic Theology*, 2:545). Augustus Strong also pointed out that the message of Christ is not limited to Christendom. (*Christ in Creation and Ethical Monism*, 104).

At the forty-first annual meeting (November 1989) of the Evangelical Theological Society, James A. Borland delivered the presidential address.[18] In his address, Borland illustrates the stance that Pinnock is reacting against. After raising a series of "informed" questions that he asks of all religions, Borland contrasts the gospel and world religions in regards to their Christology, their understanding of the nature of persons, and their soteriology. Based on this contrast, he concludes that the world religions are in total antithesis to Christian doctrine in each of these categories. However, it is the third point of Borland's address that provides the clearest illustration of the exclusivism, that Pinnock is reacting against. The subtitle of his third section is, "Everyone Must Hear and Believe the Gospel to Be Saved."

> The means of securing salvation has always been faith. But the actual content of faith—that is, what must be believed—has changed with the progressive nature of God's revelation . . . Since Calvary, the unchanging required content of one's faith is the gospel. Nothing else saves, while all else damns. No substitutions, additions or imitations are permitted. Any other gospel is not another that can save. It only brings with it an anathema (Gal 1:6–9).[19]

In conclusion, Borland claims that if evangelicals embrace any position other than exclusivism in regards to the recipients of salvation, missionary zeal is diminished and the helpless are left hopeless.[20]

In the spring of 2002, the *Southwestern Journal of Theology*, the journal for Southwestern Baptist Theological Seminary's School of Theology, devoted the entire issue to the theology of religions, and Ebbie C. Smith contributed the initial article.[21] Smith presents an exclusivist approach. While the article does provide some valuable insights, it illustrates some of the problems created by evangelicals, and others, in this field of theology. After a brief introduction to the theology of religions, Smith claims "Ronald Nash slices to the heart of the issue with his question, 'Is Jesus the only Savior?'" Smith then outlines his own taxonomy.

> This article . . . accepts only two major categories: (1) the "wider-hope" theories (pluralism and inclusivism); and (2) *the exclusivist position that Jesus Christ is the one and only Savior, whose salvation can be attained only by a direct response, during*

---

18. Borland, "Theologian Looks," 3–11.
19. Ibid., 9.
20. Ibid., 11.
21. Smith, "Evangelical Approach," 6–23.

lifetime, to the message of the historic, risen Christ as presented in the Christian gospel.[22]

He then addresses both "wider-hope" theories before presenting his own position of exclusivism. Unfortunately, Professor Smith's assessment of these theories is flawed because some of his claim statements are, at best, inconsistent with claim statements we have already seen by evangelicals. For example, Smith says that "inclusivism believes salvation is possible through the Non-Christian religions."[23] However, as the Manila Declaration points out, religions do not provide salvation, only God does. Evangelicals agree that God has provided salvation only through the son Jesus Christ. However, the major flaw in Professor Smith's assessment is his failure to distinguish between the issue of agency (Jesus Christ is the one and only Savior) and the issue of recipients of salvation (salvation can be attained only by a direct response, during one's lifetime, to the message of the historic, risen Christ). Notice how he defines his own position of exclusivism.

> The exclusivist (particularist, Restrictivist) position contends that salvation is received only through an explicit act of repentance and faith directed to the Living Christ during the believer's lifetime in response to the revealed message of the gospel. Ronald Nash forcefully expresses exclusivism's conclusion, "Evangelicals believe that Jesus is the only savior. There is no other savior and no other religion, we believe, that can bring human beings to the saving grace of God." Exclusivism answers the question, "Is Jesus the only Savior?" with an unmixed and uncompromising "Yes."[24]

Smith makes the mistake many have made as they work within the theology of religions, and that is to conflate issues within the discipline.[25] However, Smith's article is not without valuable insights.

Smith identifies nuances within his own position of exclusivism, and these nuances form four distinct groups. There are the rigid exclusivist, which Pinnock appears to view as the only type; the uncertain exclusivists,

22. Ibid., 7 (italics original).

23. Ibid., 12.

24. Ibid., 13.

25. This is not to deny the interrelatedness of the issues. They are connected. "Doctrine is organic. Rather than comprising a loose collection of scattered ideas, theology properly done is a whole, so that the position a person takes on one doctrine affects conclusions in other areas as well" (Erickson, *How Shall They Be Saved?*, 14–15). However, one should not work out one area of theology and assume they have a complete picture. The various ideas must be individually examined, and only then can they fit together as a whole.

the hopeful exclusivists; and the realistic exclusivist. "Rigid exclusivists see such a radical difference in Christianity and other religions that they ascribe neither value nor truth to the other faiths."[26] Smith suggests that Harold Lindsell represents this position. Furthermore, Smith believes that some rigid exclusivists hold this position because they embrace a limited atonement view. Some writers "are classified as 'uncertain exclusivists' because they express less than a clear, straightforward conviction of salvation only through the gospel of Christ."[27] Smith places individuals such as Karl Barth and E. Luther Copeland in this group.[28] Other exclusivists, whom he calls hopeful exclusivists, maintain "that Christ is the only Savior, [but] still hold the hope that God will successfully extend salvation to much of humanity."[29] After surveying the positions of Carl Braaten and Lesslie Newbigin as representative of this position, Smith continues to present other forms of hopeful exclusivism.

> Another option for hopeful exclusivism is that of "reflective agnosticism." John Stott seems to fit into this category as he cherishes the hope that a majority of humans will be saved—although he does not know exactly how this will happen. Loraine Boettner and Bruce Demarest both hold out some hope that God may have some way of dealing with the lost . . . Alister E. McGrath has another hopeful suggestion. He says that in places where the Word of God is not, or cannot be proclaimed by human agents, that "God is not inhibited from bringing people to faith in him, even if that act of hope and trust may lack the fully robed character of an informed Christian faith." The doctrine of prevenient grace, says McGrath, has been severally neglected in the theology of mission.[30]

The position of hopeful exclusivism sounds very much like the position advocated by those evangelicals who contributed to this field prior to the

---

26. Smith, "Evangelical Approach," 16.

27. Ibid., 17.

28. "Copeland[, a Baptist theologian,] explains his own view in terms of a somewhat uncertain exclusivism. He clearly states his belief that divine revelation exists in the whole of human culture, including the non-Christian religions. He further declares that some, perhaps many, who never hear the Christian Gospel in this life will be saved whether or not they profess the beliefs of the Christian religion. Copeland adds that no one is saved apart form the redemptive work of God in Jesus Christ. Some may hear and reject the gospel and still be saved because they reject it for valid ethical reasons" (ibid., 17).

29. Ibid., 17–18.

30. Ibid., 19.

1980s and reflects the inclusivism of some contemporary evangelicals. The final type of exclusivist identified by Smith is the realistic exclusivist.

> They stand on their belief in the total authority and reliability of biblical revelation and find no genuine promise of salvation apart from an explicit faith in Jesus Christ. Realistic exclusivists find in Scripture no promise of a second chance, postmortem evangelism, or salvation in the other religions. Realistic exclusivists refuse to promise anything not directly promised in Scripture. Their realistic stance finds its foundation in the acceptance of biblical teachings on salvation and lostness. They are, however, realistic enough to accept God's sovereignty to work outside their understanding and provide other ways.[31]

In this group, Smith places Hendrik Kraemer, John Newport, and James Leo Garrett Jr.[32] While Smith claims that rigid exclusivists "have too little respect for the world religions" and that hopeful exclusivists offer hope for which there is no evidence, realistic exclusivists are more faithful to "sound biblical interpretation and evangelical theology."[33] While his conflating of issues flaws Smith's article, the article does suggest that there are different forms of exclusivism about recipients of salvation. Furthermore, the form of exclusivism that Smith refers to as "hopeful exclusivism" may properly be referred to as inclusivism. Smith's broadening of the notion

---

31. Ibid., 20. Regarding Garrett, "he teaches that Christian salvation comes only through personal faith in the incarnate, crucified, risen Christ. Demonstrating his exclusivist convictions, Garrett says that there is no way for a Buddhist, a Hindu, or a Muslim to appropriate the saving grace of Jesus Christ while remaining in his/her own religion. Garrett's most helpful aspect is his emphasis that the church's proclamation should be exclusivist so as not to promise salvation outside the conscious acceptance of Jesus and the gospel. He goes on to state that in God's sovereign freedom, he might effectually work outside the boundaries of exclusivism. Garrett is actually calling for humility on the part of those who follow the exclusivist position" (ibid., 21).

32. While Smith does not refer to William Lane Craig, Craig's position can be understood as what Smith calls a realistic exclusivist stance. While Smith does not refer to William Lane Craig, Craig's position can be understood as what Smith calls a realistic exclusivist. "Since Jesus and his work are historical in character, many persons as a result of historical and geographical accident will not be sufficiently well-informed concerning him and thus unable to respond to him in faith. Such persons who are not sufficiently well-informed about Christ's person and work will be judged on the basis of their response to general revelation and the light that they do have. Perhaps some will be saved through such a response; but on the basis of Scripture we must say that such 'anonymous Christians' are relatively rare. Those who are judged and condemned on the basis of their failure to the light of general revelation cannot legitimately complain of unfairness for their not also receiving the light of special revelation had they received it" (Craig, "No Other Name," 186).

33. Smith, "Evangelical Approach," 22.

of exclusivism opens the door for us to mention three other evangelical theologians who further the discussion. Those theologians are Culpepper, Erickson, and Sanders.

In an article in which he reviews *The Myth of Christian Uniqueness: Toward a Pluralistic Theology of Religions* (edited by Hick and Knitter) and *Christian Uniqueness Reconsidered: The Myth of a Pluralistic Theology of Religions* (edited by D'Costa), Robert Culpepper offers a tentative approach to this area of theology.[34] He begins by clearly stating that the basic issue has to do with Christology. "In Jesus Christ God acted decisively for human salvation: to do something which needed to be done, which had never been done before, and which would never be done again."[35] "It is . . . to proclaim the unique and decisive revelatory act of God in Jesus Christ and its salvific significance for all humankind."[36] Culpepper acknowledges that his position is that of exclusivism.

> Yet I am contending for—and let this be clearly understood—
> *an open-ended exclusivism*. It is not our responsibility to make pronouncements concerning the eternal destiny of those who through no fault of their own have never heard the Gospel. The matters are in God's hands, not ours.[37]

Because salvation is a gift from God, there is no room for arrogance among those who have received the gospel message, and there is no "need to denigrate the faith of others. We should imitate Jesus, who welcomed every sign of faith that he saw outside the household of Israel (Matt 8:5–8; 15:21–28)."[38]

Millard Erickson summarizes the Protestant exclusivist position:

1. All humans are sinners who live apart from God. This combination of disbelief and disobedience means that they are under God's condemnation.

2. Even those who have never heard of Jesus Christ are responsible for their sins and guilt. There is a genuine general revelation of God in nature and in the human personality, and from this all persons know God sufficiently so that they should have been able to respond positively to him, but have in fact suppressed this truth.

---

34. Culpepper, "Lordship of Christ," 311–20.
35. Ibid., 318.
36. Ibid., 319.
37. Ibid., 320.
38. Ibid., 321.

3. Salvation cannot be by works. It is only available through God's merciful, gracious provision in offering Jesus Christ as a sacrifice for the sins of all humankind.

4. In order to be forgiven and saved, it is necessary to understand the basis of this salvation, in other words, to have the special revelation that gives knowledge of the gospel.

5. No one is innocent. Because all have sinned, the question of the condition of the unevangelized is not a question of the innocent. All deserve divine judgment. If God were to give each person what he or she deserves, none would be saved; all would be lost.

6. Adherents of other religions, no matter how sincere or committed, are spiritually lost unless they come to belief in Jesus Christ.

7. Death brings to an end the opportunity for accepting Jesus Christ, and thus for eternal salvation. The decisions made in this life have eternal consequences.

8. Jesus Christ's return will be followed by a great judgment, at which point persons will be consigned to eternal fellowship with God if they have accepted Christ, or to eternal separation from God and to eternal punishment if they have not.

9. In light of the foregoing, Christians have an obligation to take the good news to unbelievers by telling them of Jesus Christ.[39]

In an article published in 1988, John Sanders asked the question "Is belief in Christ necessary for salvation?"[40] The major question, according to Sanders, is, "Will God extend the opportunity of salvation to those who have never been presented with the proclamation of the person and work of Jesus Christ?" Within evangelical circles, Sanders identifies three responses:

> (1). Some maintain that the unevangelized are forever lost. (2). Others hold that the unevangelized will receive a future chance after death to hear and decide concerning Christ. (3). Some believe God separates the unevangelized into saved and lost depending upon the response they make to the limited information they have concerning God.[41]

All three of these responses have one point in common: "It is *only* through Christ that any man can come to a personal knowledge of, and fellowship

---

39. Erickson, *How Shall They be Saved?*, 61–62.
40. Sanders, "Is Belief in Christ Necessary, for Salvation?," 241–59.
41. Ibid., 242.

with, God, and *only* through his life, death and resurrection that any man can come to an experience of salvation."[42] The first response is clearly the response of exclusivism. Sanders points out those arguments for this position that are based upon Scripture contain logical errors.

> Such statements as "No one comes to the Father except by me" (Jn 14:6), and "there is no other name by which you must be saved" (Acts 4:12) certainly teach that any who receive final salvation do so only because of the atonement of Jesus. But it is not certain from these passages that one *must* hear of Christ in this life to obtain salvation. They simply say there is no other way to heaven except through the work of Christ; they do not say one has to know about that work in order to benefit from the work. Furthermore, Romans 10:9 could be summarized as saying, "If anyone receives Christ, then he will be saved," but this proposition cannot, according to the rules of logic, be converted to read, "If anyone does not receive Christ, then he is lost." Again, the statement "All who receive Christ will be saved" is not synonymous with "All who do not receive Christ will be lost." The argument, 'If you accept Christ then you will be saved. You did not accept Christ. Therefore, you are lost" is fallacious.[43]

Furthermore, according to Sanders, when exclusivists use scriptural phrases such as "call upon the name of the Lord" (Rom 10:14) to name a necessary condition of salvation, they are missing the intent of those passages. Sanders claims, "Calling upon the *name* of God has not so much to do with using a specific title of God as it does with placing yourself at God's mercy ... To 'call upon the name of the Lord' refers to asking God for forgiveness and help."[44] The second position, a future second chance, is on solid ground theologically, but Sanders maintains that it is weak biblically. "On biblical grounds it is quite uncertain whether 1 Peter or the doctrine of Christ's descent have anything to do with a future opportunity to hear the gospel."[45] The third "position maintains that the unevangelized are saved or lost depending on their response to the light they have."[46] Sanders cites three major forms of arguments to support this position. He also notes several of the major criticisms of this position.

42. Ibid., 242.
43. Ibid., 246–47.
44. Ibid., 247 (italics original).
45. Ibid., 252.
46. Ibid., 252. Sanders cites the following individuals as holding this view: Justin Martyr, William Booth, G. T. Shedd, A. H. Strong, G. Campbell Morgan, E. J. Carnell, William Dyrness, and C. S. Lewis.

The first type of support Sanders provides for this position is biblical. To "call upon the name of the Lord" is to request mercy from God. Furthermore, "general revelation reveals enough about God to enable us to make a faith response to God since it reveals God's power and divinity (Rom 1:20), goodness (Acts 14:20), and glory (Ps 19:1)."[47] In addition, Sanders claims that the Old Testament gives examples of God's gracious activity toward those outside of Israel (Deut 2:5ff. and Amos 9:7). Finally, according to Sanders, Peter's statement "God is not one to show partiality, but in every nation the man who fears Him and does what is right, is welcome to Him" (Acts 10:34–35) supports this third position. Sanders believes that the person who fears God is one who trusts and obeys God to the extent of the revelation that one has. Citing F. F. Bruce, Sanders says that the idea of doing what is right must be understood in the widest possible sense. It is not restricted to obedience to the revelation at Sinai, but obedience to God's general revelation.

> The fear and righteousness which Cornelius possessed did not come about entirely on his own initiative, rather, these effects are signs of the work of the Holy Spirit in the lives of the unevangelized. God is at work whenever a person is searching for him, helping them to understand whatever revelation they have, convict them of sin, and come to faith in the true God.[48]

The second type of support provided by Sanders for this third position is theological. Sanders maintains, "that the "gospel" does not always refer to the message about Jesus but has a broader meaning which may include even general revelation (Rom. 10:18)."[49] A second theological argument, according to Sanders, claims that saving faith does not necessarily require explicit knowledge of Jesus, but means trusting God. Sanders claims, "knowing about and having faith in the God who raised Jesus is one sure way of appropriating salvation but it is not the only way. We must be careful not to place constraints on God's mercy and activity where He does not."[50]

Sanders's third type of evidence for his position that God separates the unevangelized into categories of saved and lost based on the response they make to the limited information they have about God is historical. If God at times works through general revelation to reach individuals, then we ought to find historical evidence for this. Sanders refers to the findings of anthropologist Don Richardson for an example of this historical evidence.

47. Ibid., 253.
48. Ibid., 254–55.
49. Ibid., 255.
50. Ibid., 257.

According to Richardson, numerous cultures possess redemptive analogies that illustrate God working among those ignorant of the true God.

> [Richardson] places these cases into three categories: (1). Peoples of the vague God—those who know something of the true God and desire to serve him but are hampered by lack of knowledge—like the Athenian, Inca, Santal, and Gedeo peoples; (2). Peoples of the lost book—those who are looking for special revelation (a book) which was lost to them—like the Karen, Kachin, Lahu, and Maga peoples; (3). Peoples with strange customs—those with practices which graphically portray redemption and forgiveness—like the Sawi, Dyak, and Asmat peoples.[51]

As Sanders says, "God has not been sitting idly by waiting for missionaries to take special revelation to the unevangelized . . . God has been very active in bringing salvation to the peoples of the world who have never heard of Christ."[52]

Sanders cites the four basic objections to his position: (1) this position suggests a salvation by works, (2) it gives too much credit to general revelation and human ability to understand salvation, (3) passages like 1 John 5:12 deny the possibility of salvation without knowledge of Jesus Christ, and (4) this position makes missionary activities insignificant. Sanders maintains that each of these criticisms is wrong. To the first criticism he points out that in his position, salvation is still based upon the work of Christ. The second criticism is flawed because his position claims, "we still would not know we were forgiven unless God told us by special revelation."[53] The third criticism fails because it fails to understand that all believers—Christians, those of Old Testament times, or unevangelized people of faith—have Christ implicitly. For Sanders there are still good reasons to continue missionary activities. "(1). God commands us to go!; (2). Those who are not searching for God need to be challenged to do so; (3). Unevangelized believers need the clearer revelation of God's love, assurance, and will for their lives."[54]

Like Pinnock and Sanders, Terrance Tiessen does not embrace an exclusivist stance regarding the recipients of salvation.[55] However, his rejection of that position differs in a number of ways. First, he does not reject the Augustinian tradition. He embraces monergism, which maintains "that

---

51. Ibid., 258.
52. Ibid.
53. Ibid., 259.
54. Ibid.
55. Tiessen, *Who Can Be Saved?*

everything comes about because God has determined that it will occur."[56] Second, he claims, "The possibility and the process of salvation are no different for infants and the mentally incompetent than for competent adults."[57] Finally, instead of working with the threefold typology, Tiessen proposes his own categories: ecclesiocentrism, agnosticism, accessibilism, religious instrumentalism, and relativism. For Tiessen, these categories are flexible enough to be functional given the array of issues that arise within the theology of religions. The following characteristics of each position do not capture Tiessen's full understanding of the category but focus on the relevant aspects pertinent to who the recipients of salvation are.

> *Ecclesiocentrism*: Characterized particularly by the conviction that ever since Christ ascended and sent the Holy Spirit, only those who hear the gospel can be saved. This means that the possibility of salvation is coextensive with the presence of the church, which makes the church and its gospel proclamation essential to God's work of salvation. (32–33)
>
> *Agnosticism*: Characterized by the conviction that the Scriptures do not clearly indicate that none of the unevangelized are ever saved; hence does not know for sure that God has means by which to save people who do not hear about Christ. (33)
>
> *Accessibilism*: Asserts that Jesus Christ is exclusively God's means of salvation and that the covenantal relationships God established with Israel and the church, in working out his saving program, are unique and unparalleled. There is biblical reason to be hopeful about the possibility of salvation for those who do not hear the gospel. Do not restrict God's saving work to the boundaries of the church. God makes salvation accessible to people who do not receive the gospel. No religion saves—only God. (33)
>
> *Religious instrumentalism*: Goes beyond the accessibilist and argues that God's salvation is available through non-Christian religions. (33–34)
>
> *Relativism*: Salvation is universally accessible through the various religions that are part of the divine program. All religions are, more or less, equally true and are paths to salvation. (34)

---

56. Ibid., 18. Monergism stands in contrast with synergism. According to the latter position, "events occur through a cooperation of God and his creatures, such that God does not always have his way" (ibid., 18). In evangelical circles these two position are frequently referred to as Calvinism and Arminianism.

57. Ibid., 25.

Tiessen points out that Harold Netland's definition of inclusivism most closely fits his own category called religious instrumentalism; however, others define inclusivism in a way that is more compatible with accessibilism. Tiessen's own stance regarding the recipients of salvation is that of accessibilism.

Stanley Grenz provides another example of an evangelical theology that is inclusive regarding the recipients of salvation.

> Like exclusivists, [evangelical inclusivists] are firm in the conviction that Jesus is God's unique means of salvation; eternal life comes only through Christ. What sets them apart from their exclusivist colleagues is their willingness to affirm the possibility of salvation for those who have not had an opportunity to respond to the Christian gospel. Salvation is not dependent on explicit faith in Christ but comes through personal commitment to the God who saves through the work of Jesus Christ. Those who never hear the gospel may nevertheless enjoy eternal life if they respond in faith to the revelation they do have.[58]

As he explores "Jesus' mission in the divine program," Grenz carefully points out that as Messiah, Jesus "will save his people—and indeed the whole world—from their *sins*."[59] Furthermore, as the Son of Man he ""was given authority, glory and sovereign power," so that "all people, nations and men of every language"" will worship him.[60] Grenz claims, "Christ's reconciling work . . . has cosmic implications," such as "reconciliation of humankind with the entire creation."[61] "In the end, we humbly conclude that no other religious vision encapsulates the final purpose of God as we have come to understand it. Both the divine diagnosis of the human predicament and the ultimate answer are given in Christ."[62] This finality of Christ, for Grenz, means that through Jesus "we discover the truest vision of the nature of God."[63] This position does not deny that other religious visions occur, but those visions are not as clear or they point to another God.

There is another distinct group of evangelicals working to develop an inclusivism regarding the recipients of salvation, and these are Pentecostal theologians such as Amos Yong and Veli-Matti Kärkkäinen.[64] Building upon

58. Grenz, "Toward an Evangelical," 53.
59. Grenz, *Created For Community*, 133 (italics original).
60. Ibid., 134.
61. Ibid., 145.
62. Grenz, "Toward an Evangelical," 63.
63. Ibid., 64.
64. Kärkkäinen, *Introduction to the Theology of Religions*; Kärkkäinen *Trinity and*

the works of Georges Khodr, Stanley Samartha, and Jacques Dupuis, their project is to explore whether a pneumatological approach to the theology of religions will illuminate God's work in other faith traditions. As Amos Yong says, "I do maintain . . . that discerning the presence and activity of the Spirit in the religions is central to this endeavor and that we are in desperate need of more adequate categories in order to conduct more viable theological comparisons across religious lines."[65]

Before we evaluate the contribution of North American evangelicals regarding the recipients of salvation, it is important for us to see how some evangelicals have answered two relevant questions: What is meant by salvation? and, How does one appropriate the atonement provided by the cross event? The first question has already been answered in passing but needs to be the point of focus now. In the opening of this essay, we stated,

> Evangelicalism, like other Christian theologies, understands salvation to be a process that includes justification, sanctification, and glorification. It is a process capturing at the same time both a here-and-now and a not-yet understanding. While the need for salvation is rooted in the fall, whereby sin entered the world, and while salvation influences the recipient's life in the world, salvation is not culminated until the eschaton, when God completes glorification and brings about a new heaven and a new earth. An individual, evangelicals hold, is justified when he/she accepts or appropriates the atoning work of Jesus Christ. Upon being justified, the believer becomes part of the bride of Christ, the church universal. Justification is understood to be immediate and does not necessarily involve external signs. The process of sanctification is that process of becoming more mature in his/her relationship with God, becoming more Christ-like.[66]

While for some conservative Christian groups salvation may be understood in a negative way (that is, salvation is *from* sin, *from* condemnation, *from* punishment in hell), evangelicals emphasize a positive attitude toward the nature of salvation. Salvation is *into* a relationship or community that proclaims the rule of God. For the evangelical, salvation is that process of being restored to fellowship with the true God. It is a process involving both here

---

Religious Pluralism; Kärkkäinen, *One with God*; Kärkkäinen, "Toward a Pneumatological Theology of Religions"; Kärkkäinen, "Surveying the Land and Charting the Territory of the Spirit"; Yong, *Discerning the Spirit(s)*; Yong, *Beyond the Impasse*; Yong, "Turn to Pneumatology"; Yong, "Not Knowing Where the Wind Blows"; Yong, "Whither Theological Inclusivism?"; Yong, et al., "Christ and Spirit."

65. Yong, *Beyond the Impasse*, 454.
66. See p. 58 above.

and not-yet benefits for the believer. It is a process providing community between believers with the true God, among believers, and between believers and the rest of creation. It is a process moving participants into deeper and more mature relationships of community.

How does one appropriate the work of the cross? Evangelicals must maintain the exclusivity of the cross, but appropriation of the work accomplished there might be wider than historically conservative Christians have thought. After examining the biblical requirements for salvation as outlined in both the Old and the New Testaments, Millard Erickson concludes, "There is certainly a need of awareness of and repentance for one's sin. This also means an awareness of the consequences of such sin for the person's relationship."[67] Erickson points out that in both Testaments an understanding of the inability of the individual to appease God, a turning away from self-reliance, and a trusting in God's mercy are biblical requirements for salvation. This raises the question, do the biblical requirements for salvation require an explicit knowledge of Jesus Christ and his atoning work, or can these requirements be met through implicit faith? This primary question distinguishes those evangelicals who embrace an exclusivism regarding the recipients of salvation from those who embrace an inclusivist stance.

Pointing to Paul (Rom 1:18–24), Erickson believes that if general revelation provides adequate knowledge to be condemned, then it must also provide adequate knowledge in order to satisfy the biblical requirements of salvation.

> It must be correct to say that on some level persons responding to the God of general revelation are genuinely responding to the true God. It also must be deemed to be the case, however, that while the knowledge of this God may not include all the details about him . . ., the conception of God should not be contradictory to the nature of the true God. Thus, one could not have been an "implicit Jehovist" while worshiping Baal, for instance. This would be true of the worship of man of those in other world religions. And it must be borne in mind that this implicit faith will always involve the idea of salvation by grace, which in its genuine form is so rare among devotees of the world religions. It must always be an abandonment of reliance on anything other than the grace of God himself.[68]

Erickson also asks of those who require an explicit knowledge, "how much must one know, understand, and believe? Must one understand the

---

67. Erickson, *How Shall They Be Saved?*, 192.
68. Ibid., 194–95.

incarnation . . . ? How orthodox must this understanding be?" Erickson concludes, "Perhaps there is room for acknowledging that God alone may know in every case exactly whose faith is sufficient for salvation."[69]

As we move into the evaluatory section of this essay, a preliminary comment will be insightful. Writing for *Christianity Today*, Roger Olson discusses the division within evangelical theology toward the close of the twentieth century.[70] After identifying four minimum characteristics of an evangelical theology, he notes the two basic parties that threaten to end their theological consensus.[71] One party he describes as the traditionalists; the other party he calls the reformists. "Their differences lie in divergent *mindsets* toward a variety of fundamental issues, including *theological boundaries, the nature of doctrine, progress in theology*, and *relating to nonevangelical theologies and culture in general*."[72] For example, regarding theological boundaries, one party views the church as a bounded set. This party wishes to specify who is "in" and who is "out." The boundaries are concrete and firm. The other party views the church as a centered-set. "Risking ambiguity about boundaries—who is 'in' and who is 'out'—they insist on keeping the boundaries open and relatively undefined."[73] Olson cites both Pinnock and Grenz as examples of reformist evangelical theologians who "look to the future and seek change within continuity for the sake of continuing evangelical vitality and viability."[74] This divide, according to Olson, is problematic and potentially destroying the fiber of evangelicalism.[75] However, his assessment may be seen as ignoring the history of evangelicalism in America.

69. Ibid., 195.

70. Olson, et al., "Forum: The Future of Evangelical Theology," 40–48.

71. The four minimum characteristics are (1) "It looks to the Bible as the supreme norm of truth for Christian belief and practice"; (2) "It holds a supernatural world-view that is centered in a transcendent, personal God who interacts with, and intervenes in, creation"; (3) "It focuses on the forgiving and transforming grace of God through Jesus Christ in the experience called *conversion* as the center of authentic Christian experience"; and (4) "It believes that the primary task of Christian theology is to serve the church's mission of bringing God's grace to the whole world through proclamation and service" (ibid., 40).

72. Ibid., 41 (italics original). In spite of these differences, both parties, Olson emphasizes, are working within the evangelical paradigm.

73. Ibid., 42.

74. Ibid. We must be careful and not assume that the lack of unison among evangelicals regarding the recipients of salvation is simply the traditionalist versus the reformist. Olson clearly places Millard Erickson within the traditional camp; however, it was Erickson who cautioned against closing the door of salvation to all but those who confess the name of Jesus.

75. W. Gary Phillips referred to this divide as a watershed. "Within evangelicalism, the exclusiveness of Jesus Christ—as both the *ontological* and *epistemological* basis for

Robert Johnston presented part of that history, and a backdrop for Olson's model.[76] According to Johnston, the first-generation evangelicals after World War II exhibited bounded-set thinking. Individuals such as Carl F. H. Henry exhibited "a strong sense of correctness about their theology. [As a result], they lived out their vocation as guardians of a received body of truth."[77] Other early evangelical theologians, such as Edward Carnell and Bernard Ramm, "while holding to revelation as a bounded set of truths, sought early in the post-war period to move evangelicalism beyond its divisiveness and belligerence on the one hand, and its anti-modernism on the other."[78] However, according to Johnston, a second generation of evangelicals emerged, who were more interested in focusing on central issues than in drawing the boundaries that determined who was in and who was out.[79] This group was operating with centered-set thinking.

Whether Johnston's picture of first-generation versus second-generation evangelicals or Olson's traditionalist versus reformist evangelicals is adequate, what is significant about the current situation is that the disagreement within contemporary American evangelicalism is over foundational issues. The lack of unison is more foundational than the terms "traditionalist" and "reformist" might suggest. The lack of unison is rooted in fundamental presuppositions, which results in divergent mindsets. Olson believes that North American evangelicalism will suffer because of these divergent mindsets; however, other disciplines have had such disagreements and have benefited because of the disagreements. For example, consider the discipline of logic, in which a similar disagreement regarding sets arises.

Within contemporary logic, we find two major competing theories: classical or Aristotelian and intuitionalism. This disagreement can be illustrated by considering the logical principle known as the law of the excluded

---

salvation—may become a watershed issue" ("Evangelicals and Pluralism: Current Options," 242).

76. Johnston, "Orthodoxy and Heresy," 7–38.

77. Ibid., 14.

78. Ibid., 18.

79. David Allan Hubbard, who became president of Fuller Theological Seminary, listed these central doctrines as Trinity, revelation, creation, fall, incarnation, cross, resurrection, Holy Spirit, the church and its mission, and consummation. "Evangelical theology's shift to defining orthodoxy in terms of a centered set has reinforced and solidified changes that transitional theologians Carnell and Ramm struggled to affirm: (1) an openness to the wider church through dialogue and civility; (2) an openness to the wider culture as a source for theological reflection and renewal; (3) a commitment to doing theology in community; and (4) an openness to theological creativity within a continuing commitment to Scripture's authority" (ibid., 26).

middle.⁸⁰ Within classical logic, a statement is either true, e.g., P, or it is false, e.g., $\sim P$. There is no middle ground. The set of truth-values for a given statement is bounded; it contains a finite number of members. However, intuitionalists, while accepting the law when dealing with a finite set, will reject the law of excluded middle when considering an infinite set. Their set theory is not as restricted as the Aristotelian approach. For example, consider the sentence "There is an odd number that is perfect".⁸¹ If this sentence were true, then it would mean that we could run through the odd numbers and find one that is perfect, e.g., P. However, what would it mean to deny this sentence? Since the set of numbers is infinite, the denial could not mean that we will not find an odd perfect number. For the intuitionalist, it means that the idea of an odd perfect number is a contradiction, which is not simply a denial of P. Notice, within a finite set, intuitionalists will accept P or $\sim P$, but because their understanding of sets is not bound by a finite number of members, they will reject this law of logic in cases where the set contains an infinite number of members. Within logic, this divergent mindset has become a gold mine. Without the classical mindset, logic would lack its necessary groundings. However, because individuals such as L. J. Brouwer and his student Arend Heyting challenged the classical mindset, new areas of logic such as multivalued logic and fuzzy logic have been developed. Logic has profited because of the divergent mindsets. These divergent mindsets are the result of disagreements at the level of fundamental presuppositions. In one case, a set is bounded; it contains a finite number of members. In the other case, a set is not bounded; it may contain an infinite number of members, in which case the focus at times becomes a specific part of that set.

Now back to North American evangelicals and their theology of religions regarding the recipients of salvation. Some evangelicals see a defined boundary between those with whom God is working and those whom God is not. For these evangelicals the Christian church is the group with whom God is currently working. The recipients of salvation are Christians, followers of Christ. In order to be a follower, the recipients must have heard the gospel message (i.e., the story of Jesus) and accepted that message. However, other evangelicals understand God's mercy to be wider than the church. The set with which this group of evangelicals is working does not have defined boundaries. They do not deny that if we are dealing with the church, a finite

---

80. In classical or Aristotelian logic the laws of excluded middle and noncontradiction are considered foundational truths. Intuitional logic questions these laws in some cases. See Dummett, *Elements of Intuitionism*.

81. "A perfect number is defined as an integer that is equal to the sum of all its own divisors except itself. Thus, 6 is a perfect number because 6 = 1 + 2 + 3" (Anderson and Johnstone, *Natural Deduction*, 124–25). The number 28 is another example.

set, salvation is obtained by naming the name of Jesus as Christ. However, they maintain, God works in many ways and, typically, in ways that are compatible with the culture or information available to the individuals.[82] While the discipline of logic has benefited because of divergent mindsets, will an evangelical theology of religions benefit because of these divergent mindsets within evangelicalism?

Internal Consistency

Unlike the issue of agency of salvation, there is not a singular response by North American evangelicals regarding the recipients of salvation. Rather we have seen two basic responses to this latter issue, and within each response, numerous nuances clearly complicate the question of whether the evangelical response to the issue regarding the recipients of salvation is internally consistent. However, while the situation is complex, some surprising discoveries can be found as we assess the evangelical response in light of this criterion.

Our initial assessment might suggest that the exclusivist stance regarding the recipients of salvation is very consistent as long as we exclude some of its nuances such as rigid exclusivism.[83] The reasoning for this initial assessment develops through three distinct threads. First, there is biblical evidence that those who name the name of Jesus Christ and are his followers are recipients of salvation.

John 3:15–18

> [15]that whoever believes in him may have eternal life." [16]For God so loved the world that he gave his only Son, that whoever believes in him should not perish but have eternal life. [17]For God sent the Son into the world, not to condemn the world, but that the world might be saved through him. [18]He who believes in him is not condemned; he who does not believe is condemned already, because he has not believed in the name of the only Son of God.

---

82. It can be argued that even those who operate within a bounded set accept the position that God always works with individuals within their own cultures and understandings. For example, all the evangelical theologians whom Olson identifies as traditionalists understand that while the Scriptures are inspired of God, God did not supersede the culture in which the revelation was given. Rather, God chose to communicate the message typically without violating the individual's personality, knowledge, or culture.

83. This exclusion would include infralapsarianism and limited atonement positions, which many evangelical exclusivists would understand to be problematic both for scriptural and theological reasons.

John 5:24

> Truly, truly, I say to you, he who hears my word and believes him who sent me, has eternal life; he does not come into judgment, but has passed from death to life.

John 6:35, 47

> [35]Jesus said to them, "I am the bread of life; he who comes to me shall not hunger, and he who believes in me shall never thirst. [47]Truly, truly, I say to you, he who believes has eternal life.

John 11:25–26

> [25]Jesus said to her, "I am the resurrection and the life; he who believes in me, though he die, yet shall he live, [26]and whoever lives and believes in me shall never die. Do you believe this?"

John 15:4–5

> [4]Abide in me, and I in you. As the branch cannot bear fruit by itself, unless it abides in the vine, neither can you, unless you abide in me. [5]I am the vine, you are the branches. He who abides in me, and I in him, he it is that bears much fruit, for apart from me you can do nothing.

John 20:31

> but these are written that you may believe that Jesus is the Christ, the Son of God, and that believing you may have life in his name.

Rom 10:8–13

> [8]But what does it say? The word is near you, on your lips and in your heart (that is, the word of faith which we preach); [9]because, if you confess with your lips that Jesus is Lord and believe in your heart that God raised him from the dead, you will be saved. [10]For man believes with his heart and so is justified, and he confesses with his lips and so is saved. [11]The Scripture says, "No one who believes in him will be put to shame." [12]For there is no distinction between Jew and Greek; the same Lord is Lord of all and bestows his riches upon all who call upon him. [13]For, "every one who calls upon the name of the Lord will be saved."

2 Cor 5:17

> Therefore, if any one is in Christ, he is a new creation; the old has passed away, behold, the new has come.

Ephesians 1:13

> In him you also, who have heard the word of truth, the gospel of your salvation, and have believed in him, were sealed with the promised Holy Spirit . . .

Historically, it may be argued, the church took the position that those outside the church are lost and condemned already—"outside the church there is no salvation." For example, consider Louis Berkhof's description of the position taken by the early church fathers.

> In harmony with the New Testament statement, that man obtains the blessings of salvation by "repentance toward God, and faith in our Lord Jesus Christ," the early Fathers stressed these requirements . . . Faith was generally regarded as the outstanding instrument for the reception of the merits of Christ, . . . It [salvation] was understood to consist in true knowledge of God, confidence in Him, and self-committal to Him, and to have as its special object Jesus Christ and His atoning blood.[84]

Salvation is available only to individuals who know Jesus Christ and his redemptive act upon the cross. General revelation, which is available to all, could not provide adequate content for salvation. Only special revelation could provide that information. Furthermore, given the success of Augustine's understanding of human nature over Pelagius' position, the church came to embrace human nature as depraved and unable to attain any spiritual good. As Pinnock claimed above, the evangelical movement for the most part accepted this Augustinian stance. Finally, the evangelical church in North America has been committed to missions and evangelism, key components of their theology. It has been assumed that an exclusivist stance regarding the recipients of salvation validates both evangelistic and mission activities. Furthermore, it may have been assumed that an exclusivist stance regarding agency of salvation necessarily entails an exclusivist stance on this issue of recipients. However, does the evidence support the initial assessment that exclusivism is internally consistent? For this initial assessment to be internally inconsistent, we need to show that it is impossible to embrace the basic tenants of evangelicalism and this position at the same time.

---

84. Berkhof, *History of Christian Doctrines*, 203.

However, if it is possible to hold those basic tenants as true and exclusivism as true, then we must understand the position as being internally consistent.

Before continuing our investigation regarding consistency, it may be beneficial to begin by examining the assumption presented above that an exclusivist stance regarding agency of salvation entails an exclusivist stance on this issue of recipients. This assumption can be clarified by asking two questions, which are equivalent but helpful for understanding the assumption. First, is it necessarily the case that the first stance implies the second stance? That is, does the second stance regarding recipients always follow from the stance regarding agency? Second, is it not possible to hold the first position and not embrace the second? The first question is important because if it is true that it is necessarily the case that the first stance implies the second stance, then our taxonomy presented in essay 2 lacks the simplicity we prefer in a good model. Instead of offering a complex model in which it is possible to mix the categories of pluralism, inclusivism, and exclusivism relative to the issue under discussion, we need only to have the simpler taxonomy first presented by Race. Given the simpler model, if one is an exclusivist regarding agency, then one is an exclusivist regarding the recipients. This simpler model was rejected because we did find evangelicals who hold one position regarding agency but a different position regarding the recipients of salvation.

However, this reaction is descriptive in nature and not prescriptive as the sentence of entailment suggests. To say that it is necessarily the case that the first stance implies the second stance is to make a prescriptive claim. After all, those evangelicals who hold an exclusivism regarding Jesus Christ but who take an inclusivist stance regarding the recipients of salvation might be thinking illogically. Therefore, to offer a counterexample that is descriptive may miss the point. If a descriptive counterexample cannot count against the claim, then we might ask what evidence we have to accept the claim that it is necessarily the case that the first stance implies the second stance. Is the sentence an analytical truth? No, for we can assume the negation of the claim, and it does not result in a reductio ad absurdum.[85] Hence, the descriptive counterexample may provide evidence against the claim. This brings us to the second question: is it not possible to hold the first position and not embrace the second? Since this question is equivalent to the first question, it also is not an analytic truth, so descriptive evidence is allowable. Obviously, it is possible to embrace an exclusivist

85. The claim can be symbolized as $\Box\,[(\forall x)\,(\forall y)\,(Ex \supset Ey)]$, where E stands for exclusivism, x represents agency, and y represents recipients. Its denial, i.e., $\sim\!\Box\,[(\forall x)\,(\forall y)\,(Ex \supset Ey)]$ when tested does not result in a contradiction, as we would expect if the original claim was an analytical truth.

stance regarding agency, while embracing a nonexclusivist stance regarding the recipients of salvation. Therefore, we are not logically or empirically restricted to the narrower taxonomy.

This brings us back to our initial assessment that the exclusivist stance regarding the recipients of salvation is consistent with basic evangelical thought. If we limit our understanding of basic evangelical thought to the issues of biblical testimony, historical practices, and missions as a crucial element of evangelicalism, then the exclusivist stance is consistent. However, should more be taken into account? Since bounded-set thinking is a presupposition of the exclusivist stance, we might ask whether it is consistent with evangelical thought. This bounded thinking requires explicit faith in Jesus Christ, but as Millard Erickson points out, we do not know precisely how much knowledge is required for explicit faith, nor do we know the details of the content of that knowledge. As we saw, Erickson concludes, "Perhaps there is room for acknowledging that God alone may know in every case exactly whose faith is sufficient for salvation."[86] If Erickson's conclusion is representative of evangelical thought, then the bounded-set mentality is inconsistent with evangelicalism. The bounded-set, whether we are considering rigid or realist forms of exclusivism, is inconsistent with evangelicalism. The former does not reflect the openness of evangelicalism that distinguishes itself from fundamentalism. The latter, while taking the Scriptures seriously—as all evangelicals wish to do—does support a God-in-the-box mentality. Evangelicals, while maintaining that the Scriptures are accurate presentations of God's person and message, acknowledge that God is greater than the portrayal found in Scripture. God's ultimate being is not inconsistent with the portrait given in the Scriptures, but there is more to God than what is illustrated in the Scriptures. As a result, exclusivism regarding recipients of salvation must be rejected as being inconsistent with evangelicalism.[87]

If this conclusion is accurate, the question regarding why it is such a common stance among North American evangelicals must be asked. There are several possible explanations for this inconsistency. First, many evangelicals have not seriously considered the issues regarding the theology of religions. This lack of study is partly explained by the fact that evangelicals did not enter the dialogue until relatively recent times. In addition, many

---

86. Erickson, *How Shall They Be Saved?*, 195.

87. This is not the only approach one might take to suggest that the exclusivist stance on this issue is inconsistent with evangelicalism and basic Christianity. For example, Thomas Talbott argues that given the basic essence of God as love and Paul's understanding of election, exclusivism is inconsistent with Christian beliefs (Talbott, "Love of God and the Heresy of Exclusivism," 99–112).

evangelicals who are already in some time of ministry find very little time to explore this new area within their own theology. Second, because it was originally assumed that a three-tier taxonomy captured the options and evangelicals could not embrace anything else but an exclusivism regarding Jesus Christ, many may have assumed they had no options regarding the recipients of salvation. A third possible explanation may be found in the long-standing cooperation between fundamentalism and evangelicalism as they combated theological liberalism prior to World War II. It is possible that this stance of exclusivism regarding recipients of salvation held by some evangelicals is a residue from the period when North American evangelicalism and fundamentalism were joined together. If this is correct, then Phillips's suggestion that this issue "may become a watershed issue" has been realized and it becomes a point of distinction between fundamentalist and evangelicals as they move into the twenty-first century.

Now the question is whether the inclusivist stance held by some evangelicals is internally consistent. The centered-set mindset is consistent with evangelical thought; however, the issues of biblical evidence, historical precedence, and implications for evangelism and missions must be examined.

Regarding biblical evidence, while the Scriptures do not give examples of individuals who are saved by means of general revelation, we must not make too much of this fact.[88] An argument from ignorance is generally considered poor reasoning. Furthermore, if we consider the basic purpose of the Scriptures, then it is even less surprising that they do not present such examples.[89] However, the following passages may offer hope for those who do not have special revelation, or have not been evangelized.

Gen 9:8–16

> [8]Then God said to Noah and to his sons with him, [9]"Behold, I establish my covenant with you and your descendants after you, [10]and with every living creature that is with you, the birds, the cattle, and every beast of the earth with you, as many as came out of the ark. [11]I establish my covenant with you, that never again shall all flesh be cut off by the waters of a flood, and never again shall there be a flood to destroy the earth." [12]And God

---

88. Some inclusivists suggest the "holy pagans" such as Abel, Cornelius, Enoch, Melchizdek, Noah, and Job are examples. However, these attempts are in most cases inappropriate. "Most of the Old Testament people who are outside of Israel and yet evidence a proper relationship to God all had special revelation in some form" (Tiessen, *Who Can Be Saved?*, 149).

89. Second Timothy 3 suggests that the primary purpose of Scripture is to equip believers.

said, "This is the sign of the covenant which I make between me and you and every living creature that is with you, for all future generations: ¹³I set my bow in the cloud, and it shall be a sign of the covenant between me and the earth. ¹⁴When I bring clouds over the earth and the bow is seen in the clouds, ¹⁵I will remember my covenant which is between me and you and every living creature of all flesh; and the waters shall never again become a flood to destroy all flesh. ¹⁶When the bow is in the clouds, I will look upon it and remember the everlasting covenant between God and every living creature of all flesh that is upon the earth."

Jer 29:13

You will seek me and find me; when you seek me with all your heart . . .

Matt 25:31–46

³¹"When the Son of man comes in his glory, and all the angels with him, then he will sit on his glorious throne. ³²Before him will be gathered all the nations, and he will separate them one from another as a shepherd separates the sheep from the goats, ³³and he will place the sheep at his right hand, but the goats at the left. ³⁴Then the King will say to those at his right hand, 'Come, O blessed of my Father, inherit the kingdom prepared for you from the foundation of the world; ³⁵for I was hungry and you gave me food, I was thirsty and you gave me drink, I was a stranger and you welcomed me, ³⁶I was naked and you clothed me, I was sick and you visited me, I was in prison and you came to me.' ³⁷Then the righteous will answer him, 'Lord, when did we see thee hungry and feed thee, or thirsty and give thee drink? ³⁸And when did we see thee a stranger and welcome thee, or naked and clothe thee? ³⁹And when did we see thee sick or in prison and visit thee?' ⁴⁰And the King will answer them, 'Truly, I say to you, as you did it to one of the least of these my brethren, you did it to me.' ⁴¹Then he will say to those at his left hand, 'Depart from me, you cursed, into the eternal fire prepared for the devil and his angels; ⁴²for I was hungry and you gave me no food, I was thirsty and you gave me no drink, ⁴³I was a stranger and you did not welcome me, naked and you did not clothe me, sick and in prison and you did not visit me.' ⁴⁴Then they also will answer, 'Lord, when did we see thee hungry or thirsty or a stranger or naked or sick or in prison, and did not minister to thee?' ⁴⁵Then he will answer them, 'Truly, I say to you, as you did it not to one of the least of these, you did it not to me.' ⁴⁶And

they will go away into eternal punishment, but the righteous into eternal life."

John 3:18–21

[18]He who believes in him is not condemned; he who does not believe is condemned already, because he has not believed in the name of the only Son of God. [19]And this is the judgment, that the light has come into the world, and men loved darkness rather than light, because their deeds were evil. [20]For every one who does evil hates the light, and does not come to the light, lest his deeds should be exposed. [21]But he who does what is true comes to the light, that it may be clearly seen that his deeds have been wrought in God.

Acts 2:17

And in the last days it shall be, God declares, that I will pour out my Spirit upon all flesh, and your sons and your daughters shall prophesy, and your young men shall see visions, and your old men shall dream dreams.

Acts 10:34–35

[34]And Peter opened his mouth and said: "Truly I perceive that God shows no partiality, [35]but in every nation any one who fears him and does what is right is acceptable to him.

Acts 17:24–30

[24]The God who made the world and everything in it, being Lord of heaven and earth, does not live in shrines made by man, [25]nor is he served by human hands, as though he needed anything, since he himself gives to all men life and breath and everything. [26]And he made from one every nation of men to live on all the face of the earth, having determined allotted periods and the boundaries of their habitation, [27]that they should seek God, in the hope that they might feel after him and find him. Yet he is not far from each one of us, [28]for 'In him we live and move and have our being'; as even some of your poets have said, 'For we are indeed his offspring.' [29]Being then God's offspring, we ought not to think that the Deity is like gold, or silver, or stone, a representation by the art and imagination of man. [30]The times of ignorance God overlooked, but now he commands all men everywhere to repent ...

Rom 1:18–23

> [18]For the wrath of God is revealed from heaven against all ungodliness and wickedness of men who by their wickedness suppress the truth. [19]For what can be known about God is plain to them, because God has shown it to them. [20]Ever since the creation of the world his invisible nature, namely, his eternal power and deity, has been clearly perceived in the things that have been made. So they are without excuse; [21]for although they knew God they did not honor him as God or give thanks to him, but they became futile in their thinking and their senseless minds were darkened. [22]Claiming to be wise, they became fools, [23]and exchanged the glory of the immortal God for images resembling mortal man or birds or animals or reptiles.

Rom 2:13–16

> [13]For it is not the hearers of the law who are righteous before God, but the doers of the law who will be justified. [14]When Gentiles who have not the law do by nature what the law requires, they are a law to themselves, even though they do not have the law. [15]They show that what the law requires is written on their hearts, while their conscience also bears witness and their conflicting thoughts accuse or perhaps excuse them [16]on that day when, according to my gospel, God judges the secrets of men by Christ Jesus.

1 Cor 15:10–11

> [10]But by the grace of God I am what I am, and his grace toward me was not in vain. On the contrary, I worked harder than any of them, though it was not I, but the grace of God which is with me. [11]Whether then it was I or they, so we preach and so you believed.

Phil 2:12–13

> [12]Therefore, my beloved, as you have always obeyed, so now, not only as in my presence but much more in my absence, work out your own salvation with fear and trembling; [13]for God is at work in you, both to will and to work for his good pleasure.

James 4:8

> Draw near to God and he will draw near to you. Cleanse your hands, you sinners, and purify your hearts, you men of double mind.

Rev 20:12–13

> ¹²And I saw the dead, great and small, standing before the throne, and books were opened. Also another book was opened, which is the book of life. And the dead were judged by what was written in the books, by what they had done. ¹³And the sea gave up the dead in it, Death and Hades gave up the dead in them, and all were judged by what they had done.

While the above passages do not provide "proof-texts" to support the claim that implicit faith or faith based on general revelation may result in salvation, they at least offer hope for those who do not "name the name of Jesus Christ."[90]

If there is scriptural support for the inclusivist stance regarding the recipients of salvation, is there historical precedence for contemporary evangelicalism to embrace this position? In order to show there is historical precedence, we do not need an exhaustive list of individuals who embraced the position that became known as inclusivism. Such a study would take us far from the intent of this project. Rather what is needed to establish a historical precedence is to provide a few examples.[91] The first historical precedence for contemporary evangelicals working in the theology of religions is that set of evangelical theologians cited in the second essay of this volume. There were several evangelicals who suggested that while salvation

---

90. "What renders problematic the position that persons cannot possibly be saved through implicit faith is Paul's statement about those who have general revelation being without excuse (Rom 1:20). In other words, if the are condemnable because they have not trusted God through what they have, it must have been possible somehow to meet his requirements through this means. If not, responsibility and condemnation are meaningless. What therefore must be the case is not that on the basis of the internal law persons actually fulfill that law. Paul seems to be saying more than that no one fulfills the laws given to Moses, but that no one *can* be thus saved (Gal 2:16, 21). If this is the case, then we must ask how one is saved, and the answer is that the law serves to make people guilty, to make them realize their need of grace, thus, to bring them to Christ (Gal 3:24–25). Similarly, if individuals, on the basis of the inner law, come to realize their own sinfulness, guilt, and inability to please God, then that law would also have the effect of bringing them to grace" (Erickson, *How Shall They Be Saved?*, 194).

91. Some of the theological positions taken by several of the evangelical theologians may be raised as objections for embracing inclusivism. For example, Pinnock's rejection of Augustinian theology in favor of Pelagius, or John Sanders's entertainment of open theism, or Grenz's attempt to work within postmodern thought all leave mainstream evangelicals uneasy. However, the stance of inclusivism regarding recipients of salvation does not entail any of these moves. Consider the theologies of Ramm or Tiessen: both maintain positions that mainstream evangelicals find sound, yet both men are open to the possibility of salvation outside the church.

was possible only because of the work of Jesus Christ, the efficacy of that work may be extend to the unevangelized because of the mercy of God.

Just as evangelicalism can be distinguished from fundamentalism because of the former's willingness to acknowledge the contributions of the Enlightenment, Zwingli's theology is often distinguished from the theology of other Protestant reformers because of his acknowledgement of the value of the humanism of his day. Defining true religion as worshiping God and being obedient to God, Zwingli embraced a position that while salvation was made possible only because of Jesus Christ,

> many besides Christians, and quite independently of Christian revelation, had been religious in this sense . . . He maintained that they were saved as truly as Christian believers . . . God, he taught, had revealed Himself, not only through Christ, but in many other ways. From the beginning He has been making His will known to men, and has had His true worshippers and obedient children.[92]

Zwingli's theology is an example of inclusivism regarding the recipients of salvation from the Protestant Reformation period.

Moving back to the church fathers, both Clement of Alexandria and Justin Martyr held positions similar to the contemporary stance of inclusivism regarding the recipients of salvation. For example, one of the central issues that Clement is grappling with in *The Stromata* is the issue of God's relationship to non-Christians. Throughout this text, Clement maintains that God is actively pursuing all individuals. God embraces some via the gospel message, but others are nourished differently. "For each soul has its own proper nutriment; some growing by knowledge and science, and others feeding on the Hellenic philosophy."[93] In Book VII, Chapter II, Clement tells us:

> Now that which is lovable leads, to contemplation of itself, each one who, from love of knowledge, applies himself entirely to contemplation. Wherefore also the Lord, drawing the commandments, both the first which He gave, and the second, from one foundation, neither allowed those who were before the law to be without law, nor permitted those who were unacquainted with the principles of the Barbarian philosophy to be without restraint. For, having furnished one with the commandments, and the other with philosophy, He shut up unbelief to the Advent. When every one who believes not is without excuse. For by

---

92. McGiffert, *Protestant Thought before Kant*, 65.
93. Clement of Alexandria, *Stromata*, bk. 1, ch. 1, 300.

a different process of advancement, both Greek and Barbarian,
He leads to the perfection which is by faith.[94]

Whether we find Clement's understanding of general revelation plausible, it is clear that there is historical precedence from the early church fathers for the contemporary stance of inclusivism regarding the recipients of salvation. While God is Lord of all, Clement acknowledges that not all have faith; hence, he is not a universalist but does claim that some are brought to a saving faith without knowing the content of the gospel message.[95]

For evangelicals the primary objection to the inclusivist position is that it is inconsistent with the missional focus of evangelical thought. The reasoning claims that if God does allow individuals to be saved without understanding the gospel message, then the thrust of missions by evangelicals is misguided. However, the reasoning continues, the thrust is not misguided because the church is commanded by Christ to evangelize and make disciples. Hence, according to this reasoning, God does not operate by inclusive means. Clearly, for the evangelical who embraces the inclusivist stance, the second premise is true. What is questionable is whether the first premise is true. Does inclusivism regarding recipients of salvation undermine the missional focus of the church?

If salvation pertained only to the eschaton, then possibly a case could be made for ceasing missional activities—assuming inclusivism is true. However, evangelicals, as we have seen, understand salvation as both a here-and-now as well as a not-yet notion. Clearly salvation includes an eschatological aspect, a future relational experience with God. However, salvation also has a here-and-now aspect. Because of this aspect, an inclusivist stance on this issue does not undermine missional activities. Rather it stresses the importance of continued missional activities. Missionaries meet physical needs whether they include operating orphanages or caring for AIDS patients or setting up temporary shelters for earthquake victims. Missional activities may include working for social justice, in which North American evangelicals are very active.[96]

Even if inclusivism is true, missions still must address spiritual needs. If a person comes to adequate salvific knowledge based on general revelation

---

94. Ibid., 526.

95. "But He is the Saviour of those who have believed, because of their wishing to know; and the Lord of those who have not believed, till, being enabled to confess him, they obtain the peculiar and appropriate boon which comes by Him" (ibid., 525).

96. In an interview with Stephen Monsma, research fellow at the Paul B. Henry Institute for the Study of Christianity and Politics at Calvin College, Agnieszka Tennant concludes that "Monsma proves that evangelicals are more active in welfare-to-work programs than any other religious group" (Tennant, "Social Justice Surprise," 44).

or at least information apart from the gospel message, that person may be aware of their own sinfulness, their utter dependence upon God for salvation, and may trust that God will supply their needs, without understanding the need has been met or knowing the personal nature of how God met the need. They may not be aware of the Spirit's ministry, or the power of the Spirit's indwelling, or any of the numerous other benefits God bestows as part of salvation.[97] The missional focus is still important because the gospel message provides not only hope for tomorrow but also hope for today. Furthermore, missions can help educate the indigenous peoples so they in turn can contextualize their new understanding of God's mercy within their own culture. An inclusivist stance regarding recipients of salvation does not undermine the evangelical efforts in evangelism and missions.[98]

Viability

While the inclusivist stance regarding the recipients of salvation is consistent with evangelical thought, is it a viable position? The viability of this stance for an evangelical theology of religion is very good. While it is not the most important reason this stance has good viability for evangelicals, it is important to note that in the preface of this project we stated that while evangelical theology is diverse, it exhibits a commitment to the Christian Scriptures, an evangelistic thrust, and a level of theological tolerance. This stance promotes continued work in all three areas. It promotes further work not only in these areas but also in areas such as the work of the Spirit throughout the world. Evangelical theologians such as Yong and Kärkkäinen are exploring the work of the Spirit of God in ways evangelicals have

---

97. Lewis Sperry Chafer identified thirty-three positional truths that God bestows upon those who are saved. These benefits are intended to enable the created to have a fuller relationship with their Creator here and now. "These positions are known only through a divine revelation" (*Salvation*, 59). Without continued mission work, it is possible to possess these benefits and not be able to apply them because the recipient may be ignorant of them.

98. Sir Norman Anderson offered four reasons why a form of inclusivism should not lead to a diminution of missional activities. "First, we are under orders, explicit and unequivocal, to go to all the world with the good news. Second, a man such as we have discussed may indeed have found God's mercy, but desperately needs teaching, heart assurance, and a message he can communicate to others . . . Third, if we consider what enabled us ourselves to give up attempting to earn salvation and put our entire trust in the mercy of God, would we not—almost invariably—say that it was hearing the good news of what Christ has done, the very message which the apostle was commanded to preach in Corinth? . . . Fourth, can we deny others the present experience of joy, peace and power which a conscious knowledge of Christ, and communion with him, alone can bring?" (*Christianity and World Religions*, 155).

not considered and, hence, are making valuable contributions to evangelical thought.[99] This stance also suggests that evangelicals reexamine their understanding of general revelation. (This is the focus of the second part of this volume.)

If inclusivism regarding the recipients of salvation is the stance evangelicals should take in their development of their theology of religions, then part of the new research must be a renewed commitment to interreligious dialogue. From the beginning of the church, Christians have historically been involved in interreligious dialogue. However, whether intentional or the product of not being around individuals of other faith traditions, North American evangelicals had become isolationists. Pragmatically, North American evangelicals no longer have the excuse of not being able to engage in dialogue with individuals of other faith traditions. If inclusivism, on this issue, is true, then evangelicals have theological reasons that require them to return to the round table.[100] This stance also suggests the nature of this dialogue: it must be open, honest, respectful, and from a position of commitment.[101]

This stance is viable because of the new research and activities it promotes, and it also underscores that it is God who saves individuals. Religions do not save. God chose to provide atonement for sin through the cross-event of Jesus Christ. While the Christian faith may be the normative means by which God brings individuals to a saving faith and the fullest self-revelation by God, God is not limited to the actions of the church. The church is privileged to be a tool of God's workmanship, but the church is only a tool. It is God who is redeeming the cosmos and restoring fellowship between Creator and creation.

Harmony between Empirical Knowledge and Presuppositions of Position

One of the strongest arguments for evangelicals to embrace the inclusivist stance regarding recipients of salvation is their presupposition that God is greater than their theology. In addition, there is empirical evidence that

---

99. Kärkkäinen, *Pneumatology*.

100. Jones, *Christ at the Round Table*. See also Tennent, *Christianity at the Religious Roundtable*.

101. This is not to suggest that evangelicals have not recently been involved in interreligious dialogue; rather, it is to underscore the need for more participation by evangelicals. Evangelicals such as Norman Anderson, Kenneth Cragg, Stuart Hackett, Terry Muck, and Stephen Neill have been involved in this dialogue.

suggests God is at work even with the unevangelized. Millard Erickson captures the first point as he addresses some common errors that are made in attempting to develop a theology of God. "One [of the common errors] is an excessive analysis, in which God is submitted to a virtual autopsy. The attributes of God are laid out and classified in a fashion similar to the approach taken in an anatomy textbook."[102] Donald Bloesch points out that the Bible presents God as "Creator of the universe and Lord of history."[103] This presentation, among other things, includes the relation between Creator and creature.

> In the biblical view God created the world out of love, not metaphysical necessity. The world does not simply proceed from the Logos, but it is an act of the freedom of God. The freedom of God, indeed, is another way to express his sovereignty. God's freedom means that he is grounded in his own being, is determined and moved by himself. This is to say, God exists in and of himself and cannot be explained by any prior cause.[104]

While evangelical theologians must speak of God, they wish to retain the biblical understanding that God is beyond or greater than whatever they say about God. As a result, they must avoid declaring, "here is how God must do things" in areas that God has not provided adequate self-disclosure. While the Scriptures do speak of heaven and hell, they do not provide a clear picture of the limitations of the wideness of God's mercy. As a result, an inclusivist stance that permits God to provide salvation to whomever God chooses ought to be embraced. This should not hinder evangelism or missions but rather encourage those who are obedient and go, for they will understand that God is already at work.

This leads to the second point; there is empirical evidence that God is at work—even with the unevangelized. The church, both local and universal, seems to be the norm of God's activity today. However, God is not limited to a thriving, healthy bride of Christ to accomplish the work God wishes done. Following the defeat of Chiang in 1949, Mao Tse-Tung established one of the most powerful political parties ever to exist. In spite of repeated attempts to eradicate Christianity from mainland China, the cultural revolution failed to impede God's working among its citizenry.[105] Evidence

---

102. Erickson, *Christian Theology*, 291. An evangelical theology proper ought to promote a clearer understanding of God in order to promote a "closer personal relationship with" God.

103. Bloesch, *Essentials of Evangelical Theology*, 1:25.

104. Ibid., 26.

105. "In 1950 there were approximately one million baptized Protestant Christians

today indicates that the Spirit of God worked among the Chinese people to continue the work that God had begun prior to 1950.[106] Similar stories come from Eastern European countries that fell under the rule of communism.[107] Of course, these are examples of God's working in areas that had already been introduced to the gospel message. However, Don Richardson writes of what he calls the Melchizedek factor. Because of general revelation, individuals who have yet to be introduced to the gospel message are already prepared for that message. After a discussion of how first-century Gentile culture had been prepared by Greek philosophy for the gospel message, Richardson asks a series of questions and then follows with a bold claim.

> Do you not feel a certain question rising now within you? It cannot be avoided—if the Almighty ordained God-and-Christ-foreshadowing metaphors and concepts to facilitate the redemptive process in one Gentile culture—that of the Greeks—could He not also have manifested a similar providence within other Gentile cultures as well? Perhaps even in all of them?

In other words, has the God who prepared the gospel for the world also prepared the world for the gospel? If he has, then the current assumption, held by millions of believers and nonbelievers alike, that pagan people cannot understand and generally do not want to receive the Christian gospel, and that it is therefore unfair (and almost more work than it is worth) to try to get them to accept it, must be a false assumption.

> In the rest of this book . . . I will prove this assumption to be false. God has indeed prepared the Gentile world to receive the gospel.[108]

While Richardson's accounts are anecdotal in nature and may not "prove" his thesis, they do suggest that God has not been without witness and that God has been involved with groups of people that lie outside the covenantal lineage of Abraham.[109]

---

in China, more than 2,000 ordained Chinese ministers and 10,500 evangelists. By 1966, all the 11,470 churches and 7,500 evangelistic centers in existence when the Communists took over, had been closed" (Wang, *Chinese Church that Will Not Die*, 6). For a scholarly study of religion in China see Yao and Badham, *Religious Experience in Contemporary China*.

106. During a recent visit my wife and I had the opportunity to visit and worship in Chinese churches in Beijing and Harbin.

107. Paulson, *Beyond the Wall*.

108. Richardson, *Eternity in Their Hearts*, 27–28.

109. Evert D. Osburn builds on this concept: "Anthropological studies have revealed that the Yoruba people of Nigeria worship a Supreme Being whom they call

Relation to Other Alternative Positions

The evangelical inclusivist stance relating to salvation's recipients may be assessed in several ways. One way to assess evangelical inclusivism in terms of salvation's recipients is to compare and contrast the evangelical form of inclusivism with the inclusivism of someone like Gavin D'Costa, a Roman Catholic. There are several problems with this option. First, there is not a singular evangelical form of inclusivism, just as one could not assume D'Costa represents all Roman Catholic inclusivists. There are several problems with this option. First, there is not a single evangelical form of inclusivism, just as one could not assume D'Costa represents all Roman Catholic inclusivists. Furthermore, while North American evangelicals are working on developing forms of inclusivism that are consistent with their evangelical heritage, that work is still in its infancy. A second option is to allow a nonevangelical, a pluralist, to assess the evangelical stance in relation to other positions.

Chester Gillis provides this approach as he asks if evangelical inclusivism is progressive or a betrayal of the evangelical stance.[110] Gillis begins by applauding the move by some evangelicals.

> The limited participation by evangelicals (conservative or otherwise) in intra-religious dialogue, and the exclusion of them from interreligious dialogue arranged by pluralist-minded theologians, has plagued the dialogue process itself, and virtually conceded the territory to moderate and liberal theologians representing theologies that, to varying degrees, conflict with evangelical theology.[111]

He points out that if Christian theologians are truly going to make progress with intra- and interreligious dialogue, then evangelicals must be included in those dialogues. The inclusivist stance does promote such involvement. However, Gillis warns evangelicals who wish to participate in these dialogues that it is inappropriate to use such dialogues for proselytizing.

> Dialogue is to be a truth-seeking adventure . . . Many religions make truth claims, and each in accord with its insight, revelation,

---

Olodumare. Olodumare is known as the Creator (cf. Isa 40:28), the Most High (cf. Ps 91:1), and the King who dwells in the heavens (cf. 113:5). He possesses all superlative attributes, executes judgment (cf. 75:7), is the discerner of hearts who sees both the inside and outside of man (cf. Heb 4:12–13), and he alone can accomplish his work merely by speaking (cf. Gen 1:3ff.). Olodumare is the all-powerful Creator who deserves to be worshiped by mankind. He cannot be represented by images, but he can be approached as the Father. It is not when the Yoruba tradition about Olodumare originated, but "research has shown that the High God (of the Yoruba) was not a later insertion through contact with Western Christianity'" ("Those Who Have Never Heard," 367).

110. Gillis, "Evangelical Inclusivism," 138–50.

111. Ibid., 140.

> prophecy or enlightenment is entitled to do so . . . Dialogue is the very process that challenges those claims to truth by counter-claims, additional evidence, different perspectives, and other hermeneutics. Through the dialogue process it is possible . . . that one's understanding of the truth may change.[112]

Gillis's warning is initially puzzling. North American evangelicals, for example in the field of philosophy, have illustrated their willingness to engage in serious truth-seeking dialogue, and have changed positions when the evidence so warrants. Furthermore, they have done so without using the dialogues as opportunities to "preach." However, since evangelism is a foundational belief for evangelicals, they have been willing to share the hope that is within, when asked. If Gillis's description of dialogue were taken seriously, then one would expect change might occur on both sides of the dialogue. For example, if an evangelical and a Sikh were in dialogue about their respective positions on salvation, the Sikh and the evangelical would be expected to provide an accurate account of their own particular position. For the evangelical not to give an accurate account would be intellectually dishonest. However, shall we charge them with "preaching," if they give a full account? This seems to be Gillis's charge. However, his charge to evangelicals who engage in dialogue goes beyond this. His warning regarding change is based on an assumption that if evangelicals pursue truth in interreligious dialogues, then they will be led to embracing pluralism. This assumption is no better founded than is an assumption that pluralists when pursuing truth will become inclusivists. Meaningful dialogue, whether it is intra- or interreligious, requires both parties to approach the dialogue with an openness to learn. Given the work done by evangelicals in the field of philosophy, there is hope that evangelical theologians will learn to engage in meaningful, open dialogue.

While the work of individuals such as John Sanders and Clark Pinnock have brought the field of theology of religions into the evangelical camp, there is much work yet to be done by evangelicals in this area. It affects their doctrines regarding God, Christ, humanity, salvation, the church, as well as evangelical approaches to missions. We must remember that ultimately salvation is up to God. It is God's decision who is saved. It is God's decision to determine the content of "saving faith." If the Bible is understood as presenting redemption history, then evangelicals must not forget the focus of that redemptive history—God. While the creation benefits, redemptive history is to unveil the glory of God.

> O the depth of the riches and wisdom and knowledge of God!
> How unsearchable are his judgments and how inscrutable his

---

112. Ibid., 144.

ways! For who has known the mind of the Lord, or who has been his counselor? Or who has given to him that he might be repaid? For from him and through him and to him are all things. To him be glory for ever. Amen. (Rom 11:33–36)

Now to him who is able to strengthen you according to my gospel and the preaching of Jesus Christ, according to the revelation of the mystery which was kept secret for long ages but is now disclosed and through the prophetic writings is made known to all nations, according to the command of the eternal God, to bring about the obedience of faith—to the only wise God be glory for evermore through Jesus Christ! Amen! (Rom 16:25–27)[113]

As a result, evangelical theology must not be so tight as to dictate the limits of God's mercy and grace.[114] Furthermore, if evangelical theology is to be exclusivistic regarding the agency of salvation but to take the stance of inclusivism regarding the recipients of salvation, then evangelicalism must develop a better understanding of how individuals with only implicit faith arrive at that form of faith. Evangelical theologians such as Amos Yong are exploring this area by focusing on the work of the Spirit of God.[115] However, other aspects of general revelation must also be explored.

---

113. The motif of unveiling the glory of God is found throughout the Christian Scriptures, e.g., Exod 16:7; 24:16; 40:34; 1 Chr 16:24; Ps 8:1; 19:1; 29:1; 50:15; 106:47; Isa 12:5; 24:15; 35:2; 40:5; 44:23; 45:20–25; 49:3; 60:7; Ezek 3:12; 10:18; 28:22; 39:21; 43:2; Luke 5:26; 7:16; John 12:28; 13:31; 14:13; 15:8; Acts 11:18; 1 Cor 6:20; Eph 1:11–14; Phil 2:13; 4:20; Col 1:27; 2 Thess 1:9; 2:14; Heb 13:21; 2 Pet 1:3; Jude 24–25; Rev 14:7; 15:4.

114. While writing from an exclusivist's position, W. Gary Phillips offers three warnings for evangelicals who take the inclusivist stance. "First, they must be cautious about labeling speculations (even those they deem probable) as certainties. Second, they must be cautious about the extent to which their inclusivism becomes a component within their apologetics. Third, they should guard against the assumption that God *must* have some special arrangement for the unevangelized, because otherwise, as they argue, God would then be less worthy of worship, and is less just and loving than humans" ("Evangelical Pluralism," 153). While this writer does disagree with Phillips's exclusivism, he does agree with Phillips's warnings. The inclusivist stance is embraced as the best possible inference, given the evidence. If inclusivism is taken dogmatically or used to promote a devaluation of missions or evangelism, then inclusivism has clearly led its adherents against the biblical mandates. To maintain that God *must* act in a particular way is to deny the very character of God—if the God of the Scriptures is to be God, then God must be sovereign. The inclusivist stance regarding recipients of salvation does not entail a violation of Phillips's warnings.

115. Olson, "Wind That Swirls Everywhere," 53–54. The article focuses on the project of Amos Yong and claims that "most of his writing falls into the category of *theologoumena*—theological explorations of new ways of looking at old questions" (ibid., 54).

Part 2
Reconstruction Proposal

5

Biblical Materials

An Evangelical Perspective

One of the common threads of evangelical theology is its commitment to the Christian Scriptures. As we begin the "Reconstruction Proposal," the Bible must be at the starting point for developing any Christian theology that is considered evangelical. The focus of this chapter is to present some of the relevant biblical materials and show some of the implications they may have for developing an evangelical theology of religions.

However, before we can begin to look at the biblical materials, two important methodological assumptions must be acknowledged. Like all readers, evangelicals are influenced by philosophical presuppositions. As we saw in the previous essay, evangelicals prefer interpretations of Scripture that are consistent with orthodoxy instead of interpretations that result in nonorthodox stances. Furthermore, evangelicals believe the Christian Scriptures to be the written Word of God. Evangelicals presuppose that God is a self-disclosing God, and that one of the mediums through which God has chosen to be revealed is the Christian Bible.[1] While evangelicals may differ on the finer issues of hermeneutics or the nature of inspiration, they agree that while the Christian Scriptures do reflect the historical and cultural settings

---

1. "Revelation is, in truth, the central pillar of biblical religion. Around the living God's disclosure of his own reality, purpose, and activity range all the special affirmations of Judeo-Christian theology. Biblical assertions of the creation of the cosmos, of the future judgment and the future life, of the divine salvation of sinners, of the meaning and worth of human existence in the days of our years, turn ultimately on the self-unveiling God who confronts his fallen creatures as their Creator, Redeemer and Judge" (Henry, *God, Revelation and Authority*, 409). Evangelicals frequently understand the Bible as one of several mediums through which God is self-revealed. The Christian Scriptures and the person of Jesus Christ are understood as "special revelation," while nature and human conscience are understood as "general revelation." The latter form of revelation will be the focus of chapter 8.

of the various human writers, God is ultimately its source.² Since the Scriptures have this divine-human authorship, they are both prescriptive and descriptive. The Scriptures provide, as it were, a window through which we can begin to know the mind and acts of God.³

Given the purpose of this chapter, the biblical materials presented are selective and not exhaustive, nor should the comments made regarding the selected materials be considered complete. Our goal in this chapter is simply to see some of the biblical materials for constructing an evangelical theology of religions. From the Old Testament, two sets of materials will be presented: the first representing the earliest period of biblical materials and the second representing Hebraic thought from the late monarchy. From the New Testament, the materials will be drawn from the Pauline literature of Colossians and Romans.⁴

---

2. While J. I. Packer's *"Fundamentalism" and the Word of God* is an older work, it is considered a classic statement of the evangelical view of Scripture. "It is customary to use the term *inspiration* to refer to the divine origin of Scripture . . . When we use the phrase "inspiration of Scripture," the noun may be taken either passively, as meaning "inspiredness," or actively, as denoting the divine activity by which God-breathed Scripture was produced. In this sense, inspiration is to be defined as a supernatural, providential influence of God's Holy Spirit upon the human authors which caused them to write what He wished to be written for the communication of revealed truth to others . . . Inspiration did not necessarily involve an abnormal state of mind on the writer's part, such as a trance, or vision, or hearing a voice. Nor did it involve any obliteration or overriding of his personality. Scripture indicates that God in His providence was from the first preparing the human vehicles of inspiration for their predestined task, and that He caused them in many cases, perhaps in most, to perform the task through the normal exercise of the abilities which He had given them" (Ibid., 77–78). Packer proceeds to argue that "because Evangelicals hold that the biblical writers were completely controlled by the Holy Spirit, it is often supposed, . . ., that they maintain what is called the 'dictation' or 'typewriter' theory of inspiration—namely, that the mental activity of the writers were simply suspended, apart from what was necessary for the mechanical transcription of words supernaturally introduced into their consciousness. But this is not so" (ibid., 78–79). Other important works that present an evangelical perspective of Scripture include Henry, *Revelation and the Bible*; Orr, *Revelation and Inspiration*; and Pinnock, *Biblical Revelation*.

3. This claim the Scriptures are a window through which we can know more about God must not be interpreted as placing the Scriptures on par with Jesus Christ. Jesus Christ "is the image of the invisible God" (Col 1:15, cf. Heb 1:3, Phil 2:6, John 14:9, 1 John 1:1–3). It is through the Scriptures that we have witness of Jesus Christ.

4. Each of these voices brings controversial assumptions to the table; however, the assumptions do reflect undergird positions widely accepted in the evangelical community, but since these assumptions are not the focus of this study, they will be simply presented, and work will proceed from them. Evangelicals generally agree that the Pentateuch is attributed to Moses Mosaic authorship, and likewise that Romans and Colossians were authored by Paul to Pauline authorship. Furthermore, the two Old Testament texts are considered to represent a very early and a very late understanding

Pentateuch

In the Pentateuch, no less than sixty times do we find references to gods other than Yahweh.[5] In all but five instances, these gods are referred to by the Hebrew word *elôhîym*.[6] This word usage is significant. In the first place, *elôhîym* is the same word Moses uses when referring to Yahweh as God: e.g., Deut 29:18. Moses does not attempt to deny the existence of other gods; rather he recognized the world in which he lived, and it was a world full of gods. Moberly points out that "although the patriarchs worshipped only one God, no particular significance attaches to this; there is no implied opposition to the worship of other gods."[7] However, are these gods equal?

Edmond Jacob states that while "Yahweh does not present himself to Moses as the only God," Yahweh is different.[8] Ed Mathews supports this claim. "The Hebrews realized their religion was different from other religions because their God was different from other gods."[9] First, the patriarchs understood Yahweh as a jealous God who would not share the devotion of followers with other gods. In Gen 35, Jacob called for his household to "put away the foreign gods." The Decalogue includes God saying, "I the LORD your God am a jealous God."[10] Yahweh demanded to be the sole God of the Israelite people. Whereas gods other than Yahweh could tolerate their worshipers also reverencing other gods, Yahweh demanded sole and total attention from the Israelite people.[11] "Monotheism was in no wise a subject of factional dispute. It was the faith of a whole people, of all factions . . .

---

of Yahweh worship. Hence, they provide a broad picture of Old Testament theology. While Paul is not the only New Testament writer to address the uniqueness of Jesus Christ, e.g., the Gospel of John emphasizes this, and Colossians is not the only Pauline literature that addresses this motif, Colossians does provide a number of insights that will be significant in the development of an evangelical theology of religions. For example, Paul presents Jesus Christ as unique because of who he is and also because of what he accomplished. In the second doctrinal section of Romans (chs. 9–11), the author attempts to develop a limited theology of religions as he grapples with a Christian perspective on Judaism. This study will lay an important foundation for evangelicals working in the area of theology of religions.

5. For examples, Gen 31:30, 35:2; Exod 12:12; 15:11; Num 25:2; 33:4; Deut 7:4; 8:19; and 28:36.

6. Gen 31:19, 34, and 35 use the word *terâphîm*; Gen 12:11 uses *'êl*; and Deut 32:16 uses *zûr*.

7. Moberly, *Old Testament of the Old Testament*, 87.

8. Jacob, *Theology of the Old Testament*, 66.

9. Mathews, "Yahweh and the Gods," 30.

10. Exod 20:5 and Deut 5:9.

11. For examples see Deut 5:7 and 28:14.

From the days of Moses the one universal God was the God of the whole nation."[12] Moses partly explains this jealousy in Deut 6:14–15.

> You shall not go after other gods, of the gods of the peoples who are around you; for the LORD your God in the midst of you is a jealous God; lest the anger of the LORD your God be kindled against you, and he destroy you from off the face of the earth.

Second, the plagues in Egypt also support the claim that Yahweh is different. "The supremacy of Jehovah over the demoniacal powers of Egypt manifested itself in the very first miraculous sign, . . ."[13] Exodus 12:12 claims, ". . . on all the gods of Egypt I will execute judgment: I am the Lord." Not only is Yahweh more powerful than the gods of Egypt, but Yahweh is portrayed as greater than all other gods are.

> Who is like thee, O LORD, among the gods? Who is like thee, majestic in holiness, terrible in glorious deeds, doing wonders? (Exod 15:11)

> Now I know that the LORD is greater than all gods. (Exod 18:11)

Furthermore, the God of Moses and early Israelite thought was different because Yahweh did not want the faithful to make images of their God since Yahweh was greater than any of those images, and Yahweh understood that the faithful would be tempted to worship the images and not the living God.[14] Finally, the Shema of Deut 6:4–5 provides further evidence that the God revealed to Moses was distinct from the other gods of the region. J. Gerald Janzen suggests that the crucial word in this passage is *eḥād*, (RSV "one"). He points out that there are two basic ways of understanding this word. "The word says something about Israel's God *in se* . . .; or it says something about the claim of this God upon Israel."[15] Janzen argues persuasively that the word is best understood as saying something about Israel's God. However, if it is understood as saying something about God's claim upon Israel, then the Shema does not reveal anything new about God. This understanding underscores what is said above—Yahweh is a jealous God. However, if Janzen is correct, then it is highlighting the notion that Yahweh

---

12. Kaufmann, *History of the Religion of Israel*, 4:18.

13. Keil and Delitzsche, *Commentary on the Old Testament*, 1:477.

14. Exod 20:23. "Perhaps it [the prohibition of images] reflects the idea that an image of Yahweh would not be Yahweh, and any worship of a Yahweh image was then by definition the worship of other gods" (Curtis, "Theological Basis for the Prohibition," 281).

15. Janzen, "On the Most Important Word in the Shema," 280.

is unique, and this underscores the notion that Yahweh may be one of many gods, but Yahweh is different.

Because of this difference, Yahweh has called believers into a special covenant relationship, a relationship of loyal bonding. For the Israelite, while being respectful of other faith systems, total allegiance to Yahweh is demanded. Others may worship multiple gods, but the Israelite is restricted to the one living jealous God. This has direct implications for the development of a Mosaic theology of religions. First, the openness toward the existence of other gods suggests that monotheism is not demanded when viewing faith systems as a whole. However, for the Israelite there is a restriction to monotheism. If one does not identify with Yahweh, then there are many options open for identification; however, if one identifies with Yahweh, then there are no other options available. It is Yahweh and Yahweh alone.

This raises an interesting problem for theology. Is Yahweh for the Israelite like Ahura Mazda for the Aryans of Iran? That is, is the Israelite faith a national religion, like Zoroastrianism is for the Parsees? Given the limited Mosaic voice, it is possible to argue that Yahweh is a national God. That is, from Gen 12 through the remainder of the Pentateuch the evidence suggests that the covenant relationship is national.[16]

The Pentateuch, however, adequately supports the claim that Yahweh is greater than all the other gods are, but even this raises problems for the theology of religions. It does not deny the possibility that Yahweh is simply the name by which the supreme God is revealed to the Israelites, while to the Aryans of Iran that same God is revealed as Ahura Mazda. The Mosaic voice maintains that not all faith traditions lead to the truth, but one interpretation of the Mosaic contribution could suggest that it is not denying the possibility that there may be more than one tradition that does lead to the truth. It is possible that adherents in several faith systems worship the same God, but only refer to this deity by different names.

Listening to the Pentateuch, we found three surprising points emerge relevant to the theology of religions. First, Yahweh did not contest the claim that other gods existed. Second, monotheism was demanded for the worshipers of Yahweh, but this restriction was not binding upon other peoples. Finally, Yahweh worship could be conceived as a nationalistic practice; thus, the Yahweh cult was limited and did not deny the possibility of deliverance (i.e., salvation) for other peoples by another god or gods.[17] Salvation, or

---

16. Because of the progressive nature of biblical revelation, a theology based solely on the Pentateuch will be woefully deprived of subsequent revelation.

17. While Gen 12:3 claims that Yahweh will bless all nations through Abraham, this promise of blessing does not necessarily extend deliverance to all nations, nor does it suggest the nature of this blessing.

the fulfillment of an individual's purpose, may have different connotations in different faith systems and hence may be obtained by different means. While this later point is not what is typically embraced as evangelical theology, it is not necessarily inconsistent with it if evangelical theology is going to place an emphasis on Scripture.[18] As a final point, it should be noted that the opening chapters of the Pentateuch lay the foundation for an evangelical theology of religions. In Gen 1–3, we find four critical elements: (1) God as Creator; (2) the Creator as distinct from the created; (3) alienation, the result of sin, at three levels: the alienation of persons from God, of persons from persons, and of persons from other elements of the created world; and (4) God's promise of restoration.

Jeremiah

In this section, we will listen to a voice from the period representing the end of the Southern Kingdom (specifically found in Jeremiah) determine how the Mosaic implications are modified and suggest how this later period informs the development of a theology of religions.[19]

18. Ed Mathews aptly concludes his article on the theology of religions in the Pentateuch in the following way. "If Israel took the reality of her monotheism seriously, she had an authentic witness within pagan polytheism. If she kept at bay the voices of religious tolerance, the temptations of religious pluralism, she had an incredible purpose, a marvelous privilege . . ., she was the means of proclaiming his name "in all the earth." . . . Is that not also our calling, our purpose, our privilege?" (Mathews, "Yahweh and the Gods," 37).

19. Jeremiah the prophet spoke the word of Yahweh regarding the situation in which Judah found itself toward the end of that kingdom. Beginning his career as a prophet in 627 BCE, he saw Judah experience a brief period of independence from Assyria only to fall under the domination of Egypt and then Babylon, "before finally watching (her) destroy (herself) in a futile attempt to get free of the latter" (Bright, *Jeremiah*, xxviii). Jerusalem was destroyed by Babylon in 587, so his career extended over forty years. From this vantage point, he had access to a much better-informed theology than did Moses. Regarding the book of Jeremiah, like many of the other prophetic books, it should not be read as a history in which events are presented in a historical chronological fashion. It is a collection of topics roughly providing a structure to the text. The topics are bracketed with biographical information regarding the prophet Jeremiah or a historical appendix. (Chapters 1–25 deal with warnings and judgments. Chapters 30–33 offer a message of hope, and chapters 46–51 prophesy against heathen nations; Bright, *Jeremiah*, lix). Bright offered a similar outline in his earlier article "The Book of Jeremiah: Its Structure, Its Problems, and Their Significance for the Interpreter" (Bright, "Book of Jeremiah," 262–63). Other outlines of the book are possible. For example, Thomas M. Raitt sees the basic structure as an Oracle of Judgment in which the text offers a reoccurring pattern of "Accusation" that is followed by "Proclamation" (Raitt, *Theology of Exile*, 17). From Jeremiah we will see a transformed theology of religions emerge. (If this is accurate and we do find a transformed theology of religions emerging by the late

Jeremiah, like Moses, portrays Yahweh as acknowledging the existence of other gods. Over thirty times we find references to gods other than Yahweh in the book of Jeremiah. In most of these instances, Jeremiah uses the same term that Moses used, *elôhîym*, when referring to these other gods. Like Moses, Jeremiah uses this term to refer also to Yahweh.[20] However, by the late monarchy the revelation from Yahweh magnifies truths that Moses only suggests. As a result, we find a marked distinction in tone between Moses and Jeremiah toward other gods. While it may be argued that Moses was passive toward other gods as long as their worshipers were not Israelite, Jeremiah is anything but sympathetic to other gods, because his audience was inclined to embrace these other gods. While it may be argued that Moses was passive toward other gods as long as their worshipers were not Israelite, Jeremiah is anything but sympathetic to other gods, because his audience was inclined to embrace these other gods.

Yahweh's wrath against his people who have turned away to worship other gods permeates the book of Jeremiah. "And I will utter my judgments against them, for all their wickedness in forsaking me; they have burned incense to other gods, and worshiped the works of their own hands."[21] (This could have been spoken by Moses.) Not only had Judah turned away from Yahweh, but also with their own hands, they made the gods toward which they turned. In fact, Yahweh claims that they "have sworn by those who are no gods."[22] While Judah believes they have turned to other gods, Yahweh does not consider the objects of their worship to be gods. Their new objects of worship "did not make the heavens and the earth," and these new gods will all perish.[23] Jeremiah compares these new gods to a waistcloth that was buried in the Euphrates but now is good for nothing.[24] Jeremiah, proclaiming the word of Yahweh, claims the other gods have no value. For

---

Judahite monarchy, then this should affect our methodology for doing Old Testament theology. If different theologies emerge from different periods of time, then the Old Testament may be viewed as being inconsistent. Historically, evangelicals have denied this. A possible solution to evolving theologies is to embrace the notion of progressive revelation. Many evangelicals find this a correct approach to biblical interpretation (cf. Ramm, *Protestant Biblical Interpretation*, 101–4). Hence, while Jeremiah's theology of religions is "different" from that of Moses, the two are not necessarily inconsistent. If we embrace progressive revelation, as I believe we should, then we will probably avoid a *cross-sectional* method for doing Old Testament theology and see the various theologies as consistent.

20. E.g., Jer 2:17; 5:4; and 15:16.
21. Jer 1:16.
22. Jer 5:7.
23. Jer 10:11.
24. Jer 13.

Moses, Yahweh demonstrated this truth as Moses faced Pharaoh. However, by the late monarchy, Yahweh is no longer simply demonstrating this but proclaiming it. While Jeremiah most frequently uses the word *elôhîym* when referring to the other gods, it is significant that he also uses two other words: *hăbêl* and *shâv*. Jer 14:22 poses a rhetorical question, "Are there any among the *hăbêl* (false gods) of the nations that can bring rain?" Jeremiah is telling his audience that the worship of these false gods is unsatisfactory. They do not have any control over nature; they are empty. However, Jeremiah's tone toward these false gods is even stronger than simply calling them unsatisfactory. In Jer 18:15 he uses the word *shâv*, which the RSV translates as "false gods." In this context, the false gods are not only useless but also desolating and evil. These "null gods made them [Judah] stumble."[25] Not only do these false gods not have power over nature, but they also lead to moral ruin. For Jeremiah, these other gods are not innocent deities that those of foreign nations worship. There is an evil about them because of their influence on Yahweh's covenant people. Yahweh in the writings of Moses did not contest the existence of other gods. In Jeremiah, Yahweh again does not attempt to prove the nonexistence of these gods.[26] Rather, Yahweh calls them ineffective, unsatisfactory, and evil because of their influence upon those of the covenant.

A second relevant change can be seen in the late monarchy from Jeremiah. While it may be argued that in the Pentateuch Yahweh demanded monotheism only of the worshipers of Yahweh, thus allowing other peoples to worship their own gods, this is not the case by the late monarchy. One avenue for understanding this new attitude toward other faith systems is to notice what is said about the false prophets. False prophets were not unique to the late monarchy. Beecher claims that the false prophets were more numerous than were the true prophets.[27] However, Ronald Manahan points out that the translators of the Septuagint use the Greek word ψευδοπροφήτης (false prophets) ten times, and nine of these occurrences are in Jeremiah.[28] While the people's response to false prophets was no

---

25. Keil and Delitzsch, *Commentary on the Old Testament*, 8:300.

26. "In the age of Jeremiah such things are said of the heathen gods as leave us no doubt that the prophets had reached the idea of a theoretical Monotheism; for, e.g., these gods are named 'nothing,' . . ., Isa xli. 24; 'chaos,' . . ., Isa xli. 29; 'falsehood,' . . ., Jer x. 14; 'vanity,' . . ., Jer xviii.15; 'wind' or 'vapor,' . . ., Jer ii. 5; 'nonentities,' . . ., Ezek xxx. 13; 'no gods,' . . ., Jer ii. 11; 'abomination,' . . ., Jer xvi. 18; 'to be loathed,' . . ., Jer iv. 1; 'shame,' . . ., Jer iii. 24" (Davidson, *Theology of the Old Testament*, 65).

27. Beecher, *Prophets and the Promise*, 61.

28. Manahan points out the nine occurrences in Jeremiah are found in 6:13; 26:7, 8, 11, 16; 27:9; 28:1; and 29:1, 8 (Manahan, "Theology of Pseudoprophets," 78).

different during Jeremiah's time than it was during Moses's time, Jeremiah does confront the problem. He declares,

> the people refused correction from Yahweh (5:3), refused to repent (8:6), closed their ears against Yahweh's word (both king [36:23; 37:2–3] and subjects [7:13, 25–27] filled the temple complex with contemptible things (7:30–31), did not speak truth (6:28–30; 7:28; 8:6; 9:2–6), and sacrificed to other deities and served them (7:18; 12:6; 13:10; 18:15; 19:4; 32:29; 44:16–18)[29]

because they listened to the false prophets. Manahan concludes that we can identify a "paracovenantal" theology based on the teachings of the false prophets.[30] If we understand the theology of Jeremiah regarding the false prophets to be paracovenantal, then Jeremiah's message may be limited to Yahwehists, those to whom the covenant had been given. As we saw from Moses, Yahweh is a jealous God who demands exclusive worship from those of the covenant. However, the theology that emerges from the false prophets goes beyond Manahan's paracovenantal view.

Jeremiah speaks out "against the current prophecy of the day on three grounds: *first*, the character of its representatives; *secondly*, the substance of their message; and *thirdly*, the forms in which they gave it out as the word of Yahwe[h]."[31] If Skinner is correct, then it is possible to understand the earlier claim that by the late monarchy a new attitude had developed toward other faith systems, and this attitude was not a passive one as Moses had presented. For Jeremiah, other faith systems are viewed as false faith systems. The key to developing a theology of religions from Jeremiah, based on the false prophets, lies in Skinner's second of three points. Before addressing that point, it might be wise to indicate why the other two points are not necessarily relevant to a theology of religions based on revelation in the late monarchy. We can imagine that unlike the false prophets of Jeremiah's period, religious leaders of other faith systems do not claim their source of revelation to be Yahweh. Hence, Skinner's third point (that the false prophets claimed their messages came from Yahweh) is not relevant. Furthermore, we can imagine many religious leaders who did not worship Yahweh as being far more moral than the false prophets Jeremiah confronted. Therefore, Skinner's first point (that the character of the false prophets undermined their messages) also may be irrelevant. As a result, we should focus primarily on the substance of their message.

---

29. Ibid., 85.
30. Ibid., 95.
31. Skinner, *Prophecy and Religion*, 190–91.

Jeremiah critiqued the false prophets of his day because their message was not only different from the message Yahweh had for his people, but also it was inconsistent with the message from Yahweh. For example, the prophets promised deliverance whereas Yahweh told Jeremiah to proclaim that Yahweh was going to judge his people, not deliver them from oppression. For Jeremiah, if the message he proclaimed was from Yahweh and that message was inconsistent with a message proclaimed by another, then the latter message must be rejected as being false.[32] This provides a crucial element for Jeremiah's theology of religions. To illustrate this, consider Jer 27:1–11.

> [1]In the beginning of the reign of Zedekiah the son of Josiah, king of Judah, this word came to Jeremiah from the Lord. [2]Thus the Lord said to me: "Make yourself thongs and yoke-bars, and put them on your neck. [3]Send word to the king of Edom, the king of Moab, the king of the sons of Ammon, the king of Tyre, and the king of Sidon by the hand of the envoys who have come to Jerusalem to Zedekiah king of Judah. [4]Give them this charge for their masters: 'Thus says the Lord of hosts, the God of Israel: This is what you shall say to your masters: [5]"It is I who by my great power and my outstretched arm have made the earth, with the men and animals that are on the earth, and I give it to whomever it seems right to me. [6]Now I have given all these lands into the hand of Nebuchadnezzar, the king of Babylon, my servant, and I have given him also the beasts of the field to serve him. [7]All the nations shall serve him and his son and his grandson, until the time of his own land comes; then many nations and great kings shall make him their slave.
>
> [8]But if any nation or kingdom will not serve this Nebuchadnezzar king of Babylon, and put its neck under the yoke of the king of Babylon, I will punish that nation with the sword, with famine, and with pestilence, says the Lord, until I have consumed it by his hand. [9]So do not listen to your prophets, your diviners, your dreamers, your soothsayers, or your sorcerers,

---

32. A set of statements is considered consistent when all members of the set can be true at the same time. Hence, inconsistency occurs when it is impossible for all members to be true at the same time. Since the focus of this chapter is biblical theology, we will avoid when possible the philosophical debates that characterize the contemporary discussions about the theology of religions. Those debates will be summarized in later chapters. However, it is noteworthy that Jeremiah's position appears to oppose what is known as pluralism. He does reject the philosophical positions later developed by Kant and Wittgenstein in which all religious claims are viewed as true. For Jeremiah, if Yahweh says x, then any claim that is inconsistent with x must be false. Evangelicals typically have argued against pluralism. Two examples of this are McGrath, "Challenge of Pluralism," 361–73; and Barnes, "Why Don't They Listen?," 50–52.

who are saying to you, 'You shall not serve the king of Babylon.' ¹⁰For it is a lie which they are prophesying to you, with the result that you will be removed far from your land, and I will drive you out, and you will perish. ¹¹But any nation which will bring its neck under the yoke of the king of Babylon and serve him, I will leave on its own land, to till it and dwell there, says the LORD.'"

It is significant that Jeremiah is addressing representatives of kings that are not of Yahweh's covenant. Not only does he make demands upon them, but also he claims their own prophets and diviners are false for their message was inconsistent with that given by Yahweh. Extending this to Jeremiah's understanding of a theology of religions illustrates how much his theology had evolved from the early Israelite period. By extension, worship of other deities is considered false, worship.

There is a third change evident in Jeremiah's theology of religions. We find not only a change in tone toward other gods and in attitude toward other faith systems when comparing Moses and Jeremiah, but we also find that Jeremiah explicitly rejects a position that might have been suggested by Moses. Some may claim that in Moses we see Yahweh worship as a nationalistic practice, but Jeremiah clearly rejects this. For Jeremiah, Yahweh worship is for all peoples, all nations, and there is no deliverance apart from Yahweh. This is revealed in Jeremiah in two ways: in the prophecies against nations and in the title Yahweh bestowed upon Jeremiah.

In Jer 46:1—51:64 we are given a series of prophecies against various nations. In these prophecies, Yahweh is seen passing judgment upon Egypt, Philistia, Moab, Ammon, Edom, Kedar, Elam, and Babylon. The significance of this passage is not as a grocery list of prophetic events but rather as a demonstration that Yahweh is sovereign over the entire world. Yahweh is the Master of the Universe. The God of Judah is also God of all peoples. If deliverance should occur for these various nations, it will be because of Yahweh and not the result of their nationalist god(s). Salvation is obtained only through the one who is sovereign over all—Yahweh. Yahweh worship, according to Jeremiah, is not a peculiarity of Judah. Yahweh intends his worshipers to be represented in all nations.

The second way Jeremiah shows that Yahweh's message of deliverance is not limited to Judah but extends to all nations is through the title Yahweh bestowed on Jeremiah at the time of Jeremiah's calling. While Jer 1:4–10 tell of this personal call, verse 5 is crucial to our current point. "Before I formed you in the womb I knew you, and before you were born I consecrated you; I appointed you a prophet to the nations." Wilhelm Vischer points out that "God specifies that he appoints [Jeremiah] as prophet to the *goyim*, which means in the Old Testament the same as ἔθνη in the New Testament, the non-Israelite, non-Jewish nations."[33] However, how does Jeremiah fulfill his calling since he left Judah only at the end of his life, and how does Jeremiah fulfill his calling since most of his recorded messages are directed toward Judah? "The word that the Lord speaks to Jerusalem and Judah determines by itself the destiny of the nations. Israel is God's witness in the world. God uses Israel to reveal himself to the nations."[34] This is significant, for it has a definite implication for developing a theology of religions from Jeremiah. Yahweh is concerned for all nations and provided a witness to those nations. Jeremiah had the distinction of preparing this witness, Judah, for ministry to the nations. The Yahweh cult was not to be limited to Judah, and the salvation provided by Yahweh is extended to all peoples. We should note that portrayal of Yahweh's involvement in the deliverance of all peoples is not limited to Jeremiah. Other post-Mosaic writers, especially those of the late monarchy or the postmonarchy, also present God as involved in all nations.[35]

The late monarchy offers critical information for one attempting to develop an Old Testament theology of religions. The contemporary view of pluralism that advocates that salvation may be obtained outside of Yahweh is rejected.[36] Given a late monarchy vantage point, we can look back at the Pentateuch and see Yahweh's concern for the entire world. Yahweh is the Master of the Universe. The suggestion that Moses's theology of religions was pluralistic fails to understand the role that additional revelation brings to the Old Testament. It also is significant that based on the late monarchy theology, while pluralism is ruled out, an inclusivist theology of religions might be developed to the extent that other faith traditions are consistent with the Yahweh tradition. That is, other faith claims might be true if those claims are consistent with the claims of Yahweh. As we move into the New Testament, how does a biblical theology of religions change given the new revelation of Jesus Christ?

---

33. Vischer, "Vocation of the Prophet," 311.
34. Ibid., 314.
35. E.g., Amos 1–2; Ezekiel 25–32; Jonah; Isaiah 13–23, 66.
36. "Yahweh demanded exclusive worship and tolerated no rivals. He was unwilling to share his glory with any other 'god.' One senses that the word 'pluralism' does not exist in the divine vocabulary; indeed the spirit of religious pluralism was antithetical to Yahwism" (Chisholm, "'To Whom Will You Compare Me?,'" 67).

Colossians

Alan Race claims that the uniqueness of Jesus Christ is the "crunch issue" for Christians in the field of theology of religions.[37] In this section, we want to listen to the Pauline literature, specifically Colossians, and hear what it has to say about the uniqueness of Jesus Christ.[38] In order to accomplish the goals of this section, we will begin by collecting some of the pertinent textual evidence regarding Jesus's uniqueness in Colossians. Then we will take a closer look at several phrases Paul uses to describe the uniqueness of Jesus Christ. From this, we will then propose a limited Pauline theology, based on Colossians, of the uniqueness of Jesus Christ. This will then lead us to articulate Paul's understanding of Judaism from a Christian perspective, as seen in Romans, which will be explored in the next section.

In Colossians Paul's understanding of Jesus Christ's uniqueness is center stage (1:12–22 and 2:6–15). As we look at 1:12–22 and 2:6–15, our focus is on the theology presented by the texts regarding Jesus Christ. This theology is conveyed first by the titles assigned to Jesus Christ and second through the relationships assumed in these titles. The passages present Jesus Christ in relation to three entities: God, creation/universe, and believers' salvation/life. The following titles or phrases outline those relationships:

God

> Beloved son has a kingdom 1:13
>
> Son is the image of the invisible God 1:15

---

37. Race, *Interfaith Encounter*, 65–84.

38. While this focus will be fruitful, it does have its limitations. Much of the current discussion regarding the uniqueness of Jesus Christ is couched in philosophical arguments rather than biblical theology. As a result, that literature will not play a role in this chapter. Furthermore, the Pauline literature, while shedding light upon Paul's understanding of the uniqueness of Jesus Christ, will not provide us with a complete New Testament theology of religions. However, the value of this approach is twofold. First, if an adequate theology of religions is to be worked out in a philosophical format, that philosophical theology must be informed by a biblical theology. Therefore, this study is foundational for an evangelical theology of religions. Second, the uniqueness of Jesus Christ is a major motif in Pauline literature. This is especially true of Colossians. While his focus is not on Colossians, Robinson provides an interesting examination of the phrase "Uniqueness of Christ" (Robinson, "What Exactly Is Meant by the 'Uniqueness of Christ'?," 76–91). Finally regarding the referencing to Pauline literature, while some contemporary questions are raised concerning whether Paul himself penned those letters attributed to him, historically they have been attributed to him—directly or indirectly. That issue lies outside the scope of this project and as a result we will simply refer to them as Paul's or as Pauline literature—pointing to that group of documents traditionally understood as Paul's.

Son in the beginning 1:18

Son is the firstborn from the dead 1:18

In everything, the Son is preeminent 1:18

In the Son all the fullness of God dwells 1:19

In Jesus Christ the whole fullness of deity dwells bodily 2:9

Jesus Christ is the head of all rule and authority 2:10

Creation/universe

Son is the firstborn of all creation 1:15

In the son, all things were created 1:16

All things were created through the son 1:16

All things were created for the son 1:16

The Son is before all things 1:17

In the Son all things are held together 1:17

Through the Son all things are reconciled 1:20

Peace is made by the blood of the Son's cross 1:20

God has disarmed the principalities and powers and made public example of them, triumphing over them in Jesus Christ 2:15

Believers' salvation and life

In the son, we have redemption, the forgiveness of sins 1:14

The Son is the head of the body, the church 1:18

The Son has now reconciled us through his death, in order to present us holy, blameless, and irreproachable before God 1:22

We are to live in Jesus Christ 2:6

We are rooted and built up in Jesus Christ, established in the faith 2:7

In Jesus Christ, we were circumcised (identified) 2:11

In Jesus Christ, we were buried (identified) 2:12

God has made us alive together with Jesus Christ 2:13

God cancelled the bond of sin, setting aside the legal demands, nailing them to the cross 2:14

If the Bible is one medium through which God has chosen self-disclosure, then what do these passages tell us of the uniqueness of Jesus Christ? In answering this question, it will be prudent to avoid, if possible, a type of midrash that interprets the phrases or titles in light of a subsequently developed theology, whether that theology is traditional or nontraditional. The reason for this caution is to avoid interpreting Colossians in light of a fully developed Christology, which clearly was not developed by Paul or any other biblical writer (a concern that Race appropriately raised).[39] It is not necessary to address every title attributed to Jesus Christ. All that is required is that a sufficient sampling be reviewed to provide clues regarding the uniqueness of Jesus Christ in Colossians. Furthermore, since Jesus Christ is understood to be unique for Christians, only a couple of titles under the final category will be visited as reminders of Jesus's relationship to believers' salvation/life. Given the uniqueness of Jesus Christ as portrayed in these passages, how does it inform Paul's understanding of Judaism?

The following three phrases pertain to Jesus Christ's relation to God.

1. *Jesus Christ as the image of the invisible God* (1:15).

"Christ is described as 'the image of the invisible God,' and the word 'image' seems to include the two ideas of representation and manifestation (2 Cor 4:4; Heb 1:3)."[40] Both Lohse and Martin agree with Thomas, but they see in this Pauline phrase even more. Martin claims that

> it boldly announces that God's glory may be seen in the face of Jesus Christ (2 Cor 4:6) and His nature is revealed in one, perfect human life (John 14:9). For at the heart of this claim is the confident assertion that Jesus Christ is the true God and true man, so able adequately and finally to reveal God's hidden name and secret nature to those who confess Him as Son and Christ of God (Matt 11:25–27). He is the 'image' or visible manifestation of God not simply in that He is 'like God' or brings news from God or even a message of God. Rather it is because He is

---

39. "Without reading back into the New Testament the doctrine of later ages, what is the best way of interpreting the diverse witness to Jesus in order to assist in formulating a belief about him today?" (Race, *Christians and Religious Pluralism*, 2nd, 125). An example of midrash, which we want to avoid, may be found in W. H. Griffith Thomas as he comments on 1:13 (Beloved son has a kingdom). "Remind(s) us that the kingdom of Christ is already in existence as a spiritual reality. In the next age this kingdom will be visibly manifested, but for the present it is internal, not external" (Thomas, *Christ Pre-eminent*, 37). In this explanation, Thomas is interpreting the concept in light of an eschatological position that was developed much later in the Christian tradition. Obviously, this does not mean that Thomas is necessarily wrong, but only that if we are to avoid Race's charge of reading later doctrinal development into our initial encounter with the text, then we would be wise to first try to understand the position of the biblical writer and then from there consider subsequent developments of theology.

40. Thomas, *Christ Pre-eminent*, 41.

the objectivization of God in human life, a coming into visible expression of the invisible God that the church hails him.[41]

Lohse points out that for the early believers this phrase and the phrase "firstborn of all creation" (2:15) would be reminders of the creation story. This is significant because "as the 'image' of the invisible God, he [Jesus Christ] does not belong to what was created, but stands with the creator who, in Christ, is acting upon the world and with the world. He is absolutely superior to the cosmos."[42] For Lohse, this title is one of majesty.

2. *Jesus Christ in which all the fullness of God dwells* (1:19), and *In Jesus Christ, the whole fullness of deity dwells bodily* (2:9).

Martin sees the meaning of "fullness" as Paul's term "to assert the very truth the heretics were doubting or denying, namely that Christ is the Lord of all cosmic authority by divine appointment and that no spiritual power has independent existence outside of his control."[43] For Lohse, the phrase "all the fullness" (1:19) claims that in Jesus Christ the totality of God is found, and "the whole fullness of deity" (2:9) is stated to make this clear.[44]

3. *Jesus Christ is the head of all rule and authority* (2:10).

---

41. Martin, *Colossians*, 45.
42. Lohse, *Colossians and Philemon*, 48.
43. Martin, *Colossians*, 48.
44. Lohse, *Colossians and Philemon*, 57. "This sentence (2:9) is clearly an explanatory repetition of 1:19; 'For in him all the fullness was pleased to dwell' . . . In both verses the term 'fullness' . . . is reinforced by 'entire, all' . . . However, the genitive 'of deity' . . . more exactly determines the 'fullness' in this verse. The term 'deity' . . . should be distinguished from 'divine nature' . . . The term 'divine nature' . . . describes the character of God, divinity. The term 'deity' . . . describes the quality of being divine . . . The entire fullness of deity dwells in Christ. Therefore, only that person can be filled who belongs to this Lord—only he who is in him, who has died with him, and has been raised to new life 'with Christ' . . . While the aorist 'was pleased to dwell' . . . occurs in 1:19, here the present tense 'dwells' . . . is used to refer to the present reality. The word 'bodily' indicated that the divine indwelling is real . . . Since in Christ the entire fullness of deity dwells 'bodily,' he is the 'head of every principality and power' . . ., the 'head of the body' (. . .). This body of his is the 'church' (. . .) over which he already in the present exercises his universal rule. Therefore, whoever has been transferred into the domain of is kingdom is free from the powers which rule in the cosmos and which want to force their enslaving yoke upon men" (ibid., 100–101). Wedderburn points out "the term is . . . very much active, even dynamic, rather than passive. In the Old Testament God is one who fills heaven and earth (Jer 23.24; cf. Isa 6.3; Ps 103.24 LXX), that is, is present in them; and in the New Testament we receive from Christ's fullness (John 1:16), which as in Col 2.9–10 suggest that, because Christ has received 'fullness,' he is able to 'fill' those who receive it from him" (Lincoln and Wedderburn, *Theology of the Later Pauline Letters*, 31).

Referring to Jesus Christ as the head of all rule and authority takes us back to the poem or hymn of 1:15–20. In the hymn, Jesus Christ is portrayed as Lord over all principalities and powers. Schweizer believes that Paul cited the hymn because it was familiar to the believers at Colossae. In singing the hymn, they were proclaiming their faith, their belief in "the unique Lord of the universe . . . But the problem was how to reach this unique Lord."[45] This leads to the heresy that Paul is addressing in Colossians. Schweizer suggests that the believers at Colossae had added to their Christian faith an element of a mystery religion in which through a ritual ascension one obtains a vision of the highest God. For Paul to claim Jesus Christ as the head of all rule and authority speaks of the sovereignty of Jesus Christ, and only God is sovereign in this sense.

Jesus Christ is unique because of his relationship and identity to God. However, Paul does not limit Christ's uniqueness to this one relationship; he also develops the uniqueness of Jesus Christ by enumerating some of the relationships Jesus Christ has with the universe and creation.

1. *Jesus Christ is the first-born of all creation* (1:15).

For Thomas, "the context makes it perfectly clear that this reference to Him is to One who is separate from and above creation, and not simply a created Being. It indicates His unique supremacy over creation."[46] Martin says that Paul used this phrase to show that Jesus Christ is "Lord of creation and has no rival in the created order."[47]

2. *In Jesus Christ all things were created* (1:16), *All things were created through Jesus Christ* (1:16), and *All things were created for Jesus Christ* (1:16).

With these three propositions, we find Jesus Christ in a unique relationship to the creation. "He is seen to be at once the sphere, the agent, and the

---

45. Schweizer, "Christ in the Letter to the Colossians," 453.

46. Thomas, *Christ Pre-eminent*, 42.

47. Martin, *Colossians*, 46. Both Lohse and Martin believe this phrase clearly teaches the preexistent Christ. "The description of the pre-existent Christ as the 'first-born before all creation' . . . is not intended to mean that he was created first and thereby began the succession of created beings. Rather, it refers instead to his uniqueness, by which he is distinguished from all creation (cf. Heb 1:6). The point is not a temporal advantage but rather the superiority which is due to him as the agent of creation who is before all creation. As the first-born he stands over against creation as Lord" (Lohse, *Colossians and Philemon*, 48). "If the pre-incarnate Lord was the agent of all creation, and pre-existed before everything, it leads to the conclusion that only God can satisfactorily account for Christ's being" (Martin, *Colossians*, 45).

purpose of creation."⁴⁸ However, this relationship is complex. Lohse agrees that the statement "in Jesus Christ all things were created" is about the "unique position of the pre-existent Christ."⁴⁹ However, Lohse continues, "the use of the passive form, 'were created'... signifies that God is the creator." Furthermore, they were created through Jesus Christ. The emphasis seems to be that all things that exist in the universe were created in Jesus Christ.⁵⁰ Finally, Jesus Christ is the goal of creation.

   3. *Jesus Christ is before all things* (1:17).

If Schweizer is correct and the Colossae heresy was related to the Greek notion of elements (i.e., earth, water, air, and fire) and mystery religion, then this title becomes even more significant. This title and all other titles that Paul applies to Jesus Christ signal Jesus Christ's unique position over the universe. According to Colossians, Jesus Christ occupies a unique position: the universe has been created in Christ and by Christ; yet Jesus Christ has existed before all things.

   4. *Through Jesus Christ all things are reconciled* (1:20), *Peace is made by the blood of Jesus Christ's cross* (1:20), and *God has disarmed the principalities and powers and made public example of them, triumphing over them in Jesus Christ* (2:15).

Before presenting what these terms may have meant for Paul and the church at Colossae, I note that the phrases signal part of Jesus Christ's relationship to the universe and creation. While the next set of relational notions do relate to soteriological issues, those notions are specifically related to believers. The above three phrases also are soteriological, but are related to the cosmos as a whole. These phrases will be very important when we attempt to reconstruct an evangelical theology of religions in section 2 because they do relate to the cosmos as a whole (and so relate to general revelation) and soteriology.

Alford points out that the phrase "all things" is a reference to the universe and cannot be limited to "all intelligent beings, or all men or the whole church."⁵¹ Lohse captures the immensity of "all things are reconciled."

> In order to restore the cosmic order reconciliation became necessary and was accomplished by the Christ-event. Through Christ, God himself achieved this reconciling. The universe has

---

48. Thomas, *Christ Pre-eminent*, 42.
49. Lohse, *Colossians and Philemon*, 49.
50. Ibid., 50.
51. Alford, *Greek Testament*, 3:206.

been reconciled in that heaven and earth have been brought back into their divinely created and determined order through the resurrection and exaltation of Christ. Now the universe is again under its head and thereby cosmic peace has returned. This peace which God has established through Christ binds the whole together again into unity and underlines that the restored creation is reconciled with God.[52]

Furthermore, the cross-event had universal significance by making peace, although it was not Jesus Christ making the peace, but God the Father. "This is another reminder that the Atoning Sacrifice was not due to the love of the Son only, but also to the love of the Father."[53] Finally, the universe benefits because of the victory God established in Jesus Christ. "The main truth seems to be the completeness of Christ's victory over evil."[54]

As we have seen, Paul portrays Jesus Christ as having a unique relationship to God, as well as a unique relationship to the universe and creation. This second relationship complements and extends the first. Not only is Jesus Christ the unique self-disclosure of God, but he also has an intimacy with the universe. Finally, we find Paul showing Jesus Christ's relationship to believers' salvation and life. Because this relationship is more obvious, only three of the titles are addressed below, and even then, they are addressed very briefly.[55]

1. *"In Jesus Christ, we have redemption, the forgiveness of sins"* (1:14).

Calvin points out that this verse links redemption and forgiveness of sins. "For . . . when God remits our sins, He exempts us from condemnation to

---

52. Lohse, *Colossians and Philemon*, 59–60.

53. Thomas, *Christ Pre-eminent*, 49. "The hymn [which ends with verse 20] emphasizes the universal significance of the Christ-event by exhibiting its cosmic dimensions and by speaking of salvation for the whole world, including the whole creation" (Lohse, *Colossians and Philemon*, 60–61).

54. Thomas, *Christ Pre-eminent*, 49. The significance of 1:20 for the theology of religions is best seen when we note what Paul says that reconciliation did, in 1:22. "Son has now reconciled us through his death, in order to present us holy, blameless, and irreproachable before God."

55. In the stronger sense, Christians understand some things of the relationship between their salvation and Jesus Christ. They may not understand the various theories of this relationship, but they do understand that Jesus Christ is in some way very unique and as a result, they have salvation. In the weaker sense, to say that Jesus Christ is unique for Christians is analogous to saying Buddha is unique for Buddhist or Arjuna for Hinduism.

eternal death."[56] It is significant that the liberty we now have was procured in Jesus Christ.[57]

2. *"Jesus Christ is the head of the body, the church"* (1:18).

Interestingly, Paul modifies the hymn with which the believers at Colossae were familiar. The original hymn stated that the son is "head of the body, the universe." Paul modifies the hymn by replacing "universe" with "church."[58] The significance of this modification is less than we might surmise. "When the letter to the Colossians speaks of the church, the body of Christ that grows continually, nourished and supported by its head (2:19, cf. 1:18, 24), it is no longer, as in I Corinthians 12:14ff., the local congregation . . . , it is the universal church, growing in some way into the fabric of the whole world."[59]

3. *"Jesus Christ has now reconciled us through his death, in order to present us holy, blameless, and irreproachable before God"* (1:22).

Calvin points out that the "entire blessing of redemption consists mainly in these two things: remission of sins and spiritual regeneration (Jer. 31:33)."[60] According to this phrase, Jesus Christ through his death has made both remission and regeneration possible.

Before we move on to explore a Pauline theology of religions as presented in Romans, we may benefit from constructing a limited Pauline theology of Jesus Christ's uniqueness based on Colossians. This theology conforms to the three relational notions presented above.

Colossians sets forth a rather straightforward theology that does portray Jesus Christ as unique. While evangelicals do insist on the Christian Scriptures as foundational for their theology, they allow their understanding to be influenced by theological developments subsequent to the text.

---

56. Calvin, *Epistles of Paul the Apostle to the Galatians, Ephesians, Philippians, Colossians*, 308.

57. "Redemption is one of six words found in the New Testament to express the work of Christ: Sacrifice (Eph 5:2); Offering (Heb 10:10); Propitiation (1 John 2:2); Ransom (1 Tim 2:6); Redemption (Heb 9:12); and Reconciliation (Rom 5:11). The special thought of redemption is deliverance from slavery by means of payment (Rom 3:24), just as in verse 13 we see the corresponding thought of a victor and a rescue. The word rendered 'redemption' is significant for its emphasis on the completeness of the work. The verb 'to redeem' occurs three times in the New Testament (Luke 24:21; Tit 2:14; 1 Pet 1:18), and in each case the thought is of deliverance wrought through the death of Christ" (Thomas, *Christ Pre-eminent*, 39).

58. Martin, *Colossians*, 47.

59. Schweizer, "Christ in the Letter to the Colossians," 455.

60. Calvin, *Epistles of Paul the Apostle to the Galatians, Ephesians, Philippians, Colossian*, 315.

What is crucial here is that the Pauline literature does portray Jesus Christ as unique. How this uniqueness is understood is open to discussion and is the source of differing theologies.

For Paul, Jesus Christ is unique because of his relationship to God. We find Jesus Christ presented as the beloved Son (1:13). Morris claims, "when Paul thinks of Jesus as the Son of God, he thinks of him as occupying the highest place."[61] Paul presents Jesus Christ as a unique revelation of God.[62] To know Jesus Christ is to know God. Not only is Jesus Christ the image of the invisible God (1:15), but he is preeminent (1:18), the one in which all the fullness of God dwells (1:19; 2:9). "The pre-eminence stresses the uniqueness of Christ over everything (or in every respect), but what is the meaning of fullness (*plērōma*)? The main clue to its meaning is found in Colossians 2:9 where it means the total essence of God. All that God is, is in Christ."[63] Donald Guthrie continues, "in light of it (Col 2:9) no lesser view than the deity of Christ is tenable."[64]

While the first relational notion speaks of the uniqueness of Jesus Christ, it is the second that is even more astonishing. As Davies puts it,

> now Paul's first assertion in this passage, that Christ is the image of God, would by itself cause no difficulty, because apart from every other consideration this would be a natural designation of one who had already been called the Second Adam, being who like his counterpart would of course be in the image of God.

61. Morris, *New Testament Theology*, 41. Col 1:15–20 "refers to 'the Son of his love' (v. 13) as 'the image of the invisible God' (v. 15). 'Image' (*eikōn*) can mean a copy; e.g., the image of the emperor on a coin. But it can also be used to indicate, not dissimilarity (an image, not the real thing), but similarity (the image is exactly the same, not different). It is this second meaning that is required here. Paul is saying, not that the Son is different from the Father, but that he is exactly like him. He is, further, the 'firstborn of all creation.' This does not mean that he was the first to be created; rather it signifies that he stands in relation to the entire creation in the relationship the firstborn son has to his father's estate. In antiquity a great property involved a host of people—dependents, hired servants, and slaves—among whom there were varying orders of importance. But the father's firstborn, the son who was his heir, was the most important of all. The term *firstborn* marked a significant relation, and that is its meaning here. The Son is the most significant of all there is, because he stands in such a relationship to the Father as does no one and nothing else in creation" (ibid., 45).

62. "The idea, 'image of the invisible God,' is an astonishing thought when applied to Christ, for whatever the nuances in the word 'image' (*eikōn*) it is clear that Paul is claiming that Christ is a perfect revelation of God. Both Judaism and Christianity affirmed the invisibility of God and consequently rejected idolatry, but Christian faith is unique in considering the visibility of the invisible through his perfect likeness in Christ" (Guthrie, *New Testament Theology*, 355).

63. Ibid., 357.

64. Ibid., 358.

It is the other statements, those which assert the pre-cosmic generation of Christ and his agency in creation that occasion questioning.[65]

As Stauffer points out, "the Greek speaks of a cosmos, and for him the reality of the world is absolute. But the Bible speaks of a creation."[66] Jesus Christ is unique because of his relationship to the universe. He is its Creator.[67] "Paul's view of creation is that God is himself the Creator (Rom 1:25; Eph 3:9). However, he goes further and links Christ as an agent in creation (Col 1:15ff.). Paul sees the physical world from a Christocentric, not an anthropocentric point of view."[68] Furthermore, in light of the death of the Son (the Creator), "God reaches out to those who were once his enemies the hand of reconciliation, and the cross concludes a universal peace."[69] Stauffer picks up this theme again.

> Christ is the first-born of all creation, and in him were all things created; therefore all things have been created unto him. Christ is the ground of all being (cf. Ecclus 43.26)—whether thrones, or dominions, or principalities or powers. Therefore he is the reconciler of all. He disarms powers of hell, but he does not

---

65. Davies, *Paul and Rabbinic Judaism*, 151.

66. Stauffer, *New Testament Theology*, 57.

67. "The pre-existent one is the reflection of the divine glory, the first-born of every creature, the image that God stamps upon his creation (Col 1:15f.; Heb 1.3). God always creates by his Christ. Through him he sustains the world, through him he continues its history. In this context Paul says not only that everything was created in Christ, but also that it had is 'origin" in him . . . Christ is creation's life-giver!" (ibid., 57). "The word 'first-born' occasions some difficulty, because the statement taken on its own would seem to imply that Christ was a creature. But in view of the context this is impossible. The Creator of all things cannot himself be a creature. In what sense, therefore is 'first-born' used? Some (including the Arians) maintained that this word must be understood in terms of Proverbs 8:22, which they understood to mean that Wisdom was created. But this is possible only by ignoring the context. The word *prōtotokos* must be understood either (i) in the sense of priority to creation, thus drawing attention to the pre-existence of Christ, which is in line with his creative work; or (ii) in the sense of supremacy over creation (cf. verses 17–18). The latter idea fits in well with the main drift of the whole passage, i.e. the pre-existence of Christ. He is not the greatest among the multitude of other creatures. There is no suggestion that Paul had this in mind. He was clearly placing Christ above all creatures in the statements that follow. In a particularly full manner, he shows this in Colossians 1:16, where God is said to have created all things 'in him' (*en autō*) 'through him' (*di' auton*), and 'for him' (*eis auton*). In no clearer way could he have set Christ at the very center of creation, and in no more explicit terms could he have asserted his superiority" (Guthrie, *New Testament Theology*, 356).

68. Ibid., 137.

69. Stauffer, *New Testament Theology*, 145.

destroy them (Col 2.15). He is the universal peacemaker, and everything is included in his peace (Col 1.16, 20).[70]

Not only is Jesus Christ portrayed as having a relationship to the universe that is past tense, but also he has a continuing relationship. All things are held together in him (Col 1:17). "It is evident that Paul does not hesitate to affirm the lordship of Christ over creation, as consisting not merely in a past completed act, but in a present sovereign activity. In this dramatic way he identifies the creative activities of Christ with those of God."[71]

Finally, Colossians presents Jesus Christ as unique because of his relationship to believers and their salvation. "The Father has transferred us from the dominion of darkness to the kingdom of the Son of his love (Col 1:13)."[72] In this new position, believers find their salvation in Christ Jesus.

> Paul speaks of redemption as being 'in Christ Jesus' (Rom 3:24). Else where he declares that Christ 'redeemed us from the curse of the law,' which leads him to the other thought that he has 'become a curse for us' (Gal 3:13). Christ is linked with our justification (Gal 2:17), forgiveness (Col 3:13), and victory (1 Cor 15:57). He brought peace (Rom 5:1), hope (Eph 1:12; Col 1:27; 1 Thess 1:3; 1 Tim 1:1), sonship (Eph 1:5), the promise of life (2 Tim 1:1), eternal life (Rom 5:21; 6:23), light (Eph 5:14), and riches in glory (Phil 4:19; cf. 'unsearchable riches of Christ' [Eph 3:8]).[73]

This notion of believers "in Christ" is a favorite notion of Paul's, and is found in all of the Pauline letters except for Titus.[74] Because of being in Christ, believers are exhorted to live in him, identify with him, and acknowledge him as the head of the body, the church (1:18; 2:6; 2:11–13).

This relationship of the believer being in Christ is due to the Son's death, which resulted in our reconciliation, which in turn makes it possible for him to present us as holy, blameless, and irreproachable before God

---

70. Ibid., 224–25. Also, see Morris, *New Testament Theology*, 69; and Guthrie, *New Testament Theology*, 142.

71. Guthrie, *New Testament Theology*, 356.

72. Ibid., 319.

73. Morris, *New Testament Theology*, 51.

74. Ibid., 51.

(1:22; 2:14).[75] As Morris points out, "It was the atoning death of Christ and not his exemplary life that brought salvation to sinners."[76]

Romans

The Preacher, after his list of "a time to . . .," asked the question, "What gain has the worker from his toil?"[77] Based on the preceding materials, the apparent response to this question is, nothing. However, the Preacher continues his second discourse with a startling claim, given the preceding materials.

> I know that whatever God does endures forever; nothing can be added to it, nor anything taken from it; God has made it so, in order that men should fear before him. That which is, already has been; that which is to be, already has been; and God seeks what has been driven away.[78]

---

75. "Jesus comes into this ambiguous situation on man's behalf and gives his life 'ransom for many'. In this saying there is the basis for the teaching of the primitive Church in regard to the saving work of Jesus Christ, which can be summed up under three inclusive heads. Forgiveness of sins is redemption. In Jesus Christ 'we have our redemption through his blood, the forgiveness of our trespasses,' says Eph 1.7 (cf. 1 Cor 1.30; Rom 3.24; Col 1.14; Heb 9.15; Luke 1:68, 77; Ps 110.9). The idea of redemption can be understood in many different ways in the NT, and can mean the final deliverance from all the troubles of this world (Luke 21:28; Rom 8:23). But here the issue concerns the decisive point where the universal work of redemption comes into operation—redemption is ransom (1 Tim 2.6; 2 Pet 2.1). We were bought with a price (1 Cor 6.20; 7.23), but the price paid was the precious blood of Jesus Christ (1 Pet 1.18f.) . . . God takes his own world order so seriously that he sacrifices his son to save the world, without flouting its orders . . . In Col 2.13ff. Paul writes about blotting out of the ordinances that were against us on the cross, so that he can go on to the idea of disarming and subjection of the powers of hell (cf. 2 Tim 1.10; IgnE. 19.3). So closely do forgiveness of sins, redemption and liberation go together in his thinking. So deeply does the settling of the problem of sin concern the power relationships that obtain in universal history" (Stauffer, *New Testament Theology*, 147). "Sometimes, for example, he speaks of redemption (e.g., Rom 3:24; 1 Cor 1:30; Gal 3:13; 4:5; Eph 1:7; Col 1:14), a term we may easily misunderstand since its use concerned activities that we are not familiar with . . . Redemption means the paying of a price to set someone free (cf. 1 Cor 6:20; 7:23). No one in the New Testament ever asks the question, 'To whom was the ransom paid?' The question is illegitimate. The concern of the New Testament writers is with the costly nature of our salvation, not with any recipient of a price." . . . "Another of Paul's concepts is reconciliation, a way of looking at the Cross that nobody else in the New Testament uses . . . All of these passages point to sin as the cause of the hostility and to Christ's death as having dealt with sin. The cause of the hostility being thus removed, reconciliation takes place" (Guthrie, *New Testament Theology*, 71–73).

76. Morris, *New Testament Theology*, 66.

77. Eccl 3:9.

78. Eccl 3: 14–15.

It was the created that was driven away in Gen 3:24, and it is the creation that the Creator is working to restore.[79] The Preacher continues to claim that God would even use perversions of justice to serve his sovereign purpose (vv. 16–22). Indeed all things work toward the fulfillment of God's will. This theme is dear to the heart of Paul, who writes, "We know that in everything God works for good." Paul continues this sentence with the qualifier "for those who love God, who are called according to his purpose,"[80] and then presents his conclusion to all that he has thus far written in Rom 1:1—8:30. Salvation is a certainty for the elect (vv. 31–39). As F. F. Bruce points out, it would have been a natural step for Paul to move from this discussion of assurance that God will accomplish that which he has started to the discussion of believers fully surrendering to God as seen in 12:1—15:33.[81] However, into Romans Paul injects chapters 9 through 11, and for very good reasons.[82] These chapters do not present an aside, as it were, but present a continuation of Paul's theme of the letter.

> For I am not ashamed of the gospel; it is the power of God for salvation to every one who has faith, to the Jew first and also to the Greek. For in it the righteousness of God is revealed through faith for faith; as it is written, "He who through faith is righteous shall live."[83]

How can Christians be confident in their own salvation, which is entirely dependent upon God's mercy, if God's purpose with Israel has changed? Or as Cranfield so well puts it,

> If the truth is that God's purpose with Israel has been frustrated, then what sort of a basis for Christian hope is God's purpose?

---

79. "There is no doubt that the Preacher has modeled his view of life on the creation story in Genesis. Hence he knows that the Creator has made everything beautiful in its time, and has put eternity in Man's heart, thus binding him inwardly to himself" (Eichrodt, *Theology of the Old Testament*, 2:494). Also, see Brueggemann, *Theology of the Old Testament*, 393–98.

80. Rom 8:28.

81. Bruce, *Letter of Paul the Apostle to the Romans*, 171–72.

82. Not all commentators agree with this claim regarding chapters 9–11. "The sermon . . . starts abruptly, with no connection with what has preceded . . . But it hurts him to speak that; for, in actual fact, he sees that Israel as a people has no part at all in the blessings of the New Age that has dawned . . . The pathos of this climax lies in the fact that all the religious privileges enumerated pointed forward to the fulfillment of the whole history of Israel in the coming of the Messiah: the Messiah came—and instead of fulfillment came frustration and disaster!" (Dodd, *Epistle of Paul to the Romans*, 164–65).

83. Rom 1:16–17.

And, if God's love for Israel (cf., e.g., Deut 7.7f; Jer 31.3) has ceased, what reliance can be placed on Paul's conviction that nothing can separate us from God's love in Christ (v. 38f)?[84]

However, not only does Paul, in these three chapters, underscore why the believer can have hope for that which is unseen, but also he provides an insight that does have significance to the development of an evangelical theology of religions. It shall be proposed that based on this passage, an analogy might be developed that argues for a stance that salvation may be extended to some outside the Christian community, without making "Paul more 'multi-faith' than he was."[85] Since the Scriptures are not clear on this, we must be agnostic. However, given what is clear, we can proclaim hope based on Romans 9 through 11.

Chapter 9 begins with Paul's remorse regarding Israel. The strength of Paul's language indicates that his "great sorrow and unceasing anguish" is not to be taken lightly.[86] It is a genuine sorrow and anguish because some of his kinsmen have not embraced the Messiah, Jesus Christ. It is most significant how Paul proceeds to describe his kinsmen in the subsequent verses. "They are Israelites, and to them belong the sonship, the glory, the covenants, the giving of the law, the worship, and the promises; to them belong the patriarchs, and of their race, according to the flesh, is the Christ" (vv 4-5). Failure to appreciate these verses may lead to conclusions not present in these chapters.[87]

---

84. Cranfield, *Critical and Exegetical Commentary on the Epistle to the Romans*, 2:447.

85. Räisänen, *Marcion, Muhammad, and the Mahatma*, 5.

86. "The doubling of λύπη ("grief, sorrow, pain of mind or spirit") and ὀδύνη ("mental pain") intensifies the already strong emotive force of the affidavit. It will be no accident that the only places in biblical Greek where the two words are associated are Isa 35:10 and 51:11" (Dunn, *Romans 9-16*, 523).

87. Nygren captures the thrust of these chapters as he claims, "In the very faithlessness of man God glorifies His faithfulness" (*Commentary on Romans*, 357). However, because he fails to deal with verses 1-6, he draws a conclusion not consistent with the text: "Thus in this third part of the epistle Paul intends to show that the righteousness of faith is not contrary to God's promises. To that end he presents three main arguments. (1) He who gave the promises is God himself, who is sovereign. Thus all depends on whom God has chosen to be 'the children of promise.' When God gave the promises He determined that they should belong to those who believe in Christ. (2) When Israel, directly contrary to God, seeks for righteousness by the way of works, she makes herself responsible for her rejection. (3) And yet that rejection is not final and decisive. By this very rejection God brings about the situation necessary for Israel's final salvation" (ibid., 359). In point 1, Nygren is correct that the fulfillment of the promise is dependent upon whom God has chosen; however, verses 4 and 5 do not support Nygren's claim that the promise "should belong to those who believe in Christ." In point

Paul begins by identifying his kinsmen as Israelites. James Dunn points out that "12 of the 19 occurrences of Ἰσραηλ[ίτης] in the Pauline corpus are found in chaps. 9–11; . . . Ἰσραηλίτης is therefore deliberately chosen by Paul to evoke his people's sense of being God's elect, the covenant people of the one God."[88] Those very individuals over whom Paul has just expressed great sorrow because of their unbelief are God's elect. Furthermore, they are identified as belonging to three categories that speak of relationship with God: the sonship (or adoption), the glory, and the covenants.

As Morris points out, this is the only place in the New Testament where the expression "adoption as sons" is used in reference to the Jews. However, ὧν ἡ υἱοθεσία ("whose are the adoption") emphasizes their relationship is not of natural sonship, but of adoptive sonship: so the phrase ὧν ἡ υἱοθεσία "helps bring out the sense of election more clearly."[89] Cranfield captures the significance of this expression for Paul.

> Israel's sonship is a matter of grace, a moral relationship, not to be thought of in any naturalistic or mythological way . . . For Paul, the Israelites' adoption was a continuing reality (just as their being Israelites was) in spite of their unbelief; but we must naturally distinguish carefully between Paul's use of υἱοθεσία here of what is real objectively by God's grace but not as yet truly grasped or experienced and his use of the same word in 8.15 and . . . 8.23.[90]

Those Israelites, whom Paul acknowledges are in a state of disbelief, are claimed to belong to God not only because of God's adoptive process of

---

2, an ambiguity arises—who is doing the rejection? Nygren seems to be suggesting that because Israel chose to go in directions contrary to God, that God rejected Israel. This interpretation, while not supported by the biblical text, is commonly seen. For example, Harold Lindsell in providing the section titles, etc., for the *Harper Study Bible* titled chapter 10 of Romans as "God's rejection the fault of the Jews" (p. 1689).

88. Dunn, *Romans 9–16*, 526.

89. Ibid.

90. Cranfield, *Critical and Exegetical Commentary on the Epistle to the Romans*, 461. "The reference here is to God's gracious adoption of the nation as His son (see especially Exod 4.22ff; Jer 31.9; Hos 11.1) as the basis and beginning of the long history of His fatherly dealings with it (cf., for example, Deut 1.31; 8.5; Isa 1.2)—fatherly dealings which should have met with the response on Israel's part of reverent love, trust and obedience (cf., for example, Deut 14.1; Isa 1.2; Jer 3.19, 22; Mal 1.6) . . . Though there is a marked reserve in the OT with regard to speaking of God as the Father of the individual Israelite (Deut 14.1 stands out as the exceptional; Hos 1.10 . . . refers to the future, not the present; Ps 2.10; 103.13 show the reserve), the thought of God's fatherly relationship to the individual was to some extent implicit all along in the conception of Israel's adoption" (ibid., 461).

election, but also because they belong to the δόξα. The glory is that "outward sign of God's presence with his people, the 'visible aspect of the invisible God.'"[91] Cranfield continues,

> It is God's own manifestation of His personal presence with His people, which is always His presence in the sovereign freedom of His gracious condescension, never a presence under their control or at their disposal, which Paul here lists as one of the privileges of his fellow-Jews.[92]

Dunn claims that δόξα for Paul points to "the eschatological promise that the divine glory would be more fully and more widely revealed through Israel to the nations (particularly Isa 35:2, 40:5, 59:19, 60:1–3, 66:18–19)."[93]

Furthermore, this group of disbelievers belongs to the covenants of God. The word *berit* (covenant) appears some 286 times in the Old Testament. The term points to a binding of obligation upon parties who want to be in a relationship, usually a legal union between unequal partners, and which involves both promise and obligation.[94] New Testament commentators are not clear which covenants Paul has in mind as he declares the Israelites belong to the covenants. Whether he had in mind specific covenants, such as the Abrahamic, Mosaic, and Davidic covenants, or used the plural form to point to the two basic covenants, old and new, may not be crucial for understanding Paul's intention.[95] What is significant is that God established a covenant with those whom God chose, and while each covenant does contain conditional elements (i.e., elements dependent upon obedience by lesser members of the covenant), they all contain unconditional elements (i.e., elements dependent solely upon God's promise).[96] Furthermore, ultimate maintenance of the

---

91. Ibid., 461–62.

92. Ibid., 462.

93. Dunn, *Romans 9–16*, 526.

94. For an excellent discussion of the notion of covenant in the Old Testament, see Eichrodt, *Theology of the Old Testament*, vol. 1.

95. Abrahamic covenant—Genesis 12; 15; and 17; Mosaic covenant—Deuteronomy 28 through 30; Davidic covenant—2 Samuel 7; new covenant—Jeremiah 31 and Ezekiel 36. Since the latter covenants are amplifications of the Abrahamic covenant, they are not replacements of earlier covenant, but reconfirmations and clarifications.

96. Abrahamic covenant—conditional element: Abram was commanded to go; unconditional elements: great nation, great name, blessing for him, and blessing for all people. Mosaic covenant—conditional element: If you obey, I will bless you, but if you disobey, I will curse you; unconditional element: final inheritance. Davidic covenant—conditional element: obedience brings enjoyment whereas disobedience brings chastisement; unconditional element: kingdom to be ultimately and permanently established; new covenant—conditional element: repentance; unconditional element: the "I will . . ." found in Jer 31:31–34.

covenant relationship is based upon the character of God. Paul is not minimizing the unbelief of his fellow Jews, but rather highlighting that in spite of their disbelief, God is still faithful to God's promise. The remainder of verses 4 and 5 only continue to underscore that although Paul's fellow Jews are in a state of disbelief, they still stand in a special relationship with God. Paul ends this introduction to chapters 9 through 11 with a doxology: "God who is over all be blessed for ever" (Rom 9:5b).

The remainder of this section of Romans addresses three related issues: 9:6–29 God's mercy is greater than the human failures of disobedience and disbelief; 9:30—10:21 Israel is without excuse, but there is hope; and 11:1–36 God has a merciful plan. While the last two sections are less problematic, 9:6–29 provide a special challenge for those expecting Paul to be consistent with himself and with Old Testament teachings.[97]

Paul, in these verses, recognizes that not all Israelites are Israelites. He makes a distinction between the Israel of the promise and Israel of physical descent.[98] Boice claims, "the promises of God were not made to all the physical descendants of Abraham, but only to those whom God has elected to salvation and in whom he had therefore implanted or was implanting life."[99] Paul provides two illustrations of his point. First, he points to God choosing to work through the offspring of Sarah and not Hagar, while both are physical descendants of Abraham. His second illustration is Rebekah's twins, Esau and Jacob. These illustrations exhibit Paul's point that "the sovereign act of God in election . . . , the purpose of God which works by the principle of election might stand . . . , so likewise his plan of selecting cannot do anything other than 'stand,' i.e., prevail."[100] However, these illustrations have been misunderstood. For example, Boice uses these illustrations to teach the doctrine of double predestination or the doctrine of reprobation

---

97. It should be noted that not all biblical scholars expect Paul to be self-consistent. For example, Heikki Räisänen finds Paul to be frequently inconsistent, even within these three chapters of Romans. "It may be pointed out in passing that it is not just in his treatment of the law that Paul gets involved in intellectual difficulties. He likewise contradicts himself when discussing the not unrelated problem of Israel's reluctance to accept the gospel. In Rom 9 he resorts to the extreme explanation of divine hardening which takes place regardless of any man's doings (9.6–23), whereas he in the very next chapter puts all emphasis on Israel's own notorious disobedience. In chapter 11, at last, Paul definitely discards his predestinarian construction and replaces it with the statement that Israel's obduracy is of a temporary nature. This runs counter to 1 Thess 2.14–16 as well" (*Paul and the Law*, 264). However, some of the apparent inconsistencies may be due to misinterpretations, especially of 9:6–29.

98. Black, *Romans*, 126.

99. Boice, *Romans*, 3:1044.

100. Black, *Romans*, 129.

(i.e., "passing over of those who are not elected to salvation").[101] While many evangelicals, because of their Calvinistic leanings, might agree with Boice, it appears that Boice has missed Paul's intention. First, it is questionable whether such an interpretation is consistent with the unconditional nature of the Old Testament's covenants. Second, this seems to be a forced reading of the text, especially in light of verses 1–5.

Cranfield offers an interpretation that is viable and consistent with both Old Testament passages and verses 1–5 of chapter 9, and, as a result, the following relies heavily upon his work.

> The point Paul is making is that not all who are included in the comprehensive Israel are included also in the selective, special Israel. But this does not mean . . . that only part of the Jewish people is the elect people of God . . . This explanation of his meaning is ruled out by vv. 1–5; for it is clear that the Jews he is referring to in those verses are the unbelieving ones (for the others he has no need to grieve), and that he recognizes these unbelieving ones as his brethren . . . and acknowledges that they are still . . ., even in their unbelief, Israelites to whom the privileges belong. Paul's meaning is rather that within the elect people itself there has been going on throughout its history a divine operation of distinguishing and separating, whereby 'the Church hidden in Israel' has been differentiated from the rest of the chosen nation. All Jews . . . are members of God's elect people. This is an honour—and it is no small honour—of which no member of this race can be deprived. They are all members of the community, which is the environment of Jesus Christ. They are all necessarily witnesses to God's grace and truth. But not all of them are members of the Israel within Israel, which is the company of those who are willing, obedient, grateful witnesses to the grace and truth. But, if God's purpose of election has, from the very beginning included a process of distinguishing and separating even within the elected people, then the present unbelief of many Jews is no proof that that purpose has failed, but may be understood as part of its working out.[102]

---

101. Boice, *Romans*, 3:1051. He continues, "Reprobation is the teaching we come to specifically in Romans 9:13–18 . . . The doctrine is brought into our text by two Old Testament quotations: Malachi 1:2–3 . . . and Exodus 9:16" (ibid., 3:1059). Boice cites other passages where this doctrine is taught: "Prov 16:4; John 12:39–40; John 13:18; John 17:12; 1 Pet 2:7–8; Jude 4. In fact, verses 1–29 are the most forceful statements of double predestination in the Bible" (ibid., 3:1061).

102. Cranfield, *Critical and Exegetical Commentary on the Epistle to the Romans*, 473–74. Note Gen 16:10–14; 17:20; and 21:13–21 for God's provision for Ishmael.

For this interpretation to be viable, it is crucial that Cranfield explain Paul's two illustrations in a fashion that offers hope instead of condemnation. Regarding the first illustration, Cranfield reminds us "we must not read into Paul's argument any suggestion that Ishmael, because he is not chosen to play a positive part in the accomplishment of God's special purpose, is therefore excluded from the embrace of God's mercy."[103]

Regarding the second illustration, Cranfield's argument is much more detailed.

> What is here in question is not eschatological salvation or damnation, but the historical functions of those concerned and their relations to the development of the salvation-history . . . There is no doubt that the concern of Mal 1.2–5 is with the nations of Israel and Edom, and it is natural to suppose that by 'Jacob' and 'Esau' Paul also understands not only the twin sons of Isaac but also the peoples descended from them. But what exactly is the connection in Paul's mind between this quote [v 13] and vv 11 and 12? . . . [P]robably Paul thought of it as expressing the same truth as the words of Genesis, . . . and therefore suitable as a further and decisive corroboration of what had just been said, and in particular, of the words of Gen 25.23 . . .
>
> The word[s] . . . "love" and "hate" are . . . to be understood as denoting election and rejection respectively. God has chosen Jacob and his descendants to stand in a positive relation to the fulfillment of His gracious purpose: he has left Esau and Edom outside this relationship. But, again, it must be stressed that, as in the case of Ishmael, so also with Esau, the rejected one is still, according to the testimony of Scripture, an object of God's merciful care. That he is, is eloquently hinted by such things as the setting of Gen 27.39f (Isaac's blessing of Esau) in close proximity to Gen 27.27–29 (Isaac's blessing of Jacob), the inclusion of the detailed genealogies of Edom in Genesis 36 and I Chronicles 1, the precept of Deut 23.7 ("Thou shall not abhor an Edomite; for he is thy brother"), and the judgment of Amos 2.1–3, though, not surprisingly, the bitter hatred of Edom often felt by the Jews has also left its traces in the OT as well as in extracanonical Jewish literature.[104]

To summarize Paul's claim in 9:6–29, believers can be confident that nothing will separate them from God because that relationship is based not on human action but on the very nature of God's mercy, and that mercy is

---

103. Ibid., 475.
104. Ibid., 480–81.

greater than human failure of disobedience and disbelief. Furthermore, within God's general plan of election, which includes all the descendants of Abraham, God has chosen specific individuals through which God's ultimate promise will be accomplished.[105]

Given the above understanding of 9:6–29, the remainder of this section of Romans does not reflect the discontinuity that Räisänen suggests.[106] Paul's predestinarian language in this passage is not referencing an eschatological future but rather illustrates that God is in control to bring about God's own promise. This is reinforced by 9:30—10:21. Here Paul points out that the chosen, the elect, have had every benefit, so they are without excuse for their state of unbelief. However, even in their state of unbelief, hope is seen. Paul ends this section by quoting Isaiah 65. "But of Israel he says, 'All day long I have held out my hands to a disobedient and contrary people'" (10:21). This note of hope is continued in chapter 11. Paul begins by acknowledging Israel's failure, but their stumbling does not result in their falling from God's mercy. Rather, their stumbling is used by God to extend mercy to the Gentiles. Paul's point is not to determine who will ultimately experience glorification and who will not. That decision is God's alone and is based on God's mercy. "For God has consigned all men to disobedience, that he may have mercy upon all" (11:32). Paul understands that any

---

105. Cranfield's comments on verses 15 and 18 support his understanding of Paul's two illustrations. "v 15—It is our contention that Paul regarded these words from Exodus as an appropriate and cogent answer to the suggestion that there is unrighteousness with God, precisely because he understood them to be affirming emphatically the freedom of God's mercy (and therefore the fact that God's mercy is not something to which men can establish a claim whether on the ground of parentage or of works), and at the same time making it clear that it is the freedom of God's mercy that is being affirmed, and not of some unqualified will of God behind, and distinct from His merciful will" (ibid., 483–84). "v 18—Two contrasting forms of God's determination of men corresponding to the two different ways in which men may serve the divine purpose are indicated by ἐλεεῖ and σκληρύνει. Some serve it consciously and (more or less) voluntarily, other unconsciously and involuntarily. And men's stances in relation to God's purpose depend ultimately on God. He has mercy on some in the sense that He determines them for a positive role in relation to His purpose, to a conscious and voluntary service: others He hardens in the sense that He determines them for a negative role in relation to His purpose, for an unconscious, involuntary service" (ibid., 488).

106. "The observations made in the course of this study about Paul's self-contradictions suggests that one should hardly posit a theological development in Paul's thinking about Israel from 1 Thess to Romans. It is sufficient to note that Paul finds himself in a different situation. No wonder that precisely in issues concerning his relationship to his Jewish heritage Paul gets caught in theological difficulties. He is torn into two directions, and he is incapable of resolving the tension in terms of theological thought" (Räisänen, *Paul and the Law,* 264).

theological attempt to explain precisely the work of God is bound to fail. As a result, he ends this section of Romans with a doxology.[107]

> O the depth of the riches and wisdom and knowledge of God! How unsearchable are his judgments and how inscrutable his ways! "For who has known the mind of the Lord, or who has been his counselor?" "Or who has given a gift to him that he might be repaid?" For from him and through him and to him are all things. To him be glory for ever. Amen.[108]

In the above sections, we explored three distinct voices, looking at some of the relevant biblical materials. These biblical texts acknowledge the existence of other gods while insisting that Yahweh is superior to all and that Yahweh intends to be the God of all peoples. Furthermore, if salvation, as understood in a biblical sense, is obtained, then it is only because of Yahweh.[109] The Pauline texts present Jesus Christ as unique in both person and works, the vehicle for knowing God and for obtaining salvation, and illustrate how this uniqueness has implications for understanding other faith traditions. Furthermore, the basis for any relationship with God is God's mercy, faithfulness, and sovereignty. While the three voices do not present all of the relevant biblical materials for constructing an evangelical theology of religions, they do provide a rough theological framework in which the construction can take place. What theological framework emerged? Ethelbert Stauffer identifies two relevant points of this framework.

> Paul now writes to the Colossians, and opposes the misleading human "philosophy" of worldly elemental powers with a *christocentric "philosophy"* (Col 2.8) . . . There are cosmic powers. Paul did not contest that, but Christ was before them (Col 1.15ff.). Christ bears in himself the whole fullness of the Godhead (Col 1.19, 2.9), and his redemptive work embraces both heaven and earth (Col 1.20). The crucified has disarmed the principalities and powers, and led them in his triumphal procession (Col

---

107. For a discussion of Rom 9–11 from the perspective of a progressive dispensationalist, see Burns, "Israel and the Church of a Progressive Dispensationalist," 263–91.

108. Rom 11:33–36.

109. Defining "salvation" in the broad sense, we can say that it occurs when an individual achieves their ultimate purpose. Different understandings of what constitutes "ultimate purpose" emerge from different faith traditions. Within evangelicalism, salvation involves redemption, reconciliation, satisfaction, and justification, and results in an everlasting personal relationship with Yahweh, the Creator. This emphasis on personal relationship does not deny the sense in which salvation is eschatological, a renewed heaven and earth. The present sense and the future sense of salvation are equally embraced by evangelical thought.

> 2.15). Therefore, Christ is Lord not only of his Church, but of the whole cosmos, and all its powers (Col 2.10). In this way Paul opened the Colossians' eyes to the world-wide range of the *sola cruce* which Epaphras had preached to them. So in the same spirit that produced the movement of concentration in Galatia Paul developed now an audacious and unheard of movement of expansion (Col 1.9ff). The coming of Christ is either the center of our conception of the world, or it has no place in it.[110]

That cosmic powers exist is the first point that Stauffer identifies. The second is that Jesus Christ is Lord, not only of his church, but of the whole cosmos. He is a universal Christ. Furthermore, given Paul's hope for Israel's ultimate salvation, which is not based upon their belief or actions but on God's mercy that stimulated God's election of them, can a hopeful analogy be proposed?

Reconstructing Paul's argument in Romans, we find that Paul considers even those Jews who are in a state of disbelief as ultimately recipients of God's mercy. Even in their state, while they have not been chosen to be part of those who believe and are participating in a positive fashion to bring about God's promise, they are still part of that promise. Because they are descendants of Abraham, mercy is theirs. Can Paul's argument take us beyond what Paul has stated regarding his fellow Jews? Is it possible that God has established covenant relationship prior to the Abrahamic covenant? Clearly, Gen 9 presents an earlier covenant. God enters into a relationship with all of Noah's descendants. Furthermore, the language of Gen 3:11–24 has the benchmarks of a covenant. Is it possible that as early as the original fall, God instituted a plan to restore the broken fellowship? If this is possible, then this plan too must have been based on the mercy of God. The entire history of humankind may be understood as the history of restoration. If the salvation of Christians and Jews is not based upon their actions, then is it possible that among other faith traditions God has chosen to elect a remnant? "For he says to Moses, 'I will have mercy on whom I have mercy, and I will have compassion on whom I have compassion.' So it depends not upon man's will or exertion, but upon God's mercy" (Rom 9:15–16). While we want to avoid any attempt to put Paul into our current situation, he does exhibit several characteristics that we benefit from as we grapple with our theology of religions. First, he recognizes that ultimately salvation is dependent upon God. It is God who chooses. Because it is God who is sovereign, Paul is confident that God's promises will be accomplished. Hence, his has an optimistic hope for those of the Jewish tradition, while at the same time

---

110. Stauffer, *New Testament Theology*, 39.

he takes an agnostic stance and declares that no one is God's counselor.[111] Finally, Paul's "theology of religions" motivated him to do missions and proclaim the gospel.

These themes (i.e., that there are powers opposed to God, that the Christ-event has cosmic universal implications, and that God's mercy is the seat of all salvation) suggest that the New Testament message and its theological framework are relevant and meaningful when considering a theology of religions. In the following essay, a tentative evangelical theology of religions will be proposed.

---

111. While E. P. Sanders assumes that when Paul speaks of "faith" he always means faith in Jesus Christ, a position I will suggest is questionable, Sanders does accurately conclude that we "not put him [Paul] entirely into the strait-jacket of logical arrangement. . . . He was a theologian, in Romans 9–11, as in Romans 7, he was deeply worried about theological problems. Paul was not systematic, however, since he did not reconcile his responses to these multifaceted problems with one another. . . . He forces us, in fact, to pose an extremely serious question: must a religion, in addressing diverse problems, offer answers that are completely consistent with one another? Is it not good to have passionate hopes and commitments which cannot all be reduced to a scheme in which they are arranged in a hierarchical relationship?" (Sanders, *Paul*, 148–149).

6

An Interim Outline of Theology of Religions

A Proposed Evangelical Perspective

We have claimed that evangelical theology, though diverse, exhibits three common threads: it is committed to the Christian Scriptures, it is evangelistic, and it exhibits a level of theological tolerance absent in other forms of conservative Protestant Christianity. Given these common threads, this essay outlines an interim theology of religions from an evangelical perspective. This proposal of how evangelicals might view alien faith traditions is offered to stimulate dialogue among evangelicals and those sympathetic with evangelicalism. It will include four relevant issues: God, interreligious dialogue, persons, and salvation.[1] This proposal should not be viewed as modeling *the* evangelical position. As we have seen, evangelical theology is extremely diverse. This essay provides simply one route weaving its way through the maze of possible positions. The positions offered in this proposal do affect other areas of theology, so interested parties, in dialogue with each other, must seriously consider the implications. While that dialogue lies outside the domain of any single individual, this essay will conclude that evangelicals ought to embrace an agnostic optimism regarding their theology of religions. This stance leads to a fundamental question: How is this stance even possible for evangelicals? This question is the focus of the essays that follow.

Before moving forward, I will comment briefly on my understanding of the nature of theology. As a critical objectivist, I maintain that there is a reality that exists outside of the knower; however, while the world we experience is what is there, our knowledge of it is mediated. Hence, knowledge of the world requires analysis, which includes interpretation, inquiry

---

1. While this order of presentation may not be the typical order for developing an evangelical theology, the placement of interreligious dialogue does naturally follow the discussion of God. Furthermore, because of the development of the argument in this project, placing salvation last contributes to the flow of the reasoning.

through dialogue, and application of data. As a result, theology is a searching to understand principles that enable the knower to imitate or reflect the mind of God. This understanding is partial, for we are limited (1 Cor 13:12). Furthermore, this search is most fruitful when done in dialogue. As a result, the following is intended to promote dialogue.

God

Thomas Aquinas claims that theology is about God.[2] Theology begins with God, comes from God, and leads to God. Following Aquinas's lead, our proposal begins with God. Who is this Supreme Being that evangelicals worship? Is the God of evangelicals the same as the God of other faith traditions? In short, are all God-seekers seeking the same God? Evangelicals, as well as others, advocate that the purpose of theology is to bring appropriate glory to God. Because they do not wish to malign their God, North American evangelicals frequently assume that the God they worship is not the same God worshiped in other faith traditions. This assumption leads to a very significant stance, which affects their theology of religions. The stance goes something like this: They, Christians, worship the true God, whereas others, non-Christians, worship false Gods. Alien religions are false religions; hence, they have little or no redeeming value from this evangelical perspective. While this stance provides a clear line of demarcation, it faces a couple major obstacles that lead me to suggest that this simplistic stance is inadequate as a foundation for this area of theology. First, this position is inconsistent with another position equally held to be true by evangelicals. Second, by separating the God worshiped by evangelicals from other Gods, this position implies the existence of multiple Gods, and this implication is frequently taken to be incorrect. These two obstacles must be examined more closely.

Evangelicals are people of the book. They believe that both the Old and New Testaments are God's written message. Because they accept the Old Testament as God breathed, evangelicals believe the God they worship is Yahweh—the same God worshiped in Judaism. While Christians claim additional revelation, they acknowledge that they are worshiping the same God that Jews worship, although Christians claim that their understanding of God is more complete than Jewish understanding because of the additional revelation, Jesus Christ. Hence, some evangelicals' assumption that followers all other faith traditions are worshiping a false God does not hold. Followers of at least one other tradition (Judaism) do worship the same

---

2. *Summa Theologiae*, Question 1, Articles 1–3, and 7.

God as Christians do. If adherents of at least one alien tradition worship the same God as they do, then it is possible that followers of other traditions might also. For example, it may be possible that the supreme God of Hinduism, Parabrahma, is the same God that Judaism identifies as Yahweh. It is possible that the position of distinguishing the God of evangelicals from any other God is a problem of identity—a problem like the morning star/evening star distinction (where the same star seen at separate times of day appears to be two different stars).

While the discussion of who is being worshiped in a given religion illustrates the first problem for evangelicals, the predicament is much deeper. Individuals worship God. Institutions, such as religions, do not worship God. Evangelical theology maintains that one's membership in a religious institution does not necessarily make one a true religious adherent. That is, one may be a member of a given religion, practice the rites of that religion, and still fail to be a true believer.[3] For evangelicals, marks of a true believer may include a proper attitude or a proper intent of the heart or a particular relationship with God, none of which may be empirically verifiable. According to this view, some members of an evangelical church may not be worshiping the Christian God even though they appear to meet all external benchmarks that suggest otherwise. This acknowledgment has major ramifications for evangelicals as they consider practitioners of alien religions. If it is possible for "Christians" to worship some other God, then the question is not whether "Parabrahma" is the same as "Yahweh," but whether an individual worshiper of Parabrahma is worshiping Yahweh. An evangelical assumption that the Christian God is different from Gods of alien religions is problematic because it is extremely complex. While interreligious dialogues will not remove the complexity, without dialogue we can never begin to tackle the problem.

The assumption of some evangelicals that their God is different presents a second obstacle to interreligious dialogue. It stands as contrary to another assumption made today: that assumption is that if God does exist, then there must only be one God. That is, monotheism is assumed to be correct.

> *God* is a name, or better yet, a title, and it's a title that's generally understood to refer to a single being if it refers to anything at all. If there are two or more equally viable candidates for the title

---

3. There are religious traditions in which the practice of given rites is all that is required to be considered a true believer. These cases are the exception.

"God" then *God* does not exist, though some gods do. God, if God there be, is unique.[4]

This reminds us of J. Gerald Janzen's discussion of the crucial word *ehād* in the Shema of Deut 6:4–5, which the RSV translates as "one". Janzen points out that there are two basic ways of understanding this word. "The word says something about Israel's God *in se* . . .; or it says something about the claim of this God upon Israel."[5] The quotation from Stairs and Bernard seems to try to straddle both meanings. God is one (i.e., monotheism is correct), and God is unique (i.e., God calls for special claim upon God's people). However, as Stairs and Bernard use the word "unique," they are not using it as Janzen suggests, but rather are indicating oneness, singularity. The assumption that there is only one God is significant for the development of any adequate theology of religions.

If there is only one God, then Parabrahma is identical with Yahweh or Ahura Mazda of Zoroastrianism. All God-seekers are seeking the same God. We simply see different names used to denote the same Being. However, the biblical materials we just surveyed offer a surprising picture, which supports a position similar to that of some evangelicals. While Israelite believers are to worship one God (to practice monotheism), the Scriptures acknowledge the existence of other deities beside Yahweh. While it is possible that Parabrahma, Yahweh, Ahura Mazda, and Allah are simply different names denoting the same Supreme Being, the biblical materials open the door for polytheism. As a result, an evangelical theology of religions must hold open the possibility that the Supreme Being worshiped by Christians is not the Supreme Being of Hinduism. Yet, they must also acknowledge the possibility that they are the same. This means that evangelicals cannot initially assume either stance, but their theology of religions must reflect an agnosticism that motivates inquiry: not a hopeless agnosticism that promotes despair because no answers are possible, but a hopeful agnosticism, that promotes research. Evangelical theology of religions cannot assume an abstract position about the relationship between the God evangelicals worship and the Gods worshiped in other faith traditions. In order to develop an adequate story about other faith traditions, evangelicals will need to ask whether the God of the tradition or practice in question is the same as their God. This task is not a simple one, and it must be done with an attitude of humbleness.[6]

---

4. Stairs and Bernard, *Thinker's Guide to the Philosophy of Religion*, 2.

5. Janzen, "On the Most Important Word in the Shema," 280.

6. In Buddhist literature known as *Sutra Pitaka*, Gautama tells the story of a king who is pressed to describe Dhamma. The king, being wise, assembled all of the people

If an adequate theology of religions for evangelicals calls for careful consideration of the Being identified as God because presuppositions that paint an abstract position are dubious, there is little question for evangelicals about the relationship between God and the created. The Being that evangelicals worship as God is distinct from creation, though the agent and source of creation. As a result, evangelicals do reject any form of pantheism or panentheism.

A third stance evangelicals must take regarding the God they worship is that God is greater than any human attempt to define God. While some forms of conservative Christianity may be accused of having a God-in-the-box, evangelicals must wrestle to preserve the position that God is wholly other. However, this does not imply that nothing can be said accurately about God. Evangelicals believe that God has chosen to be self-revealing, and, as a result, accurate and meaningful truth-claims can be made about God. These claims are just incomplete.[7]

One such truth-claim is that God desires relationship with creation, which is based upon God's mercy. Whether we review the Old Testament or the New Testament, God is seen as pursuing and establishing covenant with those whom God created. It is significant to note that within the Christian worldview are two orders of things: that which is uncreated and that which is created. In short, all that is not Creator is created, and the Creator seeks relationship with all outside the Godhead. This desire for relationship is the basis for claiming that God is personal. Furthermore, God is not limited to desire relationship or community with only a specific group of people. God desires to have community with the entirety of creation. This entails that

---

of Savatthi that had been born blind. Some of the blind people were introduced to an elephant by being presented its tusks. Others were introduced by the trunk, others by an ear, or the tail, or a leg. While all were introduced to the same elephant, they were introduced to different parts. Then they were asked to describe an elephant. Each spoke only of their understanding of "elephant." They claimed an elephant to be only to what they were introduced to, nothing more. Evangelicals must be cautious because their understanding of God is limited.

7. It must be remembered that evangelicals understand revelation to be progressive and unfolding. "The Bible does not present a revelation given all at once. The truth it offers was communicated over a long time and by a very dynamic process. The text seems to breathe, to expand and contract, to grow and build toward the full actualization of salvation, the coming of God's kingdom. The truth is given dialectically in a process of conversation and refinement, which makes for a dynamic experience of interpretation. The Bible takes the form, not of a systematic theology, but of a great narrative that presents the grace of God in action for the redemption of the nations. Therefore, the truth it yields is not cut-and-dried, but balanced and nuanced. The truth is given and applied, then reinterpreted and reapplied. Older material is appealed to again and again and put to new use. Out of this process of refinement, fresh insights appear" (Pinnock and Callen, *Scripture Principle*, 201–2).

God wishes to have community with all nations, all tribes, and all people. In addition, we should understand that this community is not limited to persons but extends to the entire created order of things. Does this mean that all of the created order will participate in community with the Creator? No, but it does mean that the God of evangelicals cannot be viewed as a God who is only interested in "our little group."

The starting point for an evangelical theology of religions is an understanding that God is greater than anything they can say about God. While the Creator has chosen to reveal some things about God's nature, God is more than an itemizing of the incommunicable and communicable attributes.

> The names of God constitute a difficulty for human thought. God is the *Incomprehensible One*, infinitely exalted above all that is temporal; but in His names He descends to all that is finite and becomes like unto man. On the one hand we cannot name Him, and on the other hand He has many names. How can this be explained? On what grounds are these names applied to the infinite and incomprehensible God? It should be borne in mind that they are not of man's invention, and do not testify to his insight into the very Being of God. They are given by God Himself with the assurance that they contain in a measure a revelation of the Divine Being. This was made possible by the fact that the world and all its relations is and was meant to be a revelation of God. Because the Incomprehensible One revealed Himself in His creatures, it is possible for man to name Him after the fashion of a creature. In order to make Himself know to man, God had to condescend to the level of man, to accommodate Himself to the limited and finite human consciousness, and to speak in human language. If the naming of God with anthropomorphic names involves a limitation of God, as some say, then this must be true to an even greater degree of the revelation of God in creation. Then the world does not reveal but rather conceals, God; then man is not related to God, but simply forms an antithesis to Him; and then we are shut up to a hopeless agnosticism.[8]

The God worshiped by evangelicals is beyond comprehension, yet knowable. Berkhof's quote illustrates an assumption that evangelicals have regarding God. God is a revelatory God who has chosen to be self-revealing. Because God is self-revealing, we can know some things about God. This revelation frequently is subdivided into two types: general and special revelation. The former points to God being revealed in nature, in the general working of the

8. Berkhof, *Systematic Theology*, 47–48.

Spirit of God, and in human conscience as seen in the Noahic law.⁹ The latter points to God's self-revelation in the Scriptures, to the person and work of Jesus Christ,¹⁰ and to other modes such as personal experience (1 Sam 3:2–9; Acts 10:9–16), miracles (John 9:1–12), or prophecy (Joel 2:28—3:21).

Interreligious Dialogue

At the end of the previous essay, Ethelbert Stauffer claimed that the biblical materials offer a framework that highlights both the cosmic powers and the universality of Christ. The notion of cosmic powers unfolds in two directions. On the one hand, these cosmic powers may be viewed as deities. For example, Moses does not attempt to deny the existence of other gods; rather he recognized the world in which he lived, and it was a world full of gods. Just as Paul on Mars Hill (Acts 17) used the belief in the existence of cosmic powers as a point of dialogue, contemporary Christians can do the same. While details may differ, many of the world faith systems regard their God(s) as life-givers, as sovereign, as judge, and so forth. Given these similarities and dissimilarities, meaningful dialogue can be opened and maintained. The other direction in which cosmic powers unfold is toward the demonic, the powers and principalities, of which Paul spoke. From the most animistic to the most refined religious traditions, belief in powers that corrupt is a cornerstone to most traditions. Once again, this point of common ground becomes a foundation for dialogue. A crucial aspect of an evangelical theology of religions is to embrace a positive stance toward interreligious dialogue.¹¹

Furthermore, the theological framework sketched from Colossians presents a Jesus Christ who is Lord of the entire cosmos. He is universal.

---

9. This will be closer examined in the eighth essay of this volume.

10. Evangelicals would agree with N. T. Wright when he states, "Until we look hard at Jesus, we really haven't understood who God is" (Stafford, "Mere Mission," 40). Jesus Christ is the ultimate presentation of God presently available.

11. Various terms have been used to refer to what I am calling interreligious dialogue. It is often referred to as "multifaith" or "interfaith" dialogue. Each term elicits a connotation that is useful. "Multifaith" captures a dialogue among the involved religious traditions. 'Interfaith' points to the dialogue between. It could be suggested that "multifaith," while foundational, may focus upon sharing one's history and understanding of their given tradition. However, "interfaith" may focus on the region between the various faiths. Some of the most interesting aspects of religious dialogue is found in that space between the religions. Hence, my preference for "inter-." In some traditions, the concept of "faith" does not easily fit for some practitioners, e.g., Buddhism and Judaism; hence, the term "interreligious" is used. (I want to thank Alan Race for suggesting the various implications of these terms.)

Whether this universality or cosmic Christ concept is worked out in the form of some type of fulfillment theology[12] or within the Reformed tradition as in the work of J. H. Bavinck (cited in Tiessen),[13] it points to a belief that God has not left the world without a witness.[14] Therefore, Christians and non-Christians have enough commonality to engage in meaningful dialogue.

Because the notion of the uniqueness of Jesus Christ can and should stimulate meaningful dialogue, it is relevant.[15] Evangelicals can and must engage in interreligious dialogue. An evangelical theology does not curtail a dialogue but enriches it because an evangelical framework brings a perspective of the divine and God's activity in the world that is often not heard. Even in North America, many individuals have a misconception of evangelicalism, and unless evangelicals are willing to participate in dialogue, which requires both sharing and listening, ignorance of an evangelical theology will only continue. Furthermore, many North American evangelicals are ignorant about members of other faith traditions. By participating in interreligious dialogues, many of those misconceptions can be corrected.

If evangelicals wish to continue their mission, which provided them with their name, and be obedient to the Great Commission of evangelization and discipleship, then they must be present at the table where the conversation is taking place. Interreligious dialogue groups provide an excellent opportunity to join the conversation among individuals who are interested in God-talk.[16] However, the ground rules frequently outlined by interreligious groups for dialogue require evangelicals to learn a new way of sharing their faith.[17] In these dialogue groups, the emphasis is on sharing informa-

12. Dhavamony, "Cosmic Christ and World Religions."

13. Tiessen, "God's Work of Grace in the Context of the Religions."

14. "We would also see clear proof that God has not abandoned man, has not left himself without a witness, but is unceasingly concerned and active with man" (J. H. Bavinck cited by Tiessen, "God's Work of Grace," 250–51).

15. David Williams calls for Christians to engage in dialogue, and this dialogue is meaningful if the Christian takes a christological approach (Williams, "Salvation in Non-Christian Religions"). Also, see Cutsinger, "Uniqueness of Jesus Christ and Other Religions," 427–34; and Bloesch, "Finality of Christ and Religious Pluralism."

16. To speak of God-talk should not exclude those traditions that do not talk about "God," traditions such as Buddhism or Unitarian Universalism. In the broadest sense, God-talk refers to talking about ultimate concern or ultimate power.

17. For example, the Fresno Multifaith Exchange outlines six ground rules as part of their Mission Statement: (1) The context of the program is one of rejoicing in the faith diversity of the Fresno community. (2) The program will look for depth through teachings, shared dialogue, and social exchange. (3) There will be information sharing; there will not be proselytizing. (4) Hospitality will be simple and minimal, in keeping with the traditions of a given religion. (5) Study group members are asked to commit, as much as possible, to visits and dialogue for the entire schedule. (6) Study group

tion about one's own faith, and proselytizing is considered inappropriate. Furthermore, evangelicals must learn to listen to positions they consider wrong, whether the position is presented by a fellow Christian who is not an evangelical or by a member of some alien faith tradition. Dialogue is about listening, learning, and sharing when it is your turn. If interreligious dialogues are properly structured, all parties will have an opportunity, at some point, to share their understanding of their own faith. Participating in such dialogues, evangelicals will learn that while they may be in theological disagreement with others in the dialogue, they do share common concerns as persons who are interested in issues such as social justice or peace or correcting misconceptions that may lead to distrust or dealing with local issues like poverty, homelessness, or religious freedom. All of these are part of the Great Commission. The evangelical message is one of good news, not of pessimism. Only as evangelicals participate in interreligious dialogues will their message of optimism be realized.

Finally, if God is more than their theology outlines, and evangelicals must acknowledge that they do not have "God in the box," then by listening to others who are also God-seekers, evangelicals may learn new insights about the richness of the God they worship. The God of evangelicals is a cosmic God who loves all people. Furthermore, evangelicals may learn religious practices that their tradition has not practiced. For example, one cannot read the Psalms without realizing that meditation is an important element in worship. Yet, it is a topic evangelicals have ignored. As evangelicals listen to members of alien faith traditions talk about the value of meditation, they must ask if there is a Christian perspective on meditation and whether practicing meditation could enhance their spiritual walk. As evangelicals emphasize the importance of prayer in their spiritual walk, does meditation have a role? Or consider the Islamic understanding of charity. Evangelicals are a people who give, but too frequently it is done with much show. While being visibly beneficent may encourage others to give, is there not something valuable about giving without fanfare? Additionally, engaging in dialogue may provide, an evangelical theological insight that previously may have been overlooked. For example, these insights may be the result of the evangelical participant being forced to clarify his or her own understanding of a given theological issue in order to discuss it with members of another faith tradition. Or the insight may be taught by a member of another tradition. Evangelicals have claimed that God is greater than anything they can say about God. However, because of the influence of Greek philosophy

---

members should represent a balanced variety religiously, racially, and culturally. (Revised June 2004).

on Christianity, evangelical theology tends toward developing connotative definitions of God. As a result, evangelicals produce a God-in-the-box. Dialogues with those of the Hindu tradition about Parabrahma may shed new light on the Christian God.[18] Evangelicals, while they have something to share with those of other traditions, can learn from those outside their own faith tradition.

Persons

If an adequate evangelical theology of religions requires the starting point to be God, which leads to a discussion regarding interreligious dialogue, the third foundational area must be the nature of persons. Evangelicals, while they may disagree about the details, generally agree on four crucial issues on the nature of persons. First, persons were created for fellowship or community with their Creator. While all of creation is maximized when it is in community with God, persons, the only part of creation that is specifically made in the image of God, are unique. Second, the desired relationship between God and persons has been broken. The human race has not properly acknowledged their Creator, and by failing to do so they have failed to give proper glory to God. This broken fellowship refers to the "fall" and the need for restored community, or salvation. Third, individuals on their own are incapable of mending the gap between their Creator and themselves. Restoration is totally dependent upon God. A fourth crucial point is that as sin entered the world, so did evil. Furthermore, while individuals can strive to minimize evil in the world, and they must, human beings are incapable of eradicating evil. These convictions are essential to an evangelical theology of religions, and these same convictions create an arena for interreligious discussion. All the major faith traditions say something about the nature of persons and about the ability and inability of persons to do right; all faith traditions grapple with the problem of why there is evil in the world.

Salvation

An evangelical theology of religions must address the issue of salvation. However, it might be questioned whether evangelicals can develop a stance regarding other faith-traditions and salvation. The problem stems from the

18. Evangelicals, like many other adherents of Christianity, do acknowledge the Scriptures as the only or ultimate rule for Christian faith and practice. As a result, evangelicals who are engaged in interreligious dialogue must constantly be evaluating what they are hearing in light of their Scriptures.

stance that religions do not offer salvation. Only God saves. Furthermore, evangelicals believe that individuals, not institutions such as religions, obtain salvation by God's mercy. As a result, evangelicals will claim that no religion, not even their own, offers soteriological value. Nevertheless, soteriological issues are crucial for evangelicals and must be addressed as part of their comprehensive theology of religions.

Because of the fall and need of all persons for restoration, evangelicals must incorporate into their theology of religions several soteriological issues. Six specific issues are crucial: (1) the nature and purpose of salvation, (2) the agency of salvation, (3) salvation as a process, (4) the basis of salvation, (5) the recipients of salvation, and (6) the impact on missions and evangelism.

First, evangelicals must address how their idea of salvation differs from the end goal of other faith traditions. While most traditions may speak, in broad terms, of salvation as deliverance, the content of that deliverance is radically varied. Deliverance or salvation means something different in different traditions. For example, a Buddhist understanding of salvation or deliverance is very different from an evangelical view of salvation. In the Buddhist tradition, one loses individuality whereas in evangelicalism it is generally seen as being preserved.[19] Given different conceptions of salvation, different ways or means exist to obtain salvation. While most faith traditions have as a goal obtaining salvation, that goal is not the same point since salvation means different things to different groups. For evangelicals, as for most Christians, salvation is restored fellowship or community, not only with their Creator, but also with other persons and with the cosmos. Furthermore, salvation, while a goal, is not the ultimate goal for Christians. The *Shorter Westminster Catechism* captures the ultimate goal in its first question: "What is the chief end of man?" To which it answers, "Man's chief end is to glorify God, and enjoy him forever." Salvation or restoration of fellowship is not ultimately about us, persons, but about the Creator. This is significant because salvation must focus on glorifying God.

19. "The Rightly-Illumined One perceived all these things and thus was decisively awakened: when birth is destroyed, old age and death ceases; when 'becoming' is destroyed, then birth ceases; When attachment is destroyed, 'becoming' ceases; when craving is destroyed, attachment ceases; when sensations are destroyed, craving ceases; When contact is destroyed, sensation ceases; when the six sense organs are destroyed, contact ceases; when the physical form is destroyed, the six sense organs cease; When consciousness is destroyed, physical form ceases; when psychic constructions are destroyed, consciousness ceases; when ignorance is destroyed, psychic constructions cease. Reflecting his right understanding, the great hermit arose before the world as the Buddha, the Enlightened One. He found self (ātman) nowhere, as the fire whose fuel has been exhausted" (De Bary, *Buddhist Tradition in India, China, and Japan*, 68–69).

In essay 3 we saw that one of the six crucial elements of soteriology relevant for developing a theology of religions is the agency of salvation. We saw evangelicals taking a unanimous stance that Jesus Christ is the agency through which salvation or restoration is made possible. It is Jesus Christ and only him that provides the possibility of restoration through the atonement that he made possible.[20] An evangelical theology of religions must retain the uniqueness and singularity of Jesus Christ's work that makes restoration of fellowship or community with God possible. While the means is not open to question by evangelicals, the application of that work must be examined.

Furthermore, evangelical theologians speak of salvation not as a single event but as a multifaceted process.[21] It involves sacrifice, propitiation/expiation, reconciliation, and redemption.[22] The process ends with a fully restored fellowship, a redeemed state of being in community with God. Salvation in this ultimate or eschatological sense is commonly referred to as glorification. If salvation is merely an ultimate or eschatological accomplishment, then the task for evangelicals of making sense of how "those whom have not heard" are treated in their theology of religions is potentially very concise. However, for evangelicals, salvation is more than the ultimate or eschatological accomplishment. Salvation also includes the processional sense and the positional sense. The New Testament speaks of a believer being "in Christ," or "having been saved," or of being saved (e.g., "since you are saved").[23] These expressions and other similar ones speak of salvation in the past tense and depict a positional truth. We are justified in

---

20. Isa 53:5, Matt 20:28, 1 Cor 5:3, 2 Cor 5:21, Gal 1:4, 1 Tim 2:6, and 1 Pet 2:24. Robert Lightner says this of the substitutionary death of Jesus Christ: "He died in the place of sinners. His death was vicarious in that He was the sinless vicar intervening for man. The Savior took the sinner's place and thus acted as the sinner's substitute. The certainty and finality of this substitution is true whether anyone ever appropriates it by faith or not. In other words, its reality and value do not depend upon its application to the individual" (Lightner, *Death Christ Died*, 23).

21. Horne, *Salvation*, 34–46. Also see Bloesch, *Essentials of Evangelical Theology*, 1:149–52; or Erickson, *Christian Theology*, 917–19.

22. Evangelicals understand the atonement in terms of propitiation as opposed to Dodd's argument that in Pauline literature atonement is best understood as expiation. "The numerous passages that speak of the wrath . . . of God against sin are evidence that Christ's death was necessarily propitiatory; Rom 1:18; 2:5, 8; 4:15; 5:9; 9:22; 12:19; 13:4–5; Eph 2:3; 5:6; Col 3;6; and 1 Thess 1:10; 2:16; 5:9. So then, Paul's idea of the atoning death . . . is not simply that it covers sin and cleanses from its corruption (expiation), but that the sacrifice also appeases a God who hates sin and is radically opposed to it (propitiation)" (Erickson, *Christian Theology*, 828–29).

23. "In the primary sense, justification is concerned not with our spiritual *condition* but with our spiritual *relation*; it is not a matter of our actual *state* but of our judicial *position*" (Horne, *Salvation*, 70). cf. Rom 5: 9–21.

Christ. One benefit of this positional salvation is the permanent indwelling of the Holy Spirit. Furthermore, the New Testament speaks of a believer working out their salvation, becoming sanctified.[24] Salvation in this sense is something that is currently being performed in the lives of believers to mature them in their relationship with God. Much of this growth is possible because of the indwelling Spirit. This is the process of sanctification. The total picture of salvation, for evangelicals, includes justification, sanctification, and glorification.

An adequate evangelical theology of religions must come to grips with the nature of salvation—these three aspects—as it might apply to those of alien faiths. If salvation were only eschatological, then the development of a theology of religions might be easier. We would only need to address how those of an alien faith could have a salvific faith for which God ultimately draws them back into community. However, given the tripart understanding of salvation, the difficulty of developing a theology of religions becomes much more complicated. For example, if one indicator that an individual has been justified before God is the permanent indwelling Holy Spirit, then a theology of religions must address how the Holy Spirit might relate to some members of alien faiths. Is it possible that an individual will experience ultimate or eschatological salvation without experiencing the process of sanctification? Is it possible that one will obtain glorification but never experience the indwelling of the Holy Spirit? Traditional conservative Christianity simply maintained that those outside of camp are lost; hence, the above questions pose no problem. However, if an adequate evangelical theology of religions is going to hold out hope, then one must grapple with very difficult issues. Can one be justified—positionally be in God—without knowledge of the agency God has chosen to use? Is sanctification even possible if one is unaware of the Comforter? On the other hand, is it possible that God might have something else in place for them? As we saw in Rom 9–11, it does appear possible that God has another economy at work for those outside of Christianity.

The development of a theology of religions that takes into account the basis of salvation must address the notions of mercy and justice. How wide is God's mercy? How far does it extend? Evangelicals such as Clark Pinnock have opened the door for extending the notion of mercy beyond the boundaries traditionally accepted. However, justice must also be explored. If salvation is obtainable only by those who have been privileged to hear the Gospel and whose surroundings were conducive to acceptance of the

---

24. "Sanctification has to do with the progressive outworking of the new life implanted by the Holy Spirit in *regeneration*" (ibid., 78). cf. 2 Cor 5: 17–21.

gospel, then has justice been served? If it is impossible for some to accept the gospel because of conditions beyond their own control, is God just in condemning them to continued alienation? Traditionally, evangelicals have maintained that justice is served because those condemned are guilty, for all have sinned.[25] Is this traditional response adequate? Should God decide to open the floodgates and provide salvation to those outside the camp, has God's justice been violated? No, for Jesus Christ is still the agency, and as we saw, especially through Colossians, the work of Jesus Christ is cosmic. The ramifications of the cross-event go far beyond the Christian church. Just as Jeremiah depicted God, the God of the Bible is the God of all people.

Evangelicals have begun the discussion about the recipients of salvation.[26] While their discussion made use of the stances of inclusivism and exclusivism, we saw the two positions emerge regarding the atonement: the position of limited atonement, and the position of unlimited atonement. In that discussion, it was suggested that a more consistent stance for evangelicals to take is that of an inclusivist position that maintains that salvation may be extended to more than those within the Christian church. That is, the atoning work of Christ applies beyond the scope of his bride, the church. If salvation is to unveil the glory of God, then what greater way could God's glory be shown than a restoration of those who have no or very limited knowledge of God? While the Scriptures do give a clear formula for obtaining salvation, i.e., If you believe . . . , then you are saved, the formula does not teach, "if you do not believe . . . , then you are not saved." Given that the Scriptures are primarily for training and equipping members of the Christian church, it is possible that God has some other plan to extend mercy and justice to others.[27] However, as people of the Book, evangelicals must be cautious as they develop theological stances that may be logical conclusions from the Scriptures but are not clearly taught. In such situations, evangelicals may be optimistic about the future of those who have not heard, but evangelicals must quickly acknowledge their position is agnostic. Anything not clearly taught in Scripture must be embraced with an agnostic attitude.

Will an optimistic agnosticism affect an evangelical's understanding of missions and evangelism? Some evangelicals have expressed concern that

---

25. Saint Augustine clearly has influenced the evangelical position. Augustine embraced the position that "the reason why one person is assisted by grace, and another is not helped, must be referred to the secret judgments of God" ("On Grace and Freewill," 464). This secret judgment appears to be based upon God's foreknowledge.

26. See essay 4 "Recipients of Salvation," above.

27. "All Scripture is inspired by God and profitable for teaching, for reproof, for correction, and for training in righteousness, that the man of God may be complete, equipped for very good work" (2 Tim 3:16–17).

an optimistic theology of religions will have a negative impact on both missions and evangelism. If evangelicalism is to continue to distinguish itself from other movements within the Christian faith, it must not diminish its emphasis on either missions or evangelism. However, it is unclear why an optimistic understanding of other faith-traditions entails a diminished vision of either. On a very basic level, Christians should continue working in both areas, no matter how optimistic they understand the salvation of other religions, simply because of the Great Commission. It is something the Christian church is commanded to do.[28]

However, given the evangelical's understanding of salvation, there is even greater motivation to attend to missions and evangelism. If salvation were simply an eschatological event, then there may be no good reason, other than the Great Commission, to burden people with the Gospel message. After all, ultimate salvation is up to God and, in a maximized optimistic framework, all God-seekers will be saved. Unless there are present-tense benefits for embracing Christianity, then we should simply allow individuals to continue seeking God in their current faith. However, evangelicals believe there are current benefits for embracing Christianity. First, it is Jesus Christ who provided the means by which salvation is extended to all. Evangelicals believe that Christianity reflects God's preferred means of drawing the created back into fellowship with the Creator. Next, it is unclear whether those God-seekers who will ultimately experience salvation but are outside of Christianity have the abiding indwelling of the Holy Spirit or whether the Spirit comes and goes upon such an individual, much like it did in pre-Pentecost times. If salvation has a present-tense, working-out concept (i.e., sanctification, then having the Spirit as a constant resource is vital. Finally, evangelicals should not abandon their dedication to missions and evangelism even in light of a most maximized optimistic understanding of eschatological salvation because of their understanding of the benefits of living the Christian life today. Because they are in right relationship with God, there is unsurpassing joy, there is confidence in knowing the hope that is within them; in short, there is the fruit of the Spirit. It must be noted that while this is a call for evangelicals to embrace an optimistic position, a maximized optimistic position (i.e., all will eventually be saved) is not viable within an evangelical perspective. Some will be condemned to eternal separation. For these reasons, and others, evangelicals cannot abandon their emphasis on missions and evangelism.

In the book of Hebrews, we find God self-revealing through many and various ways, "but in these last days he has spoken to us by a Son, whom he

---

28. In 2005 the journal *Missiology: An International Review* highlighted the importance of this discussion in terms of fulfilling the Christian mission by devoting an entire issue to the relationship between missiology and the theology of religions (April 2005).

appointed the heir of all things, through whom also he created the world. He [Jesus] reflects the glory of God and bears the very stamp of his [God's] nature, upholding the universe by this word of power" (1:2–3). In chapter 4 of the same book, Jesus is presented as the way of approaching God. We who are fortunate to hear the gospel message and to live in an environment that fosters acceptance of that message rejoice, for we can heed the exhortation:

> Let us draw near with a true heart in full assurance of faith, with our hearts sprinkled clean from an evil conscience and our bodies washed with pure water. Let us hold fast the confession of our hope without wavering, for he who promised is faithful; and let us consider how to stir up one another to love and good works, not neglecting to meet together, as s the habit of some, but encouraging one another, and all the more as you see the Day drawing near. (Heb 10:23–25)

Nevertheless, if evangelicals are to develop their own theology of religions, they must acknowledge that the vast majority of persons have not lived in an environment that fosters acceptance of the gospel message. This may include individuals born and raised in North America. Furthermore, the Scriptures do teach the end of some will be the lake of fire.[29] Yet, because of the mercy and justice of God, we remain hopeful for those less fortunate. While no religion saves, not even Christianity, we remain optimistic that God's glory will be magnified by bringing to Himself those whom we least expect. However, how can we be so hopeful? How can North American evangelicals exhibit the confidence in God's faithfulness and mercy that Paul exhibits in Rom 9 through 11? Faith is never foundationless; upon what can we hope their faith is built such that God would honor this faith with salvation? In the next two essays, we will consider whether the concept of general revelation might provide some basis for our optimistic hope. Paul himself alludes to this concept in the opening chapter of Romans (1:19–23 and 2:15).

---

29. "And they marched up over the broad earth and surrounded the camp of the saints and the beloved city; but fire came down from heaven and consumed them, and the devil who had deceived them was thrown into the lake of fire and sulphur where the beast and the false prophet were, and they will be tormented day and night for ever and ever. Then I saw a great white throne and him who sat upon it; from his presence earth and sky fled away, and no place was found for them. And I saw the dead, great and small, standing before the throne, and books were opened. Also another book was opened, which is the book of life. And the dead were judged by what was written in the books, by what they had done. And the sea gave up the dead in it, Death and Hades gave up the dead in them, and all were judged by what they had done. Then Death and Hades were thrown into the lake of fire. This is the second death, the lake of fire; and if any one's name was not found written in the book of life, he was thrown into the lake of fire" (Rev 20: 9–15).

7

Basic Notion of General Revelation and Evangelical Theology

As we closed the previous essay, we asked how evangelicals could embrace an agnostic optimistic stance regarding other faith traditions. We have finally arrived at the point of asking the question, can the notion of general revelation help? Part of the motivation for this question is Paul's example in Romans. It is clear from Romans 9–11 that Paul was very optimistic about the future of his fellow Jews, and he bases this on the mercy of God, as well as on God's faithfulness. While Paul does not attempt to offer an explanation regarding how God might accomplish this (hence he is agnostic), he does intertwine these two motifs (i.e., mercy and faithfulness) with the notion of general revelation. Mercy, faithfulness, and general revelation provide the relevant theme of justice. To claim that Paul understood the notion of general revelation as a key for engaging other faith traditions is probably anachronistic. However, Paul's unawareness of the term "special revelation" does not mean that we cannot consider the notion as an aid in outlining a possible evangelical theology of religions today.

In this essay we will explore the notion of general revelation from an evangelical perspective. First, we will ask the question, what is revelation? While this question is worthy of its own study, given the purpose of the question in this essay, our response will be relatively brief and to the point. We will address how evangelicals understand revelation. Then we will ask, what is the content of revelation, specifically general revelation? Bruce Demarest provides the clearest and most important study of general revelation from an evangelical perspective.[1] As a result, Demarest will largely answer this question. However, we will suggest that while from an evangelical perspective his study is accurate, the evidence does not lead to some of the conclusions he draws about other faith traditions. As a result, in the third section of this essay we will ask, what is the purpose of revelation? This will

1. Demarest, *General Revelation*.

lead to the final section of this essay in which we will reassess the potential application of general revelation for evangelicals trying to outline a theology of religions.

What Is Revelation?

What is revelation? This question is vital because it is no longer obvious, if it ever was, to what the term "revelation" refers. John Baillie's now classic Bampton Lectures, given at Columbia University in 1954, capture some of the changes in how the notion of revelation was understood from the seventeenth century through the early twentieth century.[2] Avery Dulles's *Models of Revelation* present five different contemporary models of revelation and proposes a sixth intended to work as a synthesis.[3] However, given the intent of this essay, the question is actually, what is revelation from an evangelical perspective? Dulles identifies the model for the conservative evangelical position regarding revelation as "doctrine."

> In principle God makes himself known through nature, so that one may speak in a certain sense of natural (or "general") revelation, available always and everywhere. But because of the transcendence of God and the devastating effects of original sin, human beings do not in fact succeed in attaining a sure and saving knowledge of God by natural revelation or natural theology. The self-manifestation of God through nature has as its principal result that those who fail to know and worship God are without excuse (cf. Rom 1:20). For effective knowledge of the salvific truth, supernatural (or "special") revelation is necessary. This supernatural revelation was imparted in early biblical times by theophanic phenomena and prophetic visions, but as the revelation progressed it took on to an increasing degree the form of doctrine.[4]

H. Wayne House, past president of the Evangelical Theological Society, prefers the broader notion of revelation as "speech," but does not dispute Dulles's model for evangelicals.[5] Hence, revelation for evangelicals is essen-

---

2. Baillie, *Idea of Revelation in Recent Thought*.

3. Dulles, *Models of Revelation*.

4. Ibid., 37. Dulles's other models are: history, inner experience, dialectical presence, new awareness, and symbolic mediation, which is Dulles's own proposal.

5. House, *Charts on Systematic Theology*, 52. Other works on revelation that reflect an evangelical view but not cited below include Mavrodes, *Revelation in Religious Belief*; Swinburne, *Revelation*; and Menssen and Sullivan, *Agnostic Inquirer*.

tially God's communication to humanity. As House acknowledges, Protestant theology has primarily focused on God's communication through the Living Word, Jesus Christ, and the Written Word, the Christian Scriptures. However, Protestant theology has noted that the Scriptures refer to God's communication to humanity by means to which all persons have access to knowledge of God This is the notion of general revelation. Hence, for evangelicals revelation is God speaking, in the broadest sense of the term, to the created order. The purpose of this communiqué will be discussed below.

What Is the Content of General Revelation?

The next vital question concerns the content of revelation. Specifically, what do evangelicals understand the content of general revelation to be? It is at this point that we turn our attention to the distinguished work of Bruce Demarest. Professor Demarest begins with the question "How is God known?" For evangelicals, because of the transcendent nature of God and the sinful nature of persons, "only God can make known God."[6] Revelation is the critical doctrine for evangelicals.

> The fundamental question in theology needs to be formulated more precisely. What specifically are the sources for man's knowledge of God? Alternatively, what is the nature of revelation data? Historically, Christian theology has differentiated between general and special revelation, both as to content and focus. General revelation, mediated through nature, conscience, and the providential ordering of history, traditionally has been understood as a universal witness to God's existence and character. Through the modalities of general revelation, man at large knows both that there is a God and in broad outline what He is like.[7]

General revelation has found itself abused historically by two extremes. On the one hand, some have failed to distinguish between general revelation and special revelation.[8] As a result, there is reason to question the appropriateness of mission work to those of other faiths.[9] On the other hand, "contemporary evangelical confessionalists such as Berkhouwer and presuppositionalists in the tradition of Van Til, while granting the reality of a universal general revelation, end up with Barth in asserting that man can

---

6. Demarest, *General Revelation*, 13.
7. Ibid., 14.
8. Ibid., 16.
9. Ibid., 18.

know nothing about God save by supernatural special revelation."[10] However, the key for evangelicals must always be what the Scriptures themselves say about general revelation.

Demarest's approach to what the Scriptures say about general revelation is consistent with how most evangelicals approach the issue. Demarest first acknowledges that revelation, whether general or special, is technically a "reminiscent knowledge of God."[11] Adam and Eve had a perfect relationship with God.[12] As a result, subsequent revelation was reminiscent knowledge of God.[13] More significantly, however, is his categorization of general revelation into two camps. The first camp he calls "Intuitional Knowledge of God," and the second, "Acquired General Knowledge of God."

While Demarest's categorization of intuitional knowledge assumes that Locke's classical empiricism is false, his discussion of classical empiricism clouds the point he and other evangelicals wish to make.[14] The point being stressed is that persons are created in the image of God. There is something about personhood that reflects God. As a result, persons have an intuitive knowledge of God according to Scriptures. This leads Demarest to his thesis.

> The human mind intuitively grasps the existence of a Power, a Perfection, and a Personality who is primal, uncaused, and infinite. Man at large has no need to be introduced to God, for he intuitively acknowledges the existence of a supreme spiritual Being on whom he is dependent.[15]

Furthermore, not only do persons have a level of knowledge of God because they are created in God's image, but persons are aware of God's moral law.[16] Thus, all have knowledge that God is a moral Being.[17] Hence, according to Demarest, the Scriptures teach that persons have two innate sources of knowing about God: being in the image of God and having a conscience.

The second source of general revelation open to persons is acquired knowledge of God. This is knowledge obtained by rational inference. "Scripture supports our thesis that further truth content about God is

10. Ibid., 21.
11. Ibid., 227.
12. Ibid., 228.
13. Ibid.
14. Locke proposed that the mind initially is a *tabula rasa* upon which experience provides the data that knowledge is composed.
15. Demarest, *General Revelation*, 229.
16. Ibid., 231.
17. Ibid., 233.

acquired by rational reflection on God's general revelation in nature and history... It comes as no surprise to us that the God who created and now sustains the universe should be discerned in His work."[18] It is significant that Demarest claims that rational persons can draw conclusions "about God to varying degrees of probability on the basis of the evidence from [their] surrounding environment."[19]

Based on these two sources of general revelation, Demarest identifies twenty basic points that persons can know of God via general revelation according to Scripture.

God exists (Ps 19:1; Rom 1:19).

God is uncreated (Acts 17:24).

God is Creator (Acts 14:15).

God is Sustainer (Acts 14:16; 17:25).

God is universal Lord (Acts 17:24).

God is self-sufficient (Acts 17:25).

God is transcendent (Acts 17:24).

God is immanent (Acts 17:26–27).

God is eternal (Ps 93:2).

God is great (Ps 8:3–4).

God has a sovereign will (Acts 17:26).

God has standards of right and wrong (Rom 2:15).

God is good (Acts 14:17).

God is majestic (Ps 29:4).

God is powerful (Ps 29:4; Rom 1:20).

God is righteous (Rom 1:32).

God is wise (Ps 104:24).

God should be worshiped (Acts 14:15; 17:23).

God will judge evil (Rom 2:15–16).

Humanity should perform the good (Rom 2:15).

"In sum: God's glory (Ps. 19:1), divine nature (Rom. 1:20), and moral demands (Rom. 2:14–15) are to some extent known through general revelation!"[20]

Demarest acknowledges that some evangelical theologians do not believe knowledge is mediated by general revelation. Reformed theologians such as Barth, Berkouwer, and Van Til reject general revelation as a source of knowledge. Donald Bloesch nicely captures this position.

> Reformed theology has traditionally affirmed the possibility of a natural knowledge of God and morality on the basis of general revelation and common grace. Yet because of sin this general revelation does not lead man to God or give him a true

18. Ibid., 234.
19. Ibid., 233.
20. Ibid., 242–43.

picture of God; instead it renders man without excuse. The general revelation is the wrath of God that is revealed from heaven against "all ungodliness and wickedness of men who by their wickedness suppress the truth" (Rom 1:18). This general awareness of God does not prepare man for a special revelation but condemns him to perdition.[21]

However, for Demarest, and others such as Carl Henry, persons can know something of God based on general revelation.[22]

While knowledge about God via general revelation is possible for Demarest and Henry, evangelicals typically limit the specific implications of that knowledge. In the second essay of this volume, the Lausanne Covenant was cited. Regarding the uniqueness and universality of Christ, the covenant claimed, "We recognize that all men have some knowledge of God through his general revelation in nature. But we deny that this can save, for men suppress the truth by their unrighteousness."[23] As Demarest puts it,

> Through general revelation, man learns broadly that God both cares and judges, but he knows nothing of God's purpose for the sinner in special grace ... Through general revelation, man learns that God is august majesty and limitless power, but he is ignorant of the fact that God in grace became Man in the person of His Son. Fallen man needs special revelation to know the mystery of God's will with respect to human salvation.[24]

While Demarest represents an evangelical stance regarding general revelation that is more hopeful than the rejectionist position of Barth or the minimalist position of Berkouwer, he does not go as far as the Thomistic understanding of natural theology. For evangelicals, the Thomistic stance depreciates "the effects of the Fall on the human cognitive powers."[25] However, the question must be asked, does the evangelical stance regarding the uniqueness and work of Jesus Christ, God's desire to establish community with the created order, and the fall, which resulted in "estrangement from the divine intention of 'original wisdom' as well as 'original righteousness'" entail that salvation is not possible based on knowledge about God from

---

21. Bloesch, *Essentials of Evangelical Theology*, 1:103.

22. "Such questions bring us face-to-face with the important issues of general revelation, the divine image in man, the noetic effects of sin, and natural theology ... Man can indeed know the God of creation and created reality—not exhaustively, to be sure, but nonetheless truly" (Henry, *God, Revelation, and Authority*, 160).

23. Stott, *Making Christ Known*, 16.

24. Ibid., 249.

25. Ibid., 35.

general revelation alone?[26] There is no question that special revelation provides a more complete explanation of the salvific hope, but is it *possible* that salvation will be given to some with limited revelation? These questions lead to the next major section.

What Is the Purpose of General Revelation?

What is the purpose of revelation? Why has God chosen to be self-revealing? While much of what evangelicals have said regarding the purpose of revelation has focused on special revelation, we can see a common thread of agreement. Consider the following statements that reveal an evangelical understanding of the purpose of revelation:

- "Man can know God only as, in some way, God reveals, or makes Himself known, to man."[27]

- "*Revelation is the autobiography of God* [metaphorically speaking], i.e., it is the story which God narrates about himself. It is the knowledge *about* God which is *from* God."[28]

- "Revelation is adapted to the world of the persons to which it comes. It is concrete, historical and particular. Revelation is aptly fitted to our condition so that it might function as revelation to us. The ontological chasm was bridged by the divine willingness to stoop to the use of anthropic media, most clearly seen in the greatest of all revelation modalities, the incarnation."[29]

- "Revelation is the disclosure of the μυστηριον του θεου. What neither nature nor history, neither mind nor heart, neither science nor art can teach us, it makes known to us, (—the fixed, unalterable *will* of God to rescue the world and save sinners, a will at variance with well-nigh the whole appearance of things. This will is the secret of revelation. In creation God manifests the power of his mind; in revelation, which has redemption for its centre, he discloses to us the greatness of his heart."[30]

- "Revelation is a gracious divine activity, a free and voluntary gift, which has as its end the salvation of sinners (1 Ti 1:15)."[31]

---

26. Fackre, *Doctrine of Revelation*, 45.
27. Orr, *Revelation and Inspiration*, 2.
28. Ramm, *Special Revelation and the Word of God*, 17 (italics original).
29. Pinnock, *Biblical Revelation*, 30.
30. Bavinck, *Philosophy of Revelation*, 25–26 (italics original).
31. Pinnock, *Biblical Revelation*, 19.

- "Redemptive revelation is logically and chronologically prior to Scripture, whose task it is to make us wise unto salvation which is in Christ Jesus."[32]
- "The purpose of revelation is to enable us to know God personally (Phil 3:10)."[33]
- "Revelation is not merely the communication of truths about God but, more important, God's self-communication in act and word. Theology would know nothing of God if God had not taken the initiative to 'unveil' himself and raise the curtain on the theo-drama. Both the content and the process of divine revelation are thus essentially dramatic. God reveals himself in the history of Israel and the history of Jesus Christ through a series of communicative initiatives—some verbal, some eventful—all of which are ultimately redemptive. The 'event' of Jesus Christ stands as the culmination of a series of such revelatory and redemptive events, recorded in the Old and New Testaments, which *together* recount a single drama of redemption that is both covenantal in its focus and cosmic in its scope."[34]
- "Revelation, therefore, is narrative-specific, the story of the triune God's self-disclosure, the gift of the knowledge of God given in the history of God with human beings to human beings. The doctrine of revelation explores why we turn where we do to know who God is and what God does among us from creation to consummation. As such, the narrative of revelation is about, and coordinates with, the narrative of reconciliation."[35]

Revelation is, first of all, God self-revealing in order that the created might know God. However, God self-reveals in order that the created might be in a relationship with the Creator. After the fall, God's purpose for revelation did not change, though it did take on a new task. Reconciliation was necessary to bridge the alienation of human rebellion. The means of this reconciliation was provided in the life, death, and resurrection of Jesus Christ. However, revelation, whether general or special, has the purpose of drawing the created into community with the Creator. The Creator has engaged in communication with creation. The most significant means of communication is in the person of Jesus. However, God also has communicated through the written Word and other forms of special revelation. While these means

32. Ibid., 29.
33. Ibid., 30.
34. Vanhoozer, *Drama of Doctrine*, 38–39.
35. Fackre, *Doctrine of Revelation*, 15.

of communication or self-revealing provide fuller understanding of God's intent, they do not negate that God is revealed for some through nature or through conscience. The fall has damaged the human precondition toward spirituality and knowing God in an intimate way, but the fall has not limited God's ability to communicate. It has not limited the majesty of God to break through and speak even if the only means is that damaged broken conscience.[36] For some, the awe of a starry sky may become the symphony that God uses to communicate and draw a person into some type of community. God's providence, God's sovereignty, God's power has not been broken by human sin. If God chooses to communicate and self-reveal through the only means available for some—natural revelation—then God, the potter, has that ability. In summary, if revelation is ultimately about engaging creation in community with the Creator and if general revelation is a form of revelation, then it seems possible that God may use general revelation to draw some into fellowship. "What God wills in the face of human resistance is what God does. Thus the light that shines in creation, contrary to Berkouwer, is perceived through a human epistemological sight dimmed but not destroyed."[37] While Demarest's account of general revelation is more hopeful than other accounts, the evidence does not entail some of the conclusions he draws regarding other faith traditions.

Potential Application

In this section we will reassess the potential application of general revelation for evangelicals trying to outline a theology of religions. This reassessment will consider three relevant issues about general revelation. First, we will consider the covenant with Noah and the notion of common grace. Next, we

---

36. On one hand, this claim may not be problematic; the fall did not thwart God's ability to be self-revealing. However, on the other hand, it does take sides on a controversy between Emil Brunner and Karl Barth. "This point of contact is what theological anthropology on the basis of Gen 1:27 calls the 'image of God' in man. In this connexion we cannot possibly agree with E. Brunner . . . when he takes this to refer to the humanity and personality which even sinful man retains from creation, for the humanity and personality of sinful man cannot possibly signify conformity to God, a point of contact for the Word of God. In this sense, as a possibility which is proper to man *qua* creation, the image of God is not just, as it is said, destroyed apart from a few relics; it is totally annihilated" (Barth, *Church Dogmatics*, vol. I.1, *The Word of God*, 238). For Brunner the conscience "does not speak of God, but it is the flaming sword which drives us away from the presence of God . . . [F]aith awakens when man sees himself, not in light of conscience, but in the new light thrown upon his nature by the gracious Word of God, in Christ" (Brunner, *Divine Imperative*, 157–58).

37. Fackre, *Doctrine of Revelation*, 56.

will consider the notion of justice as it relates to general revelation. Finally, we will briefly consider the work being done by some evangelical theologians regarding the Spirit of God in relation to the theology of religions.

The notion of common grace is rooted in several biblical sources. Gabriel Fackre locates it in the covenant with Noah as found in Genesis 8.

> 6:5The LORD saw that the wickedness of man was great in the earth, and that every imagination of the thoughts of his heart was only evil continually. 6And the LORD was sorry that he had made man on the earth, and it grieved him to his heart. 7So the LORD said, "I will blot out man whom I have created from the face of the ground, man and beast and creeping things and birds of the air, for I am sorry that I have made them." 8But Noah found favor in the eyes of the LORD.

> 18But I will establish my covenant with you; and you shall come into the ark, you, your sons, your wife, and your sons' wives with you.

> 8:1But God remembered Noah and all the beasts and all the cattle that were with him in the ark. And God made a wind blow over the earth, and the waters subsided; . . . 20Then Noah built an altar to the LORD, and took of every clean animal and of every clean bird, and offered burnt offerings on the altar. 21And when the LORD smelled the pleasing odor, the LORD said in his heart, "I will never again curse the ground because of man, for the imagination of man's heart is evil from his youth; neither will I ever again destroy every living creature as I have done. 22While the earth remains, seedtime and harvest, cold and heat, summer and winter, day and night, shall not cease."

> 9:8Then God said to Noah and to his sons with him, 9"Behold, I establish my covenant with you and your descendants after you, 10and with every living creature that is with you, the birds, the cattle, and every beast of the earth with you, as many as came out of the ark. 11I establish my covenant with you, that never again shall all flesh be cut off by the waters of a flood, and never again shall there be a flood to destroy the earth." 12And God said, "This is the sign of the covenant which I make between me and you and every living creature that is with you, for all future generations: 13I set my bow in the cloud, and it shall be a sign of the covenant between me and the earth. 14When I bring clouds

> over the earth and the bow is seen in the clouds, ¹⁵I will remember my covenant which is between me and you and every living creature of all flesh; and the waters shall never again become a flood to destroy all flesh. ¹⁶When the bow is in the clouds, I will look upon it and remember the everlasting covenant between God and every living creature of all flesh that is upon the earth." ¹⁷God said to Noah, "This is the sign of the covenant which I have established between me and all flesh that is upon the earth."

However, while identifying the covenant that God made with Noah is not problematic, it is not initially clear how this covenant points to common grace. It first appears that God is making a very special covenant with Noah and his family. Furthermore, the covenant specifically promises only that God will not again curse the ground because of human sin or destroy the earth by flood. Nevertheless, Fackre sees grace.

> A narrative response to these issues lies in the opening essays of the biblical story—creation, fall and the covenant with Noah—and the corollary phase of revelation here discussed as the common grace of *preservation*. The economy of trinitarian revelation begins in the essay on creation, but includes the essay on the fall in which the original vision experiences its ocular damage and the promise to Noah of enough of the original light for the world's pilgrimage to go forward.[38]

First, Fackre sees the notion of preservation, a preservation that extends not only to all persons since Noah but beyond persons to the ground or earth. While the notion of preservation is much richer, at the heart of the notion of preservation is God's faithfulness and capacity to sustain that which God promises. For the most part, within evangelical thought there is little question regarding the faithfulness or the capability of God.[39] God will

---

38. Fackre, *Doctrine of Revelation*, 37–38 (italics original).

39. Within evangelical theology there is much debate regarding "Open Theism." David Basinger, who is one of the leading advocates, recently outlined four crucial points of Open Theism. First regarding God's power, open theism embraces a 'freewill theism: "God could be all controlling. But to the extent that God grants us meaningful freedom, God has voluntarily given up control over what will occur." Second regarding God's moral nature, open theism advocates, "because of his love for us, God has chosen never to do less than he can do to make our lives as good as possible." Third regarding God's affective nature, open theism holds that "while God's essential nature never changes, God is affected 'emotionally' by what we do—e.g., God really does rejoice and become sad in response to our actions." The fourth and most controversial element within evangelicalism is related to God's knowledge. Open theism takes the position that "God knows all that has occurred and is occurring, and can predict (but does not know) what people will freely do." (These points were presented in a paper by David Basinger at

accomplish what God wills. God's ultimate will or goal for creation is not made improbable because of human sin. God's power has not been diminished because humans now have a sin nature.

Furthermore, Fackre sees the covenant with Noah as reflecting hope based on some "original light." It is this original light, mentioned by Fackre, that is most crucial for an adequate development of common grace, which is to inform the development of a theology of religions from an evangelical perspective. Fackre identifies one source of this light, but we will suggest there are two sources for this original light. First, as Fackre points out, the narrative found in the opening pages of Genesis claims that persons are made in the "image of God," which is "God's own social Being."[40] For Fackre, this aspect of the original light provides human beings a unique freedom. "As representative and custodian of creation, the human race is called to mirror God's own watch-care of the world and capacitated to serve the divine purpose."[41] This leads Fackre to question the extent that this image of God has been damaged because of the fall.

> General revelation in Demarest's perspective means disclosure at both ontic and noetic poles. What God wills in the face of human resistance is what God does. Thus the light that shines in creation, contrary to Berkouwer, is perceived through a human epistemological sight dimmed but not destroyed. The merit of the maximalist interpretation is a recognition that noetic grace, as all grace, is *power* as well as *favour*, as befits its agent, the Holy Spirit. The power of God at this stage of the Story is the sustenance of creation in preparation for deeds and disclosures to come.
>
> ... In the covenant with Noah to be explained, "general revelation" and "common grace" are bashful not bold, far short of

---

the American Philosophical Association Meeting, Pacific Division. (The "Open" View of God: Why All the Fuss? April 2007). Some evangelicals have maintained that this position limits God's ability to fulfill promises. However, this seems to be an unfair charge against open theists. Alan Rhoda, in the same conference as Basinger, identified four core commitments of open theism. The first he identified as "Theism: God exists necessarily and possesses a maximal set of compossible great-making properties, including maximal power, knowledge, and goodness. He created the world *ex nihilo* and can unilaterally intervene in it as he pleases." Rhoda maintains that this last sentence distinguishes open theism from process theism, to which the charges seem directed. (Alan Rhoda, "Generic Open Theism and Some Varieties Thereof," April 2007). Open theism does not question God's faithfulness, but it does suggest that God's capacity to do certain things may be limited. Hence, if open theism is true, then it is possible that human sin has restricted God's ability to do what God wills.

40. Fackre, *Doctrine of Revelation*, 38.
41. Ibid., 39.

> the warrants needed for a "natural theology" that can establish by reason the existence and attributes of God, or a "natural law" that can discern in detail norms of human behaviour.
>
> In a narrative interpretation both reconciliation and revelation, the state of the image of God cannot be abstracted from the Story. What we are and what we know have to do with the forbearance of God in the unfolding of the divine purposes . . . Thus the capacities of the *imago Dei* to know and to do will be set in the midst of the sustaining promise.[42]

On the one hand, it appears that Fackre may understand common grace or general revelation as being inadequate to provide the necessary help for evangelicals dealing with the theology of religions because it is bashful and fails to provide the grounds for natural theology. This would be similar to the position taken by Bloesch: "Common grace is not the grace that saves but rather that which restrains men from sin and thereby enables them to survive in the world."[43] On the other hand, Fackre sees common grace and general revelation resting within God's forbearance in unfolding the divine purposes. If this source for the original light has not been totally destroyed, then elements of the image of God may manifest themselves in those religious traditions that claim "enlightenment" as the source of their sacred writings. If this is the case, then it may provide valuable hope for evangelicals as they construct a theology of religions. Unfortunately, we do not have clear evidence of the extent of damage to the image of God that occurred because of the fall. Evangelical theology maintains that alienation from the Creator occurred because of the fall. Furthermore, persons lack the ability to reinstate community with God on their own; they are dependent upon God for this. However, this does not entail that the image of God is so damaged that it is in effect dead.[44] If this is the only source of the original light, then we are left in a position of uncertainty.

We indicated above that the original light had two sources. The first was the "image of God" concept, which is problematic in that it is unclear how it survives the fallen state. While the first may offer assistance, it is

---

42. Ibid., 54–57 (italics original).

43. Bloesch, *Essentials of Evangelical Theology*, 1:61.

44. "If there is original sin, there is also original righteousness, if only in the form of longing for release and for fullness of existence. Whether one wishes to call this 'natural,' or whether one wishes to speak of a 'grace' that is universal and not tied to any special occasion of revelation, seems to me to be a matter of indifference. If there were no residuum of original righteousness even in fallen man, no continuing tendency to transcend toward the fulfilling of the image of God and no common grace in creation, then it would be hard to see how salvation could be possible" (Macquarrie, *Principles of Christian Theology*, 267).

the second source that offers evangelicals the most help as they reassess the value of common grace for developing a theology of religions. This second source may be called "latent revelation." Both prior to and in the covenant with Noah, God had dealings with persons. Self-revelation took place with the human race. As a result, humans had some knowledge of God. It is highly probable that this knowledge was preserved in oral traditions that were passed down from one generation to the next. We have clear evidence of oral traditions being preserved and passed on within tribal or clan societies. As the biblical narrative unfolds after the covenant with Noah, humans were dispersed around the world. With this dispersal, the oral traditions spread, but in new languages. These oral traditions were preserved, but in new perspectives of the world. Hence, the oral traditions evolved to reflect the perspectives of the new languages. Just as it is highly probable that oral traditions were developed and passed on, it is highly probable that the oral traditions that originally reflected God's self-revelation changed due to language development and distancing in time from the original revelation. It is plausible that eventually these traditions were committed to written forms. While the written forms would not be accurate presentations of the original revelation, it is possible that they contain elements of that original revelation. Evidence for this understanding of latent revelation may be found in both the anthropological and historical studies of religion. In both cases there is ample evidence of shared traditions among a wide spectrum of religious traditions. If latent revelation as described above is true, then evangelicals could expect other faith traditions to contain some truths regarding God, persons, and the cosmos so that a sincere seeker may find elements of that original encounter with God. This oral tradition is a form of common grace and may play an important role in reassessing the potential application of general revelation to the theology of religions.

A second aspect of general revelation that enters the discourse is the notion of justice.[45] Evangelicals agree that the Scriptures are clear that general revelation at least provides enough information about God and persons to imply that justice is served in the condemnation of individuals who live in rebellion against whatever knowledge of God they do have. "Ever since the creation of the world his invisible nature, namely, his eternal power and deity, has been clearly perceived in the things that have been made. So they are without excuse" (Rom 1:20). However, if general revelation brings to the table the important notion of justice, then we must ask, is justice possible

---

45. For an extended discussion of justice, see Boyd, "Divine Action/Human Replication—Applied Justice," 61–76 (reprinted in vol. 1, *Philosophically Thinking about World Religions.*)

if it only provides condemnation? Is there a correlation between *ought* and *can*? Does justice require the capacity to do something if one ought to do it?

First, some basic elements regarding justice should be set forth. Since ethicists speak of different types of justice, it may be beneficial to point out the type of justice being identified by those who claim that general revelation provides a basis for discerning justice. To claim that no one is without excuse for being disobedient to God because of general revelation suggests a form of retributive justice. Regardless of the consequences, individuals should receive what they deserve. For justice to be fulfilled, several conditions seem necessary. First, the reward or punishment must be comparatively the same as the reward or punishment other persons receive in the same situation for the same action. Second, the reward or punishment must be directed toward individual persons and not groups of persons. Third, the reward or punishment must be based on past actions of the individual and not based on some possible future event. Finally, the reward or punishment must be based on the agent's ability to do otherwise.

If justice is served in finding an individual guilty before God because one has access to general revelation (a position taken by many), then general revelation must be adequate for some type of positive response by the individuals such that they would not incur punishment but rather reward. If this is correct, then the statement made by the Lausanne Covenant must be incorrect. As we saw above, the covenant claimed, "We recognize that all men have some knowledge of God through his general revelation in nature. But we deny that this can save, for men suppress the truth by their unrighteousness." While it may be true that humans do suppress the truth by their unrighteousness, it does not necessarily follow that they must always suppress the truth. As a result, given our understanding of justice and our assumption that God is just, it is possible that some persons will respond to general revelation in a fashion that results in reward rather than punishment. It is important to remind ourselves of a point made earlier. It is God who declares salvation; it is God who makes the decision of what constitutes satisfaction and reconciliation.

Finally, as we finish our reassessment of general revelation, a third element must be brought into the discussion. Among North American evangelicals one group of theologians is making a significant contribution to the development of a theology of religions, but they not approaching the field as most have done. While this group has been mentioned in passing in previous essays, we have intentionally withheld their contribution for this very point. Although their focus has not been upon general revelation, their emphasis crosses all cultural lines, knows no religious boundaries, and as a result communicates with an audience as broad and diverse as that to which general revelation reaches. This group consists of Pentecostal theologians working to develop a theology of religions that is informed by pneumatology. Pentecostal theologians such as Amos Yong and Veli-Matti Kärkkäinen are exploring the implications of a pneumatological theology of religions.[46] Since the Spirit knows no boundaries and is actively engaged in the empirical world, this group of evangelicals believes the Spirit of God is the key for developing a viable theology of religions, which avoids the pitfalls of other approaches. Amos Yong suggests that those theologians who place an emphasis on God as Creator may have "undue optimism with regard to common grace."[47] Furthermore, those who have placed an emphasis on Jesus Christ may have "an undue pessimism with regard to theological anthropology."[48] In order to avoid the twin horns, Yong says, "My central claim, . . . , is a methodological one: that a pneumatological theology of religions not only commits but also enables us to empirically engage the world's religions in a truly substantive manner with theological questions and concerns."[49] As a result, he initially defines a pneumatological theology of religions by outlining three points.

> First, a pneumatological theology of religions is a robustly trinitarian theology . . . Second, given the contemporary situation in theological method in which emphasis is placed on local or marginal epistemologies and hermeneutics, and given the requirement for *theologia religionum* today needs to genuinely engage the world of the religions, perhaps pneumatology can contribute to this task where previous approaches have fallen short . . . This leads to a third point, that a pneumatological theology of religions allows us to ask the soteriological question within a different, and perhaps broader, framework.[50]

---

46. Clark Pinnock's own religious development has brought him into a charasmatic understanding of Christianity. Clearly, his work in the field of the theology of religions has been significant and has been documented in previous essays. Veli-Matti Kärkkäinen, currently at Fuller Seminary, has been prolific as a writer of substantial theological works. From the point of view of this writer, Kärkkäinen's greatest contribution has been historical in nature. His major contribution has been a careful examination of the work of other theologians. His work is extremely valuable; however, it appears that the work of Amos Yong represents the most creative work that aims to develop a fuller theology of religions. As a result, in the following discussion of this group of theologians, Yong is the individual looked at.

47. Yong, *Beyond the Impasse*, 21.

48. Ibid.

49. Ibid., 35.

50. Ibid., 20–21.

In order to develop this pneumatological theology of religions, Yong proposes three axioms:

1. God is universally present and active in the Spirit.
2. God's Spirit is the life-breath of the imago Dei in every human being and the presupposition of all human relationships and communities.
3. The religions of the world, like everything else that exists, are providentially sustained by the Spirit of God for divine purposes.[51]

The theological method that results from these axioms, according to Yong, is intended to move the discussion beyond soteriological questions, on which evangelicals have focused, to a more complete theology of religions that emerges "out of a genuine dialogue with the [world] religions."[52] It enables the evangelical to move beyond the impasses that have emerged in evangelical thought. Yong identifies these impasses as (1) the dualism between the uniqueness of Jesus Christ and the notion of the cosmic Christ, (2) the tension between natural revelation and special revelation, and (3) the tension between how some evangelicals have viewed non-Christian religions as false faith traditions and the sovereignty and universality of God as they relate to religious traditions.

How does this group of Pentecostal theologians, Yong specifically, contribute to our reassessment of general revelation? First and foremost, they remind evangelicals that their theology is extremely rich, and because of this richness, it is not monocolored. Evangelical theology should have a robust Trinitarian nature. Hermeneutical issues have played and continue to play an important role in the dialogue among evangelicals. As we have seen in the opening essays of this volume, evangelicals have been interested in the soteriological issue as it relates to the theology of religions, but their world has not been limited to this arena. The contribution made by this group of Pentecostal theologians requires evangelicals to recenter themselves, not only in their theology proper, but also in the area of general revelation. Furthermore, to deny any of Yong's axioms will result in denying beliefs typically held to be cornerstones of evangelical thought. However, while Yong sees his position as moving beyond the impasse created by the twin horns, it is unclear that his project is any more promising. By placing an emphasis on the Spirit, eventually he will still need to elaborate on the relationship between the Spirit and Jesus Christ, which brings him to the very problem he was trying to overcome—the tension between, on the one hand,

51. Ibid., 44–46.
52. Ibid., 19.

God as Creator and Sustainer and, on the other hand, salvation found in a universal Savior. Yong's real contribution is his reminder that evangelical theology is Trinitarian and that the Godhead functions in unison. In short, Yong's project must be applauded from an evangelical perspective; however, it is unclear that it requires an emphasis to be placed on the pneumatological element in order for the project to be successful.

Given a robust Trinitarian theology, with or without the pneumatological emphasis, evangelical theology should develop an extremely rich theology of religions based on the notion of general revelation. Since the Spirit of God is active in the world, working to restore community at all levels, it is very reasonable to expect the Spirit to use all forms of revelation—both special and general. As a result, the notion of general revelation should be potentially a major asset for evangelicals as they explore their own theology of religions.

8

General Revelation and an Evangelical Theology

In the previous essay, we concluded that the notion of general revelation could potentially be a major asset for evangelicals as they develop their theology of religions since they affirm that God is self-revealing, and while God is revealed in both the written and living Words, God is also revealed in ways accessible to all persons through general revelation. Before we apply the doctrine of general revelation to the development of an evangelical theology of religions in the next essay, we will explore three tangent points in this one. While the explorations of this essay are relevant to the development of a theology of religions that makes use of general revelation, the features are not necessary conditions for such a theology. The first tangent to be explored pertains to Tertullian's famous rhetorical question: "What does Athens have to do with Jerusalem?"[1] The second tangent to be followed relates to the theological position known as progressive dispensationalism, a position taken by a number of significant evangelical theologians. The third tangent to be explored, also related to progressive dispensationalism, will be to look closely at the Noahic covenant in order to suggest that progressive dispensationalism could make greater use of this covenant and so aid in the development of an evangelical theology of religions.

What Does Athens Have to Do with Jerusalem?

As we discussed the nature of justice in the previous essay, it was claimed that from an obligatory action, we could derive a possible action. As a result, we took the position that if justice is served because of general revelation, then it must be at least theoretically possible for a person to respond in

---

1. Tertullian, "On Prescription Against Heretics," 7.

an appropriate fashion to general revelation.[2] However, just because something is theoretically possible does not mean it is viable or practical. While it is theoretically possible for persons to respond appropriately to general revelation, it may be highly unlikely that anyone does. In order to respond appropriately, it seems one must be able to properly interpret the message of general revelation, God's communiqué to all people. Then this reasoned response must be translated into a faith response. Tertullian's separation of faith from reason supports the idea that reason is unlikely to help answer questions of faith. Hence, while general revelation may be theoretically useful in obtaining salvific knowledge of God, general revelation is of no practical use since the move from general revelation to salvific knowledge seems to entail a connection between reason and faith.

With his rhetorical question, Tertullian (c. 160–220) claims that Athens has nothing to do with Jerusalem. Since Athens represents the center for philosophy and Jerusalem the center for religion, Tertullian is claiming that philosophy (i.e., reason) has nothing to do with religion (i.e., faith). There is an abyss, which cannot be bridged, between reason and faith. This very concise claim expresses a view held by many, both within philosophy as well as religion. In philosophy, some forms of postmodernism and fideism embrace it, while in religion many fundamentalists embrace Tertullian's claim, leaving us with a necessary division between reason and faith. (Historically, the tension between faith and reason clearly predates Tertullian. We are only using Tertullian to give a face to the problem.)

First, we will suggest that using Wittgenstein's therapeutic approach to philosophical problems can dissolve the division between reason and faith. After a brief review of Wittgenstein's approach to philosophical problems, we will show how using Wittgenstein's approach can dissolve the faith/reason problem. Thus, there is no faith/reason problem as Tertullian claimed, and reason can be used to interpret properly general revelation. Hence, not only is it theoretically possible to respond in an appropriate fashion to general revelation, but also it is viable. Second, we will consider some of the evidence that allows this solution. As part of this second task, we will present evidence that appears to permit the problem to be dissolved using this Wittgenstein's approach, and we will review the two assumptions that allow the solution to work. We will not attempt to answer whether the assumptions are true, for it would take us beyond the scope of this volume. Finally, we will draw some conclusions regarding this move and suggest

---

2. The notion of appropriate response is intentionally abstract. Not all events of revelation warrant identical responses; some responses to a given revelation are appropriate while other responses are inappropriate. We must reserve the decision of what constitutes appropriateness to the one doing the revealing—God.

some implications of our exploration for the notion of general revelation. In this third task, we will highlight an interesting problem with Wittgenstein's therapeutical analysis and suggest that possibly some philosophical/theological problems are more important as problems than their solutions. From this we will conclude that the role that general revelation has in salvation cannot be affirmed or denied. This supports our previous claim that evangelicals must embrace an agnostic position toward members of other faith traditions.

For Wittgenstein, philosophical problems are primarily problems of semantics; they involve a misappropriation or misunderstanding of the language used to present the problem.

> These [philosophical problems] are, of course, not empirical problems; they are solved, rather, by looking into the workings of our language, and that in such a way as to make us recognize those workings: *in spite of* an urge to misunderstand them. The problems are solved, not by giving new information, but by arranging what we have always known. Philosophy is a battle against the bewitchment of our intelligence by means of language.[3]

That last sentence is extremely interesting. "Philosophy is a battle against the bewitchment of our intelligence by means of language." Wittgenstein's method of philosophical therapy is meant to unravel apparent problems by closely examining the language used to present the problems.

This suggests that we return to the problem that Tertullian gave us and examine the language for dissolving the tension. We might reconstruct the argument as follows:

> Philosophy and religion are distinctively separate disciplines.
>
> Philosophy deals with reason.
>
> Religion deals with faith.
>
> ∴ Reason and faith should be kept separate.

Interestingly, the first premise above does not appear in Tertullian's argument; it is assumed in order to create the tension between faith and reason. For the moment, let us allow Tertullian this assumption. At the core, then, of the faith/reason problem are the meanings of the two terms, "faith" and "reason". What is *faith*? What is *reason*?

---

3. Wittgenstein, *Philosophical Investigations*, ¶ 109. (Italics are Wittgenstein's.)

Faith is defined in many ways. It may be simply the name that we give to that unconscious, psychological, sociological, and historical conditioning.[4] Faith may be that nonrational dimension of experience that some mystics seek.[5] On the other hand, faith may be something irrational, but true.[6] Faith may be something suprarational, but true.[7] Or it may be simply a divine gift.[8] Faith may be a disposition of openness, of trust. Or faith may be defined as a state of responsible commitment. Possibly, faith may best be understood as a conjunction of several of the suggested definitions. For example, we may define faith as a disposition of openness and a state of responsible commitment.[9] Since this last definition seems to correlate well with our ordinary usage of the term, we will assume this concept of faith. We will need to revisit this assumption later.

---

4. This conception of faith is common among those holding a reductionist understanding of religion. The reductionist theories attempt to explain *why* religion developed in the first place. For Sigmund Freud, religion could easily be explained by understanding the human predicament. Primitive humans devised religion as a means to placate and overcome the darker side of their nature. As a result, the content of religion is empty even though it helped humans psychologically to have better self-esteem (Freud, *Future of an Illusion*. First published in German in 1927. Also see, Freud, *Moses and Monotheism*).

5. "Broadly speaking religious life may be divided into three periods. These may be described as the periods of 'Faith,' 'Thought,' and 'Discovery.' In the first period religious life appears as a form of discipline which the individual or a whole people must accept as an unconditional command without any rational understanding of the ultimate meaning and purpose of that command . . . Perfect submission to discipline is followed by a rational understanding of the discipline and the ultimate source of its authority" (Iqbal, *Reconstruction of Religious Thought in Islam*, 181).

6. Søren Kierkegaard defines faith as when "the self in being itself and in willing to be itself rests transparently in God" (*Sickness unto Death*, 82).

7. Clement of Alexandria claimed, "faith is superior to knowledge" (*Stromata*, II:IV, cited in Van Til, *Christian Theory of Knowledge*, 114). Martin Luther had a similar position. While knowledge is rooted in experience, "the proper realm of faith is the future, not the present or the past" (Heick, *History of Christian Thought*, 328). Also, see Rudolf Otto's discussion of Luther's position (*Idea of the Holy*, 103–4 and 204–7).

8. Paul claims that faith is a gift of God in Eph 2:8, but it should be noted that he is not referring to faith in general, but to what might be called saving faith, faith unto salvation. That is the divine gift. Paul also uses the term in the Old Testament sense (Rom 3:3; 1 Cor 1:9, 10:13; and Gal 3:9).

9. Jacob, *Theology of the Old Testament*, 174 points out that in the Old Testament faith has a threefold aspect: knowledge (which is reflected in the notion of responsibility), trust (which is equivalent to openness), and active obedience (commitment). In the New Testament this notion of faith is embraced and then extended. "In the NT faith becomes primarily faith in Jesus Christ" (Richardson, *Introduction to the Theology of the New Testament*, 20).

Reason is no less problematic. Nevertheless, we may assume that reason refers to being rational and having a consistent set of justified beliefs. A set of beliefs is consistent so long as the set does not consist of members that are self-contradictory.[10] What constitutes justified belief is an issue of epistemology, but a good starting point may be Robert Nozick's overview. It is a justified belief if it satisfies one of the following three conditions:

1. Believe h if there is no alternative statement incompatible with h that has a higher credibility value than h does, and the credibility value of h is high enough, given the kind of statement that h is, and the expected utility of believing h is at least as great as the expected utility of having no belief about h.

2. Believe h only if the decision-value of believing h is at least as great as the decision-value of having no belief about h.

3. Believe q if h satisfies 1 and 2, and q is an explicit deductive inference of h.[11]

Whether we accept this notion of justification is not critical. What is important is that this brings us to the question, what is a belief?

If reason is defined in terms of consistent, justified beliefs, and we have a basic understanding of what is meant by consistent and justified, then we must clarify our understanding of the notion of belief. Professor D. M. Armstrong, following F. P. Ramsey's approach, suggests that a belief has two components.[12] First, a belief provides a mapping. Second, this mapping is used to steer by. The term "mapping" is a concept of mathematics. While mapping occurs when a function "assigns exactly one element of a second set to each element of a first set," some mappings are not functions.[13] Mapping for Armstrong simply identifies a relationship between member(s) of

---

10. As Edward Martin pointed out in a personal e-mail (February 18, 2008), "The set itself is not what is self-contradictory. All of the members of the set may themselves not be self-contradictory. However, *together* elements from that set when grouped together, may form a contradictory diad, or triad, or etc. of beliefs. The point is that for some set of beliefs, that set is said to be logically consistent if all the beliefs could be true in the same possible world . . . [This] avoids the problems of causal inconsistency, historical inconsistency, which may not per se be 'logical self-contradictions' but may nonetheless not be able to be the case in some possible world where all the propositions in the set are true in that world."

11. While there are different views of rationality and justified belief, Professor Nozick provides a good starting point, and one that is not critical to the main point of this discussion (Nozick, *Nature of Rationality*, 85–92).

12. Armstrong, *Belief, Knowledge, and Truth*, 3.

13. Dinkines, *Elementary Concepts of Modern Mathematics*, 1:148.

one set to a member(s) of another set. P. F. Strawson points out that Gilbert Ryle described his approach to analytical philosophy as "conceptual mapping". "Maps . . . give us a representation of an area, . . . They can help us to get about. . . . [Maps provide] the notion of an abstract representation of certain relations between certain concepts made for a certain purpose."[14] That is, given Armstrong's notion of belief, the mapping provides a paradigm that gives guidance and direction for decision-making. Notice how this distinguishes a *proper* belief from a *mere* idea. While a mere idea does provide a mapping, it is not used for decision-making purposes. Consider a sentence I may have said to my son, who is living in Texas. "I believe the Cowboys will win next year's Super Bowl." This sentence suggests a number of relationships. There is the relationship between the claim and myself. There is the relationship between the Cowboys and the winners of next year's Super Bowl. The sentence provides mapping. However, the sentence probably does not qualify as a belief-claim in Armstrong's sense since it probably was not used for decision-making. However, if I uttered the sentence to my bookie as I was placing a bet that corresponded to the statement, then it would be a proper belief-claim. Thus, belief is a sufficient condition for having a paradigm and using that paradigm to make decisions, and "a mapping" and "a mapping used to steer by" are necessary conditions for a proper belief-claim. This view of belief provides a promising solution to the faith/reason problem.

If we embrace a position that faith is a disposition of openness and a state of responsible commitment and Armstrong's notion of belief, then Wittgenstein's method of philosophical therapy appears to unravel the faith-reason problem. That is, the philosophical problem confronting us dissolves by a closer examination of the language we used in presenting the problem. Thus, the faith/reason problem is a problem of semantics, and a reasoned response to general revelation is viable.

This solution simply suggests that "faith" and "belief" are equivalent. They represent two ways of pointing to the same thing—a mapping that is used for guidance. Moreover, since belief is a necessary condition of reason, the faith-reason problem is problematic, not as a controversy (a tension between the two terms) but in substance, because it attempts to create a problem where no problem exists. If the two terms are equivalent, then faith is a necessary condition of reason just as belief is a necessary condition. Hence, if you have reason, then you have faith. Thus, what does Athens have to do with Jerusalem? Without Jerusalem, Athens is not. Faith and reason are

---

14. Strawson, *Analysis and Metaphysics*, 2–3.

not only complementary in that they work together, but they are dependent upon each other when each is properly exercised.[15]

Now, is there evidence to support this move? The presumption that faith and belief are not equivalent is strongly held.

> *Belief* should be distinguished from *faith* in our common usage of the terms. Faith may entail belief—that is, the acceptance of something—but it goes beyond acceptance to actual dependence. Conversely, belief may be present without faith; that is, one may believe but not really trust.[16]

Clearly, one may believe but not really trust. For example, I believe that none of my students would ever try to cheat on an exam, but I still proctor those exams. The problem with Monk's claim is that we have a type of equivocation, if Armstrong is correct, that there are at least two types of belief. Monk is assuming just one type, i.e., belief that only maps. However, Armstrong is not the only one who acknowledges that faith and belief are related. Henry Nelson Wieman and Regina Westcott-Wieman point out that at least in religion belief is taken very seriously, and we refer to this as faith. "Faith is using a belief to appropriate a reality into one's total living. Faith is a belief one lives by."[17] Furthermore, an interesting point, though not conclusive, is that in Koine Greek (the language of the New Testament) the verb πιστεύω can be translated "I have faith in" or "I believe." The noun πίστις is translated as "faith," "belief," or "trust."[18] Walter Bauer's work supports the possibility of interpreting faith and belief as equivalent if the kind of belief is more than mere opinion or idea.[19] Furthermore, for Tertullian's argument to work it seems that his assumption "Philosophy and religion are distinctively separate disciplines" is crucial. However, is it true?

In order for the faith/reason problem to be dissolved as proposed, we needed to make two critical assumptions, both relating to the meaning of words. We assumed that faith is a disposition of openness and a state of responsible commitment. This seems quite possibly true, and at

---

15. Since belief/faith is a necessary condition for reason, if one has reason, then one has faith/belief. However, necessary conditions can exist without a corresponding sufficient condition. One can have belief, the kind Armstrong suggests, and it might be unjustified. One can have an unjustified faith. However, this is a condition we want to avoid. We want our belief/faith to be justified. Thus, in the dependency between reason and faith, they become tightly intertwined.

16. Monk, *Exploring Religious Meaning*, 130.

17. Wieman and Westcott-Wieman, *Normative Psychology of Religion*, 109.

18. Metzger, *Lexical Aids for Students of New Testament Greek*, 9.

19. Bauer, *Greek-English Lexicon of the New Testament*, 665–71.

least as plausible as any alternative definition. Furthermore, we assumed Armstrong's notion of belief, which reflects a belief that has appropriate commitment such that the belief is used to make decisions. His position appears very plausible. However, like our assumption regarding faith, if this assumption is false, then the current proposal for dissolving the faith/reason problem does not work. Both of these crucial assumptions must be carefully examined, but that examination lies outside the scope of this project.

We suggested a third problem at the beginning of this section. If we accept the evidence provided in the above line of reasoning and allow the two assumptions, including the conclusion reached, an interesting problem for Wittgenstein's approach to philosophical problems is illustrated. Wittgenstein tells us, "Philosophy is a battle against the bewitchment of our intelligence by means of language." In this section, we have engaged in a minor battle trying to overcome the bewitchment, which has placed an abyss between faith and reason. Wishing to promote both faith and reason and not to advocate a dichotomous approach to life, we rejected Tertullian's claim. We found the notion that faith and belief are synonyms to be attractive. However, even if this solution works, it does illustrate an interesting aspect, which may be problematic, with Wittgenstein's approach to solving philosophical problems. To do battle against the bewitchment of our intelligence by means of language required us to use that very element that bewitches us. Language is both the problem and the solution. Have we been bewitched by language into believing that this philosophical problem has now been dissolved? It is possibly so. If we accept this critique, it is not clear that our analysis of "faith" and "belief" avoids the charge of bewitchment. Given Jacob's threefold aspect of faith in the Old Testament (i.e., knowledge, trust, and active obedience), there appears a solution to the faith/reason problem.[20] However, the solution is a result of language. Nor is it obvious that the argument presented as supporting Tertullian's claim is valid, and even if we were to construct a valid argument, the truthfulness of the conclusion would still be open to question, primarily because of language. Furthermore, it seems that an important contribution of some philosophical problems is that they promote dialogue between interested parties. For example, is the "faith" that was suggested to be synonymous with "belief" the same kind of faith that a religious person might define as faith? Some religious persons will say yes while others will say no. To assume an equivalency between faith and reason may prematurely close the door of investigation. It may deny the possible interaction with another position regarding the relationship between the two notions. For example, Wilfred Cantwell Smith provides a position that

---

20. See p. 175 n9 above.

denies the absolute separation of faith and reason (i.e., Tertullian's position) as well as the stance that claims the two are equivalent.[21]

It may be that some philosophical/theological problems are more valuable unsolved because their very existence encourages continued exploration and dialogue. The correlation of knowledge derived from general revelation to salvific knowledge may be this very type of problem. The tension it creates and dialogue it promotes may provide a balanced stance that is optimistic without declaring knowledge that is beyond our understanding. We may be optimistic that reason can and sometimes does properly interpret and promote a positive response to the text presented via general revelation. However, because that text is not as complete as the one provided by special revelation, and because we are not clear on how incomplete understanding of the self-revealing God affects the desired relationship of community, proclamation of the gospel (the good news) must continue to go forth. A level of agnosticism must abide. As J. P. Moreland pointed out, North American evangelicals are overcommitted to the Bible.

> The very idea that one could be over-committed to the Bible may strike one as irreligious. In a sense, this judgment is just. One could never be too committed to loving, obeying and promoting Holy Scripture. In another sense, however, such overcommitment is ubiquitous and harmful. The sense I have in mind is the idea that the Bible is the *sole* source of knowledge of God, morality, and a host of related important items. Accordingly, the Bible is taken to be the *sole* source of such knowledge and authority. The Protestant principle of *Sola Scriptura* does not entail this claim . . . [T]he idea that from within the Christian point of view, Scripture is the *ultimate* authority, the *ultimate* source of relevant knowledge, does not entail that it is the *sole* authority or source.[22]

---

21. As Smith points out, "The relations between faith and belief . . . varies" (Smith, *Faith and Belief*, 15). Smith does not focus on the philosophical problem, on which our discussion focused, but on the historicogeographic context. As a result, his position suggests implications that our discussion failed to appreciate. He emphasizes the difference between "faith" and "belief" by drawing an analogy with the work of a scientist. "This faith undergirds and informs and elicits and transcends their work. Their beliefs (the concrete parts of the specific sciences of the day) come and go; but their faith, with all its ultimate ineffability, persists . . . We have discriminated between belief and faith, and have argued that belief is one among many of the overt expressions of faith. Every great religious movement has had many expressions" (ibid., 16–17).

22. Moreland, "How Evangelicals Became Over-Committed to the Bible" (italics original). For another critical assessment of the evangelical position, by an evangelical, consider Ash's *Critical Examination of the Doctrine of Revelation in Evangelical Theology*.

While special revelation provides the ultimate source for now, evangelicals must understand that not all knowledge, all things to be known, are found within the Bible. As we saw in the previous essay, the Bible itself attests to the reality of general revelation but does not spell out the extent (or the limit) of knowledge obtainable from it. As evangelicals develop their theology of religions, their methodology should reflect the tension created because of the finiteness of human understanding in relation to divine ways. The tension this creates must be embraced by evangelicals, resulting in a theology of religions that exhibits an element of agnosticism.

Progressive Dispensationalism

Evangelical theology in North America is extremely diverse and embraces several different theological schools of thought. Therefore, evangelicalism may be a counterexample to the claim that conservative Christianity is static and incapable of addressing contemporary issues. While some forms of conservative Christianity may accurately be charged with simply living in the past, contemporary evangelical thought illustrates a tension. On the one hand, evangelical theology is rooted in some static belief-claims. On the other hand, as we have seen in previous essays and will see in this section, evangelical theology is dynamic and capable of trying to make sense of contemporary culture and current issues in light of the existing state of knowledge. In this section, we will briefly consider one of those schools of theology, namely, dispensationalism. This approach to evangelical theology is highlighted for two reasons. First, dispensationalism inherently takes a positive stance toward at least one other alien faith tradition. One of the benchmarks historically for a dispensational position is the belief that those of the Jewish faith still have a glorious future as God fulfills promises made to their ancestors. Second, within dispensationalism, one form of it, progressive dispensationalism, might emphasize an important concept that will allow for greater optimism based on general revelation.[23]

23. If this sounds tentative, it is meant to be so. Progressive dispensationalism is a relatively new nuance within dispensational theology, and those theologians who are progressive dispensationalists are grappling with other issues. As a result, while this writer sees potential, at this point it is unclear whether the theological movement will embrace an optimistic approach toward other faiths. Robert Saucy, one of the major theologians behind progressive dispensationalism, does not believe progressive dispensationalism will provide valuable insights for an evangelical theology of religions. While Judaism does have a glorious future, it will be realized as Jews embrace the new covenant. Furthermore, Saucy maintains, and I believe he is correct, that the concept that allows for greater optimism is present in other forms of evangelical and non-evangelical theologies. (Personal interview with Dr. Saucy, November 14, 2007, in San

Some approaches to Christianity try to maintain that because adherents of Judaism refused to accept Jesus Christ as the Messiah, the promises given to the Jews have now been passed forward to Christians. The church, in essence, has now replaced the Jews in God's plan. This promotes an approach to the theology of religions that might acknowledge that non-Christian traditions have value, but that their value is simply historical in that they lead up to *the* true religion—Christianity. Such a position does not promote an optimistic view of other faith traditions. However, if evangelicals are to develop an agnostic optimism, then their approach must be more hopeful regarding God's dealing with Israel, specifically (and by extension with other faith traditions). Some within evangelicalism, making a distinction between Israel and the church, believe that God's promises to Israel are still with Israel. The church, while part of God's plan, does not replace Israel.[24]

The Brethren movement in Britain during the nineteenth century (also known as the Plymouth Brethren) influenced North American evangelicalism in several ways. One major influence from the Brethren movement was a theological approach known as dispensationalism. While many evangelicals reject dispensational theology, there is a large constituency of dispensationalists within the evangelical tradition.[25] One form of dispensationalism, progressive dispensationalism, may provide help for evangelicals dealing with some of the problems raised by the theology of religions. Classical dispensationalism was popularized by C. I. Scofield and the *Scofield Bible*. Its theological presentation is found in the work of Lewis Sperry

---

Diego, California). Ramesh Richard supports Saucy's skepticism regarding the value of progressive dispensationalism. Richard not only denies universalism, but any form of inclusivism. ("Soteriological Inclusivism and Dispensationalism," 85–108).

24. First, the reference to Israel should not be confused with the political institution known as Israel, but with the religious institution stemming from the Abrahamic covenant. Second, the relationship or distinction between Israel and the church is not a settled issue among North American evangelicals. "It is evident that what is now taking place is the emergence of a new phase in the history of American dispensationalism. The complexity of the situation is such that a new biblical understanding of Israel and the church, a change in the method of defining dispensationalism, and the emergence of a new dispensationalism are all interrelated features of the same phenomena" (Blaising and Bock, *Dispensationalism, Israel and the Church*, 378).

25. Common features of dispensational theology include the authority of Scripture, dispensations or various economies by which God relates to persons, the uniqueness of the church, the significance of the universal church, the significance of biblical prophecy, futurist premillennialism, the imminent return of Christ, and a national future for Israel. (Blaising and Bock, *Progressive Dispensationalism*, 13–21). For a critique of dispensationalism by an evangelical see Poythress, *Understanding Dispensationalism*.

Chafer.[26] During the 1960s and '70s, dispensationalism was revised through the work of individuals like John Walvoord, Charles Ryrie, and J. Dwight Pentecost. According to Ryrie, "A dispensation is a distinguishable economy in the outworking of God's purpose."[27] Then in the 1990s progressive dispensationalism was introduced to the evangelical community as an effort to correct what some dispensationalists saw as problems facing classical or revised versions of dispensationalism.

> Many contemporary dispensationalists argue that God works progressively throughout history, preparing, presenting and proclaiming His kingdom through human administrators. Saucy describes the present age "as the first phase of the fulfillment of the one promised Messianic kingdom." The key description is that phenomena belonging to the eschatological kingdom of God is present now. This is an inaugurated eschatology with an inaugurated kingdom rather than a wholly postponed kingdom. The kingdom comes in phases throughout history.[28]

Progressive dispensationalism claims that each dispensation presents an aspect to be found in the final state. Blaising and Bock, two leading evangelical proponents of progressive dispensationalism, contrast this new version as follows.

> Progressive dispensationalists agree with revised (and classical) dispensationalists that God's work with Israel and Gentile nations in the past dispensation looks forward to the redemption of humanity in its political and cultural aspects. Consequently, there is a place for Israel and for other nations in the eternal plan of God.
>
> On the other hand, progressive dispensationalists believe that the church is a vital part of *this very same plan of redemption*. The appearance of the church does not signal a secondary redemptive plan, either to be fulfilled in heaven apart from the new earth or in an elite class of Jews and Gentiles who are forever distinguished from the rest of redeemed humanity. Instead, the church today is a revelation of spiritual blessings which *all the redeemed* will share in spite of their ethnic and national differences.
>
> Consequently, progressive dispensationalism advocates a *holistic and unified* view of eternal salvation. God will save

---

26. Chafer, *Systematic Theology*.
27. Ryrie, *Dispensationalism Today*, 29.
28. Gerry Breshears, "New Directions in Dispensationalism," Unpublished paper presented to the Evangelical Theological Society (November 1991), 16.

humankind in its ethnic and national plurality. But, He will bless it with the same salvation given to all without distinction; not only in justification and regeneration, but also in sanctification by the indwelling Holy Spirit. These blessings will come to all without distinction through Jesus Christ, the King of Israel and of all the nations of redeemed humanity.[29]

This presentation of progressive dispensationalism is not to defend the position; such a defense is outside the scope of this essay.[30] Nor is the purpose here to suggest that only progressive dispensationalism is capable of developing an optimistic theology of religions; many of the characteristics cited below of progressive dispensationalism are shared with other theological systems. Rather the purpose of presenting progressive dispensationalism is to illustrate that within evangelical theology a major system of thought exists that may be helpful in dealing with some of the questions evangelicals face as they develop their theology of religions. Harold Netland, whom we have seen as a major contributor to the development of an evangelical theology of religions, has suggested two questions that an adequate theology of religions must address.

> First, how do we account theologically for the sheer fact of human religiosity? Why are people incurably religious? Second, how do we account theologically for the particularities of religious expression, the many diverse beliefs and practices we find among the religious traditions?[31]

While Netland's brief reply to these questions does not make use of progressive dispensationalism, this theological system may be well equipped to offer a response to these questions, and potentially provides an insight relevant in the development of a theology of religions. Before we can appreciate this insight or suggest how this type of dispensationalism might offer a reply to Netland's questions, we need to consider the classical dispensationalism of Lewis Sperry Chafer.

Regarding the term "dispensation," Chafer says, "As a time measurement, a dispensation is a period which is identified by its relation to some particular purpose of God—a purpose to be accomplished within that

---

29. Blaising and Bock, *Progressive Dispensationalism*, 47–48.

30. However, one way of evaluating a theory is to show that it has viability in dealing with specific problems. Therefore, this discussion may contribute to a defense of progressive dispensationalism. For a defense of this position, see Saucy, *Case for Progressive Dispensationalism*.

31. Netland, "Theology of Religions, Missiology, and Evangelism," 145.

period."[32] Chafer then proceeds to present seven dispensations, each having a distinct beginning and ending in time. For example, "the Dispensation of Conscience, which extended from Adam's fall to the flood."[33] All who lived during that time period belonged to that dispensation or economy. This understanding of dispensations promotes the development of static timelines that display a linear unfolding of God's redemptive plan in which one dispensation follows another. If any overlap appears among the dispensations, it is insignificant—the ending of one and the beginning of another. However, this notion of static timelines is potentially jettisoned in progressive dispensationalism. A dispensation or economy, given this recent form, applies to God's management of a group of individuals. As a result, it is at least theoretically possible that significant overlapping of dispensations will occur. With the institution of the new covenant as developed in the New Testament, knowledge of God's chosen agency for salvation (i.e., Jesus Christ—his death, burial and resurrection) is prerequisite for salvation for those in the dispensation of grace, However, God may have another economy at work for those who currently are ignorant of Jesus Christ. God determines appropriate faith, according to the economy in which the individuals finds him- or herself. While the concerns of those evangelical theologians working in the area of progressive dispensationalism has not been with the theology of religions or soteriology, it appears that their form of dispensationalism at least allows for different dispensations to be operative or binding upon different individuals at the same time. As indicated above, Robert Saucy does not believe this feature is unique to progressive dispensationalism; however, Saucy's theology may be much richer than even he understands. While other forms of theology do allow for some overlapping of God's economies, progressive dispensationalism develops those economies based upon available revelation. Hence, progressive dispensationalism has greater capacity of handling parallel and concurrent economies. As a result, progressive dispensationalism is consistent with the Pauline optimism regarding Jews in spite of their rejection of Jesus as the Messiah.[34] From God's perspective, according to this nuance of dispensationalism, the various dispensations are holistic and unified as God brings about the Divine intent. These various economies or dispensations, while appearing to be different, are part of the same plan. Hence, progressive dispensational-

32. Chafer, *Systematic Theology*, 1:40.

33. Ibid.

34. Whereas Saucy believes Paul's basis for optimism is found in a Jewish remnant embracing the new covenant, progressive dispensationalism does open the door to the claim that Paul's optimism is based on God's promise and fulfillment in relation to the economy in which the Abrahamic covenant was made.

ism might provide a valuable tool for evangelicals working in the area of theology of religions. It might provide a solution for some of the problems raised when evangelicals embrace an agnostic optimism regarding other faith traditions. However, the proposal that progressive dispensationalism may have positive ramifications for an evangelical theology of religions is not without its own difficulty.

An optimistic theology of religions does raise numerous problems for other areas of evangelical theology. This is especially true of soteriology. For example, evangelicals may hear from their pulpits, "I must accept that Jesus Christ is not just the Lord but my Lord, not just the Savior but my Savior, not just the King but my King" in order to have salvation. Or, if "response" is always the key to triggering the process of salvation (i.e., faith), then it is unclear how this proposal would work.[35]

In the remainder of this section, we will explore this problem before returning to Netland's questions for an adequate theology of religions and progressive dispensationalism. However, the nature of the problem needs first to be clarified here. Evangelical theology wishes to avoid the problem of inconsistency. Their soteriology claims that salvation is appropriated by an act of faith that accepts the atonement resulting from the work of Jesus Christ. Yet, to embrace an optimistic position toward individuals who are non-Christian and suggest that some of these individuals may experience ultimate salvation appears inconsistent. If progressive dispensationalism is accepted, is it possible for evangelical theology to embrace without being inconsistent the position that some individuals may experience salvation without an act of faith that knowingly appropriates the atoning work of Christ?

Whether progressive dispensationalism is embraced or not, evangelicals must be very careful and not claim that no one outside of the church will experience salvation. Presumably, Moses and Abraham are saved. Nor would an evangelical want to claim that those outside of Christianity cannot be saved. Both positions are inconsistent with evangelical theology. While the first case makes an institution, the church, the arbiter of salvation, in the second case a religion is what saves. However, evangelical theology, as we saw earlier, understands that only God provides salvation.[36] It is God who bestows salvation. It is God who is the arbiter of salvation. Institutions

---

35. As I stated earlier, the use of progressive dispensationalism should not be understood as a defense of that position. Such a defense is outside the scope of this project.

36. These issues were addressed in essay 3, "Agency of Salvation" and essay 4, "Recipients of Salvation." Salvation should not be limited to some future deliverance. As Elmer Martens has argued in *God's Design*, God's intent is to provide his creation with (1) deliverance, (2) community, (3) knowledge of God, and (4) abundant life. This is salvation; it is the gospel message according to evangelicals.

or religions do not save, according to evangelical thought, and the God of evangelical theology is sovereign. Yet evangelical theology also maintains that Jesus Christ is the sole agency of salvation. The Christian Scriptures do claim that if you believe in Jesus Christ—not by expressing a mere idea but rather by taking action based on the idea—you will be saved (Rom 10:9). Does this mean that if one does not believe in Jesus Christ, then that individual is not saved? From Rom 10:9, we cannot deduce this latter statement. Rom 10 declares that if one has an appropriate type of faith, then they are guaranteed salvation. While Jesus Christ is the sole agency or source for salvation, God may assign salvation based on the work of Jesus Christ, to individuals who do not have *that* appropriate type of faith—faith in Jesus Christ.[37] While this stance is not internally inconsistent, such an evangelical position may present an apparent antinomy.

It is this apparent problem that progressive dispensationalism may help address. Given progressive dispensationalism, we could understand that our theology is limited to our current place in God's overall plan. The theology of this type of evangelical thought understands that God works differently, with different economies, during different periods of time. These various workings, while different, are consistent and provide parts of the collage to be unveiled in the future eschaton. For example, in the Abrahamic covenant God promised specific things, e.g., land, a future, to the descendants of Abraham (Deut 30). These promises were repeated throughout the Torah and other writings of the Hebrew Scriptures. Did God's promises change? Did God recall or take back the promises made to the descendants of Abraham? Were those promises simply taken from Israel and given to another institution, the church? Dispensational theology, whether classical

---

37. E. P. Sanders provides an excellent argument that, for Paul in both Romans and Galatians, to have appropriate faith was to have "faith in Jesus Christ" (Sanders, *Paul*, 52–90). While Paul's meaning may be limited to "faith in Jesus Christ," the theological significance may be richer. "The reality of meaning is grounded on past action: . . . There is a determinate something 'in' the text—intended meaning—that remains fixed and unchanging throughout the history of its interpretation. Yet many interpreters are more interested in the present than in the past, and in the question, 'What does it mean, here and now, to me?' The concern for relevance—for reading with the aim of bringing a text to bear on contemporary concerns—is a concern for what Hirsch calls 'significance.' Unlike meaning, the significance of a text can change, for significance pertains to the relation between the text's determinate meaning and a larger context (i.e., another era, another culture, another subject matter)" (Vanhoozer, *Is There A Meaning In This Text?*, 259). For a brief discussion of the complexity of "meaning" see Paul Feinberg. ("Hermeneutics of Discontinuity," 109–28). Hermeneutics is definitely in the center of the fray as evangelicals debate progressive dispensationalism. That discussion, however, is beyond the scope of our current issue See Thomas, *Evangelical Hermeneutics*.

or progressive, maintains that God's promises hold and will be realized. However, progressive dispensationalism goes a step further.

For progressive dispensationalism, current features of the church-age represent elements of a future age. While God's community or fellowship with the human race has always been based on faith, the content of that faith has changed. According to Rom 10:9, the content or object of faith for salvation is Jesus Christ. However, the writer of Hebrews illustrates various objects of faith in Heb 11. While Abel had no understanding of Jesus Christ, God counted his faith as appropriate.[38] Abel had appropriately responded to the revelation that he had available. For some God's self-revelation is manifested in the person of Jesus Christ as presented in the Scriptures and lived out in the church. However, for others this self-revelation may be limited to "the heavens declare the glory of God" (Psalm 19). "There is no speech, nor are there words; their voice is not heard; yet their voice goes out through all the earth, and their words to the end of the world" (vv. 3–4). Should an individual respond in a positive way to this wordless proclamation, and God counts it as appropriate, then this individual will experience ultimate salvation. The key is that God counts a given response to revelation as appropriate. What exactly constitutes such a response we are not told. As a result, evangelicals must continue to share the good news based upon the Christ-event. For with this good news comes both a more complete revelation of how God is at work to draw the created back into community and a guarantee. "If you believe in the Lord Jesus Christ, then you shall be saved."

If appropriate response is always tied to the extent of revelation, then the importance of general revelation becomes increasingly apparent for an evangelical theology of religions. Those working in the area of progressive dispensationalism will need to expand their work beyond the Abrahamic covenant, which appears to be their starting point. Building upon their insight of an inaugurated eschatology, which claims that some characteristics of a given dispensation are types for characteristics of the final state and the singularity of God's plan for persons and the cosmos, which supports their holistic, unified view of salvation history, can dispensationalists provide answers to the two questions that Harold Netland proposed that any adequate theology of religions must address? How might they respond to Netland, assuming progressive dispensationalists can provide a response?

In a limited way, Robert Saucy is correct when he claims that progressive dispensationalism does not provide new insights to an evangelical theology of religions that other forms of evangelical (and nonevangelical)

---

38. From the hall of faith in Hebrews 11, it should be clear that what constitutes appropriate faith is a decision that only God is in position to determine. Evangelical theology must take care and not try to establish a line of demarcation that is too narrow.

theologies fail to provide, as we consider Netland's questions regarding: (1) a theological account for human religiosity and (2) a theological account for religious diversity. Progressive dispensationalism will agree with many other forms of theology that Augustine has already provided a theological account for both human religiosity and religious diversity.

> The truth is that all these actions and energies belong to the one true God, who is really a God, who is wholly present everywhere, is confined by no frontiers and bound by no hindrances, is indivisible and immutable, and, though His nature has no need of either heaven or of earth, He fills them both with His presence and His power. Yet, the Creator of every nature has so ordained that each of His creatures is permitted to have and to exercise powers of its own. Although without Him they could not exist, their essence is different from Him.[39]

The human race has a propensity toward being religious because the Creator is ever present and we are created in God's image. In this sense, progressive dispensationalism does not provide any new insights. However, Saucy's position may provide new insights of another sort.

While other approaches to theology may advocate the following three features, which are pertinent to the development of a theology of religions, progressive dispensationalism ties them together in a fashion clearly not seen in other forms of dispensationalism and possibly not seen in other nondispensational theologies. First, Saucy's position advocates a unified, holistic approach to God's plan and activities within the cosmos; however, it does not advocate for this unity based on any singularity in God's dealings. Progressive dispensationalism embraces both continuity and discontinuity in the divine plan. Hence, this form of evangelical theology does account for both human religiosity and religious diversity. Furthermore, the notion of inaugurated eschatology appears significant. Throughout the ages, as God is moving to reestablish community with the created, elements of the final state are inaugurated or instituted in various economies. While this progressive inaugurated eschatology may be seen as a source for the current state of religious diversity (i.e., God has chosen to interact differently with different groups of individuals and has instituted diverse elements of the final state), inaugurated eschatology may be more closely associated with an explanation for human religiosity. God has and is actively involved in drawing the creature back to the Creator. This activity, while unified in goal, has been manifested through various economies. Each economy having an element

---

39. Augustine, *City of God*, 141.

of the future state also establishes a special relationship between God and the recipient group.

While the above two features of progressive dispensationalism are significantly relevant to a theology of religions, it is the third feature that is most significant. If we understand that God, through human history, has interacted with the created through various economies, and that there may be significant overlapping of dispensations, then we can potentially discover a basis for optimism about those outside of the Christian church. At least at the theoretical level, it must be seen as possible that an individual living in a region where the gospel message has never been proclaimed might appropriately respond to the limited revelation provided. As a result, because of the limited information God may choose to engage that person in accordance with an economy appropriate to the available revelation. Hence, an individual may not know anything of Jesus Christ and his atoning work. That individual, while being engaged by God, could not be considered part of the dispensation of grace, but God may choose to work with the person in light of some other economy.

At first blush, this suggestion may be problematic for evangelicals for it may sound like salvation is obtainable by means other than the work of Christ. This need not be the situation. Consider the following situations. First, consider a good, righteous Jew in the first century living outside of Palestine. This individual, while never hearing of Jesus of Nazareth, appropriately responds to the Abrahamic covenant and is engaged in a relationship with God as set forth by dispensation of law. Evangelicals would not claim this person would not enter into God's ultimate rest because they lacked certain knowledge, nor would they claim this person was "saved" because of works. Even though the individual was unaware of the atonement provided by Jesus Christ, evangelicals would claim that God could appropriate the atoning work and hence bring this individual into community with the divine.

Could evangelicals embrace the same story if the individual in question were living in the beginning of the twenty-first century but still lacked knowledge of Jesus Christ? Is the time setting the issue? For progressive dispensationalists, even though we are well into the dispensation of grace, this individual appears to be living under the dispensation of law. The time issue is not the point. What should be the point, for evangelicals, is whether this individual is responding appropriately to the revelation available; at issue is the extent of revelation the individual has and their response to that revelation.

Let us consider a third scenario. This third case looks at a descendant of Noah, say two or three generations removed, but prior to the Abrahamic covenant. This descendant has faithfully remembered the stories told by his/her ancestors and in an appropriate way has worshiped and honored the God who provided their safe passage. If this individual ultimately experiences salvation, his or her salvation will again be based on an appropriate response to the revelation he or she has and God's assigning salvation based upon the work of the cross, which has yet (at that time) to occur.[40] Progressive dispensationalism, as with other approaches to theology, will have little problem with this scenario.

However, our fourth scenario, which places our individual in Janakpur, Nepal, in the nineteenth century, presents a bit of a challenge. While it is possible that this individual has knowledge of Jesus Christ, let us assume he/she knows nothing of the gospel message, nor is he/she acquainted with Abraham and the faith-traditions that derive from him. Furthermore, let us assume that this individual concludes that God (Parabrahma) does exist and has specific expectations of the followers of Parabrahma. However, the individual realizes that his right standing before Parabrahma is not the result of his performing the *puja* or ritual offerings suggested by the temple priests. He realizes that if he should experience ultimate salvation, it will be based solely upon the mercy of God. Furthermore, let us assume his understanding of God is not based on what he had been taught by the priest before the shrine known as Janaki Mandir. Rather, after much contemplation in which he both considered the cosmos around him and delved into his own psyche, he concludes that God is holy, just, all-powerful, and so forth. Furthermore,

---

40. An evangelical theology is a Christian theology, and, as a result, its focus is on the church and those believers who are in union with Christ. This union is possible because of the atoning work of Jesus Christ upon the cross (cf. essay 3). The historical event of the cross raises the question about those prior to the Christ event. As we saw previously, evangelicals take the position that God, knowing Christ's future act, counted the faith of pre-Jesus believers as appropriate for community with God. Bruce Demarest claims, "They were justified by faith, they experienced removal of the defilement of sins . . ., they enjoyed fellowship with God, and they possessed the hope of eternal life. But the fullness and perfecting of salvation as incorporation into Christ had to await the once-for-all sacrifice of the Messiah" (Demarest, *Cross and Salvation*, 339). Charles Ryrie, a dispensationalist, addresses the problem in the following manner. "The *basis* of salvation in every age is the death of Christ; the *requirement* for salvation in every age is faith; the *object* of faith in every age is God; the *content* of faith changes in the various dispensations. It is this last point, of course, which distinguishes dispensationalism from covenant theology, but it is not a point to which the charge of teaching two ways of salvation can be attached. It simply recognizes the obvious fact of progressive revelation. When Adam looked upon the coats of skins with which God had clothed him and his wife, he did not see what the believer today sees looking back on the cross of Calvary. And neither did other Old Testament saints see what we see today. There have to be two sides to this matter—that which God sees from His side and that which man sees from his" (Ryrie, *Dispensationalism Today*, 123–24).

he realizes that he, as a creature, is not worthy to stand in the presence of such an awesome God, but that God desires community with him. Is it possible that this man might be worshiping the same God who encountered Moses in the burning bush? Is it possible that he will appropriately respond to the revelation he has at hand such that God might assign salvation based upon the work of the cross of Jesus Christ? The issue, at this level, is not the probability of such an event occurring, but whether it is even possible. If it is not possible, then how is it possible to suggest that our descendant of Noah might experience ultimate salvation? If it is possible for our individual from Janakpur to experience a reestablished community with God, then what was that revelation like to which he responded? Is there a relationship between the man from Janakpur and the descendent of Noah?

Given their appreciation for God's revelation, progressive dispensationalists should be able to ask how the Noahic covenant and the scriptural references to what we understand to be general revelation relate to God's unified plan to draw the created back into community with the Creator and embrace an optimism toward those outside the dispensation of grace. Whereas other forms of theology may acknowledge the continuity and discontinuity of God's economies and that significant overlapping of these economies is possible, the notion of progressive dispensationalism should promote an optimism frequently absent in other forms of conservative Christianity.

One aspect of a theology of religions is to address how one's home tradition views other faith traditions. Given progressive dispensationalism and its notion of multiple economies, it might be reasonable to expect this form of evangelical theology to promote a position taken in some other forms of Christianity: according to such a position, other religions may be the vehicle God uses to bring a person into salvation. This may be developed in at least two directions. Taking a lead from Justin Martyr, it may be claimed that the *logos spermatikos* can be found in non-Christian religions. As a result, for example, some devout Hindus may actually be Christians even though they do not realize it. (This position was discussed in essay 4 above.) A second strategy, which illustrates an optimism due to general revelation, is identified with the "fulfillment model" of J. N. Farquhar as presented at the Edinburgh Conference of 1910 and developed in his book *The Crown of Hinduism*.[41] This approach highlights what is good and true in the world religions.[42] Both of these approaches would suggest if an individual

---

41. Farquhar, *Crown of Hinduism*. In this model, Farquhar argued that Christ fulfilled the longings and aspirations of Hinduism.

42. While the first volume of this project explores the world religions and sees much that is good and true in those traditions, readers should not conclude that this author is

in a Hindu culture experiences salvation, that it is Hinduism that provides the salvation. That is, salvation is found for the devout Hindu in the non-Christian tradition.

Given the nature of those evangelical theologians who identify with progressive dispensationalism, neither move appears plausible. (This issue must be readdressed in the following essay.) Furthermore, this optimism is not to be confused with a universalism, but is based on the possibility of multiple economies concurrently in effect and all tied together with the cross. If salvation is bestowed due to an appropriate response to the available revelation to those outside the dispensation of grace, then general revelation and the Noahic covenant may help a progressive dispensationalist to develop a theology of religions.

The Noahic Covenant and Progressive Dispensationalism

In the previous essay, we considered the covenant God made with Noah and the notion of common grace.[43] We saw that for Gabriel Fackre this covenant speaks of God's grace and preservation, and the covenant was understood because Noah and his descendants possessed both the image of God and latent revelation. In the previous section, we concluded that progressive dispensationalists should be able to incorporate the Noahic covenant as a means to understand better God's unified plan of restoration. Before we attempt to develop in the following essay an evangelical theology of religions that is heavily dependent upon general revelation, which includes the Noahic covenant, it may be beneficial to take a closer look at the covenant God made with Noah. We will begin this section by looking at a Jewish understanding of the Noahic covenant before considering its application to Christian theology.

According to Richard Elliot Friedman, "the Noahic covenant is the first of four major covenants that provide the structure in which nearly all of the [Hebrew] Bible is framed . . . The Noahic covenant promises the security of the cosmos."[44] This covenant is significant within Jewish thought

---

endorsing a form of Farquhar's fulfillment model.

43. "In the book of Genesis, creation is not presented as an independent "doctrine" but belongs in the context of an extended story that moves from the beginning toward the fulfillment of God's purpose for all creatures and the whole creation. In the narrative perspective, creation is embraced within God's covenant, specifically the Noahic covenant" (Anderson, *Contours of Old Testament Theology*, 92).

44. Friedman, *Commentary on the Torah*, 42. It may be debated that the first covenant was with Adam; however, since a covenant is typically understood to present a "new" relationship, a changed relationship, and Adam or the human race did not have a

for several reasons. To understand why this first covenant is vital for a holistic, unified picture of God's purpose, we must ask, why does God promise security of the cosmos? Was it to guarantee against God's fickleness? On the other hand, should we understand something more significant in this first covenant? Neil Gillman provides a fascinating insight into this covenant as he places it in relation to the creation.

> [The first creation story] teaches that creation involved God's forming the cosmos out of primitive chaos (i.e. darkness, the deep and the "unformed and void" as described in 1:2), that God brought order out of anarchy. The leading motif of this story is that God introduced structures, boundaries or parameters . . . This ordering work shaped the primitive, anarchic conditions that prevailed at the outset of creation . . . In Genesis 2–3, the challenge to God comes not during creation but after, through the disobedience of Adam and Eve . . . Again, only God's eternal vigilance prevents chaos from erupting again. And sometimes, as in the flood story that follows, a punishing God destroys the structures separating the waters above from the waters below (Genesis 7:11) and the flood covers the earth. At the end of the story, God promises Noah that the original structures of Genesis 1 will be re-established forever.[45]

The significance of this covenant is two-fold for Gillman. First, it indicates God's intention to not desert that which God created. Second, it lays the foundation for all subsequent covenants. It presents God as entering into a

---

previous relationship to change from, it is generally accepted that the Noahic covenant is the first revealed covenant (McComiskey, *Covenants of Promise*, 217). It may be argued that as God provided Adam and Eve with animal skins to cover themselves that a new relationship is portrayed. Hence, the first covenant is seen with Adam. Regarding the nature of a covenant, Arnold Eisen provides an efficient discussion in his article "Covenant." "The monarchs of the biblical period, . . . , entered into several sorts of covenants . . . with their peers and subjects. In one type, generally known as the suzerainty treaty, the king bound his vassals to a set of obligations, which he defined. In return, the sovereign promised nothing, except—implicitly—his own protection, conferred in return for the subjects' loyalty and trust. Parity treaties, by contrast, stipulated the mutual obligations undertaken by two equal parties. A third sort of pact, the promissory grant, presumed the inequality of the parties, but nonetheless bound the sovereign unilaterally. Out of sheer beneficence, he agreed to the performance of stipulated acts on behalf of his inferiors. At Sinai, the suzerainty model is borrowed (cf. Ex. 19–20). . . . By contrast Noah (Gen. 9:8), Abraham (Gen 15:18; 17:4), and David (2 Sam 7) are the privileged recipients of promissory covenants. God binds himself to be their patron and benefactor. Like a lover, he accepts the partner just as he is—David even in his sinfulness, the whole of humanity despite a nature that is evil from its youth" (Eisen, "Covenant," 107–8).

45. Gillman, *Death of Death*, 45–48.

relationship with the human race that promotes order and structure against the chaos from which creation emerged. It presents a God who is in control and capable of bringing order out of anarchic conditions. Furthermore, it is from this covenant that Jewish thought has developed the Noahide laws that lay the foundation for how they were to interact with non-Jews.

> The concept of Noahide law is a border concept that mediates between Judaism and the non-Jewish world in both time and space. The *Noahide* (literally, "son of Noah"), who is the subject of this law, is a designation of both the gentile who confronts Judaism in the present and all humankind before the Torah as given to Israel, separating Israel from all the other nations of the world.[46]

Thus, within Jewish theology the covenant with Noah provides a "Torah" for Gentiles. Louis Jacob explains,

> For the Rabbis, while the Torah in its totality is for Israel alone, there is a Torah for Gentiles—the seven precepts of the sons of Noah, the usual classification of which is: (1) Not to worship idols; (2) Not to commit murder; (3) Not to commit adultery and incest; (4) Not to eat a limb torn from a living animal; (5) Not to blaspheme; (6) Not to steal; (7) To have an adequate system of law and justice.[47]

Similar to Gillman's understanding of the Noahic Covenant, Christian scholars have understood the covenant as addressing God's intent to preserve the cosmos and God's intent to interact with the entire human race. As Elmer Martens observes, following the lead of Rolff Rendtorff,

> God binds himself through covenant to guarantee the regularities of nature such as day and night, seed-time and harvest. The world is stabilized through grace . . . The creation motif is thus invoked to bear on a circumstance in salvation history . . . Creation, then, furnishes something of a bedrock or ultimate event by which warrant is provided that God's action with his people can be expected to be just. The Creator God characterized by

---

46. Novak, *Jewish-Christian Dialogue*, 26. "The first explicit presentation of the Noahide laws is in the *Tosefta*, a work commonly believed to have been edited in the late second century of the Common Era. There we read: 'Seven commandments were the sons of Noah commanded: (1) concerning adjudication, (2) and concerning idolatry, (3) and concerning blasphemy, (4) and concerning sexual immorality, (5) and concerning bloodshed, (6) and concerning robbery, (7) and concerning a limb torn from a living animal'" (ibid., 27).

47. Jacob, *Jewish Theology*, 285.

justice is also the Savior God who is characterized by justice. If canonical wisdom literature does not explicitly connect creation and redemption, it nevertheless implicitly provides a compelling theological underpinning for salvation history.[48]

Walter Eichrodt speaks of God's relationship to humans as being understood in terms of two concentric circles: "the Noah covenant for the whole human race and the Abraham covenant for Israel alone. In these two forms the relationship of God to men remains eternally constant."[49] As a result, "not only the Israelites, but also the heathen stand within a God-given order which controls their relations with God; it is only within the Noah covenant, which is binding on all men, that the Abraham covenant is set up."[50] Not only does the Noahic Covenant provide a foundation for subsequent covenants, but also Eichrodt's insights may provide a similar function as the Noahide laws do within Judaism. The covenant shows that the entire human race stands in a relationship with God, and that God's desire for restoration includes all who are descendants of Noah. Roger Hardham Hooker points out that a common misconception of Christianity is that God appears only to be interested in Christians.[51] While God enters into subsequent covenants such as the Abrahamic or the New Covenant, the promises given in the first covenant are still intact and, as a result, include all individuals who are descendants of Noah. Given the Genesis story, this means that all persons since Noah are included in this first covenant.

For the progressive dispensationalist this is significant. If they are to claim an inaugurated eschatology that is being worked out through salvation history, then they cannot begin their story with Abraham, although Abraham is a significant point of divergence in redemptive history. As a result, redemption or restoration history should include the covenant made with Noah. This covenant places clearly on the table both the notions of 'image of God' and latent revelation, which are major components of general revelation and lays an important foundation upon which evangelicals can build an optimistic theology of religions.[52]

48. Martens, *God's Design*, 282.
49. Eichrodt, *Theology of the Old Testament*, 1:58.
50. Ibid., 1:414.
51. "Christians claim, or appear to claim, that God is only interested in one stream of history and in one single people within it, while he ignores other times and other people" (Hooker, *Themes in Hinduism and Christianity*, 55). Hooker sees this as incorrect.
52. In the previous essay, we pointed out that prior to and in the covenant with Noah, God had dealings with persons, and as a result self-revelation took place with the human race. God had provided some knowledge of God to humans. We speculated that this knowledge was preserved in oral traditions that were passed down from one

In addition to placing general revelation in a position of relevance when considering restoration history, God's covenant with Noah and his descendants also highlights the notion of common grace. While this common grace is not salvific grace, it is a grace available to all and establishes an order or structure, as opposed to chaos. This is significant because given a structured cosmos in which persons have the capacity of being rational, and given the evidence made available through general revelation, the progressive dispensationalist is in position to be optimistic regarding his or her theology of religions. However, given the human capacity to challenge God's order by being disobedient, the progressive dispensationalist's optimism must be tempered. God has not given the church a clear indication of what constitutes appropriate response to general revelation.[53] Hence, the evangelical emphasis upon evangelization based upon what God has revealed in special revelation is proper.

While the development of an evangelical theology of religions is not dependent upon progressive dispensationalism, it is aided by such an approach. This form of evangelical theology does enable an evangelical to develop a theology that is consistent with its historical foundation and that is balanced between being optimistic and agnostic. It is a form that gives God's communiqué via general revelation its proper recognition, assuming that progressive dispensationalists step back and incorporate the covenant of Noah into their framework. Without progressive dispensationalism, evangelicals must emphasize the agnostic aspect of their approach to other faith-traditions. The next essay we will present an evangelical theology of religions that asserts understands that even in general revelation it is God who is revealing and who is being revealed; this theology of religions is informed by an approach consistent with progressive dispensationalism.

---

generation to the next. The content of this revelation is referred to as "latent revelation".

53. Paul provides an insight into what may constitute an appropriate response to general revelation in Acts 17:27. "God did this so that men would seek him and perhaps reach out for him and find him, though he is not far from each one of us" (NIV).

9

General Revelation and an Evangelical Theology of Religions

In the closing essay of his *Theology in the Context of World Christianity*, Timothy Tennent of Gordon-Conwell Theological Seminary identifies several "emerging contours of global theology."[1] His final contour is "Theological Engagement with Ideologies of Unbelief and with Non-Christian Religions." Tennent points out that while the earliest theological formulations of the Christian church were developed in response to positions proposed within the church, the contemporary scene has changed. Today, not only evangelicals, but also the global church, are facing positions that are proposed by those outside of the church. Because of this change, Tennent maintains that contemporary Christian theology must include "a more explicit response to the challenges of world religions."[2] This enterprise, he claims, cannot be peripheral, but must be central to the theological task. He warns, "We can no longer afford the kind of entrenched sectarianism that has often characterized fundamentalism and evangelicalism. [But t]his does not mean that we must relinquish our distinctive theological convictions."[3] While Tennent does not offer an evangelical theology of religions, his work does highlight the importance of this field of theology for evangelicals, because a theology of religions focuses upon how a faith tradition understands and responds to other faith traditions.

In this project, our focus has been on North American evangelicals and their work in this field of theology. We surveyed the contributions evangelicals have made as they have explored relevant questions in this field. Furthermore, after considering some of the pertinent biblical materials, we looked at the notion of general revelation, focusing on whether general revelation can aid evangelicals as they develop their own distinctive

---

1. Tennent, *Theology in the Context*, 249–72.
2. Ibid., 267.
3. Ibid., 269.

theology of religions. Finally, in the previous essay, we considered other relevant issues, such as the importance of leaving some philosophical and theological problems unresolved, progressive dispensationalism—a relatively new nuance within evangelical theology, and the Noahic covenant as it relates to general revelation. We now ask, based upon this research, has an evangelical theology of religions emerged for North American evangelicals, which draws upon general revelation, and, if so, what does it look like? Based on our studies, an evangelical theology is beginning to emerge, although it is still incomplete.

The emerging theology may not be as optimistic or progressive toward non-Christian religions as other theological traditions within Christianity have been. However, many conservative Christians will see the emerging position as evidence of the "liberal" influence within contemporary North American evangelicalism. As we have seen, evangelicalism is extremely diverse. As a result, the position sketched below will not satisfy all evangelicals. Since progressive dispensationalism can be modified, as proposed in the previous essay, and provides important elements for a theology of religions, this nuance of dispensationalism will be assumed in the following presentation. The remainder of this essay will sketch the emerging position. We will begin with general observations in the first section. In the second section, we will expand our understanding of the role that general revelation may play in an evangelical theology of religions. The final section will focus on interreligious dialogue. We will develop a justification for this activity and the role it will perform for evangelicals and their theology of religions.

General Observations

The development of an evangelical theology of religions provides a fascinating challenge. It must be faithful to those elements that may be seen as key characteristics of evangelicalism. It must present a story of how evangelicals should understand and relate to individuals who belong to non-Christian faith traditions. These two points can create tension. The tension may exist because evangelicals, like most human beings, tend to think in terms of either/or, black/white, Christian/non-Christian, us/them, and so forth. The challenge facing evangelicals is to develop a theology that does not reject the foundational beliefs of evangelicalism but that does encourage a move beyond dualistic thinking. Krister Stendahl offers sound advice, which if heeded by evangelicals may be very helpful.[4] He proposes stepping back and looking at a wider panorama than is normal when developing a theology.

4. Stendahl, "Notes," 7–18.

For understandable reasons, evangelical theologians have focused on Jesus Christ and the Christian church. However, Jesus Christ and the Christian church are only part of a larger drama. Stendahl suggests that we can best see this larger drama as we look at the message and mission of Jesus Christ, which was the kingdom. Stendahl says,

> My guess is that this very term expressed the continuity with the old and eternal dream of God's for a mended creation, for a redeemed world. Kingdom is more than a King and a Lordship, and Reign. The kingdom of God, the kingdom of heaven, stands for a mended creation, with people and things, a social, economic, ecological reality.[5]

It is the kingdom that captures "the sweeping vision of God's total work."[6] The kingdom speaks to God's drawing the entire creation back into community with its Creator. From this reference point, the dualism frequently encountered within evangelical theology can be transcended without losing its distinctive features. The Christian church, while crucial within God's drama, is not the only act within the epic. The Christian story does contain essential elements of the epic, but God's drama is a call to the entire cosmos. The Christian Scriptures speak to this wider scope.[7] If an evangelical theology of religions is to be embraced, the evangelical community must see itself as not only part of the Christian act, but as part of the larger drama. The evangelical community must understand that while the good news they proclaim is essential in God's work of reestablishing community with the cosmos, the reestablishment is broader than the Christian church. This

---

5. Ibid., 9.

6. Ibid., 8. It should be noted that a major topic of discussion that led to the development of progressive dispensationalism was a reassessment of the concept of kingdom. "The theme of the kingdom of God is much more unified and more central to progressive dispensationalism than it is to revised dispensationalism. Instead of dividing up the different features of redemption into self-contained "kingdoms," progressive dispensationalists see one promised eschatological kingdom which has both spiritual and political dimensions . . . Progressive dispensationalists put primary emphasis on the eternal kingdom for understanding all previous forms of the kingdom including the Millennium. They make no substantive distinction between the terms kingdom of heaven and kingdom of God" (Blaising and Bock, *Progressive Dispensationalism*, 54). "If one wants to see how God accomplishes his kingdom, one must see how that program and the promises tied to it are linked together through the Scripture's description of the career of Jesus Christ" (Bock, "Reign of the Lord Christ," 37). Also see Robert Saucy, *Case for Progressive Dispensationalism*, 81–110.

7. For examples, see Gen 12:3, Ps 67:2–3, Isa 2:2–4, Isa 60:2–3, Luke 2:32, Matt 28:19, Acts 11:18, Col 3:11, and Rev 7:9.

movement of seeing itself as part of a greater drama is enhanced by the two important elements that become the focal points later in this essay.

A second general observation is that for evangelicals the other world religions are non-Christian. To suggest that adherents of other religions are anonymous Christians or that other traditions house individuals who will become Christians is an injustice to both those other traditions and Christianity. Religions, including Christianity, are culturally connected attempts to make sense of ultimate concerns. Evangelicals, as they attempt to understand religions, have three basic options available to them. First, they can assume all religions are fundamentally the same. The differences among the various traditions can be explained as cultural variances. Second, evangelicals can assume that all other faith traditions are false and contain no hope or truth. Christianity is an anomaly among the world religions, for it has the truth. Finally, they can assume that while the various non-Christian religions may contain some religious truths and spiritual benefits, they fail to provide the foundational component that makes it possible for persons to reestablish community with God. Once again, in this option, Christianity as a religion is an anomaly, for it claims that the foundational component for reestablished community is Jesus Christ. This third option is the stance most consistent with the evangelical theology we have seen portrayed in the previous essays.[8]

Furthermore, the previous essays have suggested that an evangelical theology of religions must maintain a level of agnosticism. An evangelical theology must acknowledge its limited nature when addressing areas in which we do not have complete, or clear, revelation. An evangelical theology of religions must be agnostic in the sense that it cannot declare the mind of God beyond what God has chosen to reveal in a clear fashion. However, because evangelicals understand God to be a God of justice and mercy, and because the Scriptures do clearly declare that some outside of the Christian

---

8. Evangelicals have rejected the first stance for three basic reasons. First, the various faith systems do portray radically different pictures on issues that are crucial to given faith traditions. Second, this position may lead to an adoption of positions that have been considered heretical by mainstream Christianity. Third, this position may lead to a less than respectful position toward other faith systems by denying essential characteristics that make each a distinct faith tradition. This is a problem with any reductionistic approach to religion. While we did see those who are identified with evangelicalism holding the second stance, it was claimed that if evangelicals are to develop a theology of religions, this second stance must be rejected as being inconsistent with their basic theology. While there is a long history of Christians taking this route, it does not fit with an evangelical worldview. Furthermore, this position fails to acknowledge the common ground found among the various traditions. Typical of a fundamentalist approach to Christianity, this route tends to put God into a box and claims that those who hold the "truth" know God better. Truth is defined by what they hold to be true.

church are saved, an evangelical theology of religions must be optimistic. We have cited examples of individuals such as Abraham and Moses who are outside the church, but the Scriptures speak about their being saved. (We will say more on this point.) This optimism cannot be converted into a form of universalism because the Scriptures do indicate that some will not be saved. However, God's goodness is not limited to members of the church; it extends to all. Therefore, an evangelical theology of religions must be both agnostic and optimistic.

The fourth general observation is more specific than the preceding three. An evangelical theology of religions begins with an understanding of Christianity as based in Jesus Christ. As Harold Lindsell claims, "The deity of Christ is the foundation of the Christian faith. The denial of it invalidates the entire structure of Christian theology."[9] To claim members of other faith traditions as anonymous Christians is to deny the very foundation of evangelical thought and to deny these other traditions their own voices. Since they deny the deity of Christ, they must be non-Christian if an evangelical understanding of Christianity is embraced.[10] The Manila Manifesto proclaimed this uniqueness of Jesus Christ.

> We affirm that the Jesus of history and the Christ of glory are the same person, that this Jesus Christ is absolutely unique, for he alone is God incarnate, our sin-bearer, the conqueror of death and the coming judge . . . We affirm that other religions and ideologies are not alternative paths to God, and that human spirituality, if unredeemed by Christ, leads not to God but to judgment, for Christ is the only way.[11]

While an evangelical theology of religions will embrace these affirmations, it will point out that some of the conclusions drawn within the manifesto must be challenged. The manifesto explains,

> because men and women are made in God's image and see in creation traces of its Creator, the religions which have arisen do sometimes contain elements of truth and beauty. They are not, however, alternative gospels. Because human beings are sinful,

---

9. *Harper Study Bible*, (footnote for John 20:28), 1621.

10. This claim statement is not beyond controversy. Within the Christian church there are individuals who do deny the deity of Jesus Christ. That dialogue is outside the scope of our present discussion. An evangelical theology of religions must stay focused upon coming to grips and interacting with positions proposed by those outside the church, i.e., with other faith traditions.

11. Stott, *Making Christ Known*, 231.

and because "the whole world is under the control of the evil one," even religious people are in need of Christ's redemption.[12]

An evangelical theology will embrace this assessment. However, this assessment continues, "We, therefore, have no warrant for saying that salvation can be found outside Christ or apart from an explicit acceptance of his work through faith." An evangelical theology of religions will embrace this conclusion, but only up to the disjunctive. While evangelical theology does claim that salvation for all is based upon the work of Christ, it acknowledges that some, presumably Abraham and Moses, for example, are saved without explicit knowledge of his work. In this sense, an evangelical theology of religions must go beyond the Lausanne movement of 1974–1989. While the deity of Jesus Christ and the atonement, made possible because of his death and resurrection, are foundational, and while explicit acceptance of his work may be required to be a Christian, salvation is not limited to Christians. God is at work in the entire cosmos, not just the Christian church.

Let us return to our fourth scenario introduced in the previous essay. This individual was in Janakpur, Nepal, in the nineteenth century, and according to the scenario had no knowledge of Jesus Christ, nor was he familiar with Abraham and the faith traditions that derive from Abraham. According to evangelical theology, this individual is not a Christian, nor is he an anonymous Christian. However, according to the scenario, this individual concluded that God does exist and has specific moral expectations of God's followers. Furthermore, he realized that his right standing before God is not the result of his performing ritual offerings, but is based upon the mercy and grace of God. The individual believed that God is holy, just, all-powerful, and so forth. According to the scenario, the individual realized that he was not worthy to stand in the presence of God, yet God desired a relationship with him. In the scenario, his knowledge of God was not based on the teaching of the local priests but upon contemplating the cosmos and carefully attending to his own conscience. While his culture and religious background fostered an attitude of seeking God, his answers were primarily found as he considered what we have referred to as general revelation. Part of this revelation may have been latent revelation, which had been preserved by oral tradition before it became part of the teachings of his own religion. In the previous essay we asked, is it possible that he may appropriately respond to the revelation he has at hand such that God might assign salvation based upon the work of the cross of Jesus Christ? Is it possible that this individual possessed an appropriate faith?[13] Evangelical

12. Ibid., 235.
13. "For by [faith] the men of old received divine approval" (Heb 11:2).

theology must acknowledge that it is possible, given this scenario and the biblical evidence of salvation given to individuals between Noah and Abraham and beyond. Furthermore, given the flexibility of progressive dispensationalism, God may accept his faith as appropriate even though he has no knowledge of Jesus Christ. As a result, the evangelical response is not necessarily bleak, for while evangelical theology is Christocentric, it also is Trinitarian. The work of God is not limited to the atoning work of Jesus Christ, but includes the work of the Spirit by which God draws individuals into community. It is possible that the individual from Janakpur arrived at his understanding of God and himself via the cosmos and self-examination because of the moving of the Spirit of God, much like Abraham or Moses arrived at appropriate faith.

We must consider one last scenario. Our last individual has the last name of Singh. While he was born in India, as a young man he traveled to the United States and is now a faithful, devout member of the Nanak Sar Gurdwara in Fresno, California. Even though he has lived in North America for many years, his knowledge of Christianity is filtered through his Sikh worldview. He is ignorant of the atoning work of Jesus Christ. However, like our individual from Janakpur, he has come to understand God as holy, just, all-powerful, and merciful. He understands that God desires to have a special relationship with him and that relationship is based in God's mercy and grace, not his membership in the Khalsa.[14] Mr. Singh came to an understanding similar to the one reached by our individual from Janakpur. While all thought project scenarios are hypothetical, they are still real possibilities. It is conceivable that this individual, while in North America, might embrace a worldview closer to one held by his counterpart in Janakpur rather than a worldview held by someone attending Campus Bible Church, also in Fresno. A progressive dispensationalist would allow that rather than dealing with Mr. Singh as if he had a strong knowledge of Christ's work, as his North American neighbor might who attends Campus Bible Church, God may interact with Mr. Singh in ways more consistent with the ways God dealt with those after Noah but before Abraham. The same Spirit who illuminates individuals to understand their sinfulness before God and how the atoning work of Christ is applied to them by God such that they appropriately respond to the New Testament message also illuminates those whose current available revelation is limited to general revelation.

---

14. Those of the Sikh tradition who desire membership in the Khalsa undergo a special baptism and are required to wear five specific items: *kachh* (a pair of underwear), *kanghā* (a wooden comb), *karā* (a steel bracelet), *kes* (uncut hair), and the *kirpān* (dagger). (McLeod, *Sikhs*, 45).

Our fifth and final general observation draws attention to the pragmatic nature of evangelical theology. Evangelical theology is church oriented and seeks to be practical. Therefore, an evangelical theology of religions must be able to address, not only a theoretical assessment and response to faith traditions as religions, but also faith traditions practiced by individuals. According to evangelical theology, God seeks individuals, not institutions, such as religions. As a result, an evangelical theology of religions will focus on individuals and their relationship or community with God. As human institutions, religions themselves are not the focus of an evangelical theology of religions. The focus is upon individuals who practice other religions. While the Christian Scriptures clearly indicate, "if one believes in Jesus Christ, then one is saved," and "for all have sinned and fallen short of the glory of God," the Bible also presents a merciful, just God who knows the intent of the heart, the inner being, and judges based on that. An evangelical theology of religions seeks to understand God's potential interactions with individuals of non-Christian religions, and describes how evangelicals ought to interact with those individuals. It must strive to understand the intent of a worshipper and be capable of asking practical questions such as, is it possible that the God worshiped by an individual member of another religion is the same God who reached out and provided the means of reestablished community through Jesus Christ? Or, what can the evangelical church learn about spirituality or practices of spirituality from an individual outside of the Christian church? Questions such as these do not solicit easy answers.

In order for evangelicals to develop a theology of religions consistent with their fundamental beliefs and the above general observations, two elements are critical. First, a broader understanding of the value of general revelation is necessary. General revelation, including latent revelation, provides an explanation of how non-Christian traditions or individuals within those traditions can possibly possess knowledge of God and other spiritual insights. Second, evangelicals must increase their participation in interreligious dialogue if they are to gain any understanding of individuals from other faith traditions. While some may claim that interreligious dialogue is not part of a theology of religions, given their emphasis on individuals, dialogue is crucial for evangelicals. Dialogue provides the opportunity to gain an understanding of others. Hence, participation in interreligious dialogue seems to be a necessary condition in order to make appropriate assessments of those who belong to other traditions. These elements form the focal points of the next two sections of this essay.

Expanding General Revelation

North American evangelicalism has begun its struggle to work through the issues of a theology of religions. This project has seen some of those birth pangs, but the focus of this project has been on whether the notion of general revelation can be helpful as evangelicals develop their own theology in this area. The position that has emerged claims that general revelation can be helpful, but it will require evangelicals to embrace a new perspective about general revelation. They must broaden their understanding of the value of general revelation. Its value is greater than merely providing judgment. General revelation is not an insignificant form of revelation.

We have seen that North American evangelical theology, though diverse, exhibits three common threads: it is committed to the Christian Scriptures, it is evangelistic, and it exhibits a level of theological tolerance absent in other forms of conservative Protestant Christianity. While other forms of Christianity may also be committed to the Scriptures, for evangelicals the commitment is based on their understanding that it is the inerrant, inspired written word of God.[15] The Bible is the result of divine special revelation. As a result, the biblical materials must play a major role for evangelicals developing a theology of religions. Furthermore, we have seen evangelicals, such as J. P. Moreland, maintain that *sola scriptura* does not entail that all truth is found in the Scriptures. There are true propositions that are not found in the Bible. We also have seen that evangelicals are evangelistic because they understand that human history is also redemptive history. God desires community with creation and is working to reestablish that relationship, which was lost in the fall. Evangelicals understand the agency by which God provides that reestablishment to be Jesus Christ. It is in Jesus Christ that God has bridged the estrangement between the Creator and the created. Furthermore, the Christ-event is not only sufficient for reestablishing community for some, but it is cosmic. Its work of atonement is for all creation. Hence, the evangelical proclamation of the good news is cosmic. Evangelical theology exhibits a level of theological tolerance. Not only is the movement itself theologically diverse, but it acknowledges that other faith traditions may possess religious truths, so long as those claims are consistent with the biblical materials. Since

---

15. The Evangelical Theological Society cites two doctrinal criteria in its constitution. "Article III. Doctrinal Basis. The Bible alone, and the Bible in its entirely, is the Word of God written and is therefore inerrant in the autographs. God is a Trinity, Father, Son, and Holy Spirit, each an uncreated person, one in essence, equal in power, and glory" (http://www.etsjets.org/about/constitution/). While many Christians today challenge these doctrinal criteria, the defense of either lies outside the scope of this project.

the biblical materials are God's inerrant, inspired written word, when properly interpreted, they present religious truth. However, evangelicals do not believe they are the sole guardians or advocates of spiritual truths. These three benchmarks of North American evangelicalism provide the basis for suggesting that evangelicals can develop an optimistic theology of religions, but they must be agnostic regarding precisely how God will bring all to pass and the wideness of God's mercy.

The notion of general revelation is capable of making sense of the various religious faith traditions and avoids assuming other traditions are without hope or truth. General revelation refers to God's unveiling that is available to all persons and stands in contrast to special revelation, but when properly understood is consistent with special revelation. When we consider general revelation, we typically think of nature, human conscience or reason, God's providence, and the general working of the Spirit of God. The Scriptures attest to general revelation, and evangelicals, as we have seen in the previous essays, have considered it as they have worked to develop an evangelical theology of religions. Some of the most creative and promising work by evangelicals in this area is being done from a pneumatological approach.[16] Apart from the movement of God, there cannot be any theology. Evangelicals working within the discipline of philosophy have also contributed much, which aids in the development of an evangelical theology of religions. However, there is an aspect that falls under the category of general revelation, which has not been adequately explored by evangelicals and which may provide much help in the development of an evangelical theology of religions. This aspect is the latent knowledge from original revelations that were preserved through oral traditions and potentially preserved in the written scriptures of other faith-traditions. While the Noahic covenant promises that God will never destroy the created order by flood, the covenant is much richer than this. As we saw in the previous essay, God is reaching out to all of creation through this covenant. It is conceivable that God's interaction with Noah, for example, was developed into oral traditions, and these oral traditions were transmitted down through Noah's descendants. That transmission from one generation to the next may have become part of the warp and woof of subsequent human conscience. As a

---

16. Some evangelicals do view this movement as potentially problematic. "There are an increasing number of theologians who want to separate pneumatology from Christology. According to this view, if pneumatology is divorced from Christology then a new understanding of Christianity's relationship to the world religions might emerge" (Cole, *He Who Gives Life*, 199). While Cole's own position on the *filioque* debate is more Eastern than Western, he maintains, "in the economy of salvation pneumatology must not be divorced from Christology."

result, latent revelation may have been preserved in that aspect of general revelation known as conscience. Furthermore, it is also plausible that this latent revelation may have been partly preserved in some of the earliest written texts such as the Vedas.[17] While the source may have been lost, elements of the message may have been preserved and God, being God, is capable of breaking through and communicating even through these fractured remnants. As a result, we would expect to find remnants of latent revelation in other ancient traditions.[18]

Furthermore, we suggested in the previous essays that progressive dispensationalism offers several interesting and viable elements for the development of an evangelical theology of religions. This theological stance acknowledges that God engages individuals differently depending on the extent of their available revelation. While Robert Saucy, a major advocate of progressive dispensationalism, agrees with the previous sentence, he denies the following sentence. Since God engages individuals in ways that reflect their available revelation, it follows that if an individual responds appropriately to general revelation, if that is all they have, their response may be counted as appropriate faith. As a result, the notion of general revelation is a major asset for evangelicals as they develop their own theology of religions. Saucy, and others within the evangelical camp, as well as other theologies, object and claim that even with the existence of general revelation, the human race is incapable of appropriately responding to it because they are spiritually dead. The effects of the fall are not only cosmic, but also total. However, this response seems inconsistent with their acknowledgement that the Spirit of God must illuminate any revelation if that revelation is to

---

17. "In the beginning the Golden Embryo arose. Once he was born, he was the one lord of creation. He held in place the earth and this sky. Who is the god whom we should worship with the oblation? He who gives life, who gives strength, whose command all the gods, his own, obey; his shadow is immortality—and death. Who is the god whom we should worship with oblation? He who by his greatness became the one king of the world that breathes and blinks, who rules over his two-footed and four-footed creatures—who is the god whom we should worship with the oblation?" (Doniger, trans., *Rig Veda* [10.121.1–3], 27).

18. For example, three basic approaches have been taken to explain similarities found between Indian thought and Biblical concepts. Following Justin Martyr's notion of *logos spermatikos*, K. P. Aleaz is an example of the first basic approach (Aleaz, *Role of Pramānas in Hindu Christian Epistemology*; Aleaz, *Gospel of Indian Culture*; and Aleaz, *Christian Thought through Advaita Vedā*). J. N. Farquhar and his optimistic fulfillment theology illustrate the second approach (Farquhar, *Crown of Hinduism*). Also see Appasamy, *Temple Bells* for this approach. The third approach uses general revelation to find points of theological or philosophical convergence. This position is illustrated by work of P. Johanns, and represents the approach suggested as possible in the above discussion (Greeff, ed., *To Christ through the Vedanta*). Also see Hooker, *Themes in Hinduism and Christianity*.

be properly understood, and that same Spirit is capable of engaging individuals who have no knowledge of the Christian gospel.

From an evangelical perspective, there is little question whether the fall was cosmic, and because of the fall it is impossible for humans to be righteous before God on their own. The human race, from an evangelical perspective, cannot restore the broken fellowship. However, this does not entail that humans cannot respond appropriately to general revelation, including latent revelation preserved by oral tradition and later incorporated into sacred texts. The key does not lie with the creation, with human beings, but with the Creator. Revelation, whether special or general, is God revealing something that otherwise could not be known by the created. It is God who is communicating. It is God who is illuminating the communication. For evangelicals, God is still communicating through the written and living Word. If God is capable of communicating today through these communiqués, then why should we think God could no longer communicate through nature or an individual's conscience or even other sacred texts that may include latent revelation? If evangelicals believe, as they do, that God is able to break through human sinfulness and communicate through the written Word, then is it not possible that the same God could use general revelation to break through and touch an individual who does not have access to that written Word? God is not silent just because the created is out of fellowship and lacks information that most evangelicals take for granted. It is still the same God who illuminates "God so loved the world . . .," which results in a declaration of faith, that illuminates an individual who upon examining the visible creation perceives God's power and divine nature (Rom 1:20). If the one communicating is the same and is not limited by the method of the communiqué, and if God does successfully use Scripture to communicate today with the created, then the divine can still reveal through general revelation. General revelation cannot be viewed as an inferior revelation. It is one of God's communiqués.

Interreligious Dialogue

The twenty-first century brings many new challenges for all faith traditions. Some of those pressing issues are problems faced by all traditions. What do we do about ecology? What do we do about poverty? How can faith traditions best approach the devastation of AIDS? What do we do with the increased secularization of our communities? These social issues require a global approach if progress is to be made concerning them. This global approach will require representative members of many faith traditions working together.

However, only when each faith tradition struggles through and begins to formulate its own theology of religions can the leaders of exhibit the appropriate respect and trust that is necessary to have significant dialogue, resulting in progress regarding such social issues. As long as mistrust and misunderstanding exist among members of differing religions, mutual global solutions will be wanting. As a result, the development of a theology of religions is foundational for tackling some of the contemporary social issues.

A theology of religions requires an appraisal of other faith traditions and individuals within those traditions.[19] For the evangelical, this appraisal must be done from an evangelical perspective. However, evangelicals cannot assume an either/or, us/them mentality as they engage followers of non-Christian traditions and the ideas advocated by these individuals. An evangelical perspective must leave open the possibility that members of other faith traditions possess truth, may enlighten evangelicals in some area(s) of spirituality, and may be in community with God. Yet, evangelical theology cannot simply embrace all religious positions as equal or, even, acceptable. Like the Bereans (Acts 17), evangelicals believe they must examine what those outside the Christian faith are advocating. Part of this assessment by evangelicals requires comparing the claim statements in question with the Scriptures. Evangelicals do hold the Scriptures to be the final authority in spiritual issues. However, this comparison is not necessarily without problems. Because the worldviews and cultures behind some world religions are so different from those of most North American evangelicals, a necessary element of their assessment must be interaction and dialogue with followers of those faith traditions. For evangelicals, dialogue is essential for their theology of religions. Some Christian traditions are quite familiar and comfortable with other worldviews, and dialogue may not be necessary for these traditions. However, North American evangelicals, for whatever reason, tend to be unfamiliar with those whose systems are different from their own. As a result, until dialogue is entered into, evangelicals cannot adequately assess the claim statements of other world traditions.[20] Through interaction and dialogue, evangelicals may be in a

---

19. This is part of the reason that this current volume, *An Evangelical Theology of Religions*, follows a volume called *Philosophically Thinking about World Religions*.

20. For example, throughout this project, we have used the word "salvation." Different worldviews and cultures may use the same terms, but upon examination it may be discovered the meanings are very different. For North American evangelicals, this term points to both the present and future community with God in which an individual is realized fully. Other traditions may use the same term, but it may point to a loss of individualization. Or, upon examination, evangelicals may discover that the same proposition is being expressed, but because of cultural differences it is expressed via different words and pictures. This understanding can only be obtained through dialogue.

better position to assess accurately those claim-statements held by individuals of other faith traditions.

Interreligious dialogue provides an opportunity for evangelicals to engage in dialogue with adherents of other faith traditions. Evangelicals such as David Hesselgrave and Terry Muck have encouraged their fellow evangelicals to participate in such dialogues; but many evangelicals have not experienced interreligious dialogue. Many evangelicals have failed to see this opportunity as one of high priority. This failure may be partly due to an evangelical misconception about how interreligious dialogues work. Given their the tendency to think dualistically and the lack of experience in such dialogues, evangelicals may be prone to have a pessimistic attitude toward the process or those who engage in such dialogue.

While some objections to interreligious dialogue are based on misconceptions or ignorance, other objections have more theoretical or practical bases.[21] At a recent philosophy conference, the following argument was presented:

> In a free society, some members will choose to embrace a faith-tradition, a religion.
>
> Furthermore, not all members who choose to embrace religion will embrace the same religion or the same understanding of a given religion.
>
> Therefore, in a free society we will have a diverse religious mix among its members.

From this it was concluded that meaningful dialogue is a necessary condition in a free society for a good society. Two major objections were raised concerning this line of reasoning. First, it was claimed that a meaningful dialogue requires a willingness to engage another and that both parties must be open to changing their stances. The objection continued that religious people, specifically evangelicals, are not open to such change. Hence, devoutly religious individuals cannot engage in meaningful interreligious dialogue. The second objection was that even if an individual could engage in such a discussion, most would not because it makes them vulnerable:

---

21. The objections discussed below were raised in response to two of my papers recently presented at different conferences. The first paper was "An Interim Outline of Theology of Religions: A Proposed Evangelical Perspective," presented at the Central Valley Philosophical Association meeting in Visalia, California, in October 2007. The program title then was "The Free Society and the Good Society." The second paper was "Teaching Them to Obey: Interim Theology of Religions," presented at the Evangelical Theological Society meeting in San Diego, California, in November 2007. The program theme then was "Teaching Them to Obey."

they risk hearing something that would cause them to reconsider their own position. This vulnerability is dangerous. Hence, they would not engage in such dialogues. The first objection may be taken as a theoretical objection, whereas the second is a practical objection.

First, it is unclear that the a priori assumption that "meaningful dialogue requires a willingness to change" is correct. However, dialogue is not debate. In a debate, one enters the fray in order to win, but this is not necessarily true of some dialogues. In a Socratic dialogue, a participant enters the dialogue with the understanding that he or she may be incorrect regarding some relevant issue. Hence, a participant engages in dialogue as a means of pursuing truth and is willing to experience a global change (i.e., conversion to a new worldview) should the evidence justify such a move. In fact, one enters a Socratic dialogue with the hope of discovering truth in order to change from a false belief to a truth belief. Global change is the desired outcome of such dialogue. For example, as an epistemological fallibilist, I understand that I have been and can still be wrong on any number of beliefs that I hold to be true. This includes those claim statements that I hold to be properly basic beliefs. A willingness to listen and to learn from others is an important consequence of my fallibilism. Paul suggests that if one could disprove the resurrection of Jesus Christ, then we should abandon the Christian faith (1 Cor 15). Evangelicals, of all people, should be known as people who place truth over tradition. Interreligious dialogue may lead to global change, but global change is not entailed by the event of dialogue. Even in a Socratic dialogue, global change should not occur until truth is discovered, which may not happen in any given dialogue. This does not mean that one must remain steadfast until total truth is obtained. As Karl Popper pointed out, the key in some cases is moving toward the truth.

Another form of the theoretical objection to interreligious dialogues draws upon the fact that dialogue does entail at least the possibility of local change (i.e., while the worldview is unaltered, an element of that worldview is impacted). While some dialogues may have a goal of changing someone's stance, there exist forms of meaningful dialogues in which the purpose is simply to clarify a position. Some may engage in a given dialogue in order to understand better their own position or possibly that of another tradition. However, it must be pointed out that even in these types of dialogue a change might occur. After all, I may have a particular stance on the faith-tradition x; I may believe x to be a false religion. For example, it does not lead to community with God as it proclaims. Furthermore, upon dialogue with a member of x, I may still believe x is false. However, I may now appreciate a particular aspect of that tradition. Hence, change has occurred. So the objection may be modified to suggest that "meaningful dialogue" may entail at least a local change but does not entail a global change. So on one level, the theoretical objection may have raised an important point. Meaningful dialogue cannot take place with parties who are not willing to listen and learn from one another. This point seems to be true. Evangelicals must embrace a positive or optimistic stance toward interreligious dialogue in which they are willing to listen and learn from those of other traditions.

The second or practical objection to interreligious dialogue is equally forceful and is implied by the first objection. As a colleague pointed out, "Entering dialogue makes one vulnerable; dialogue really does involve the risk of hearing something that may indeed change us." This colleague explains:

> if evangelicals, or anyone else, enter dialogue, the very entry into and participation makes one vulnerable to change, and so the willingness to enter dialogue *ipso facto* involves the willingness to change. So I am agreeing with [the previous objection] that willingness to change is necessary for true dialogue, but disagreeing that evangelicals enter dialogue with no real willingness to change . . . People know intuitively that if they listen, they may be affected by what they hear, and they will not be able to completely control the effect.[22]

For example, as I engage in dialogue with a member of some other faith-tradition, I may discover a truth that I did not expect. Such vulnerability may lead to a global change, or it may be more localized. I may discover that the followers of a given religion are not at all the type of person they are portrayed to be by the media or my pastor. They are human beings like me. They face the same challenges of life as I do. They are committed to their faith tradition just as I am. They are . . ., and the comparison goes on.

I may find the practical side of dialogue exposes me to new ideas that challenge my system and thus makes me vulnerable. As a result, the objection claims those who are very committed to a given faith tradition will not enter into dialogue. However, is it being "very committed" that leads them to not engage in dialogue, or is it fear of being vulnerable or fear of being asked a question for which they lack an answer or, possibly, a lack of confidence in their own message? Both of these objections—the theoretical and the practical—point to real issues; however, neither undermine a call for engaging in dialogue. If evangelicals wish to develop an evangelical theology of religions, they must be willing to make themselves vulnerable and be open to learn from others. The key for evangelicals is to be open and then examine the Scriptures, testing what is heard (Acts 17).

22. James Druley, e-mail message to author, October 29, 2007.

While it may be the case that evangelicals have been reluctant to make themselves vulnerable, evangelicals are not any different from other faithful members of a given faith tradition. Most who are committed to some stance find change or vulnerability difficult. But in spite of this general reluctance, unlike some other forms of conservative Christianity, evangelicalism has a record of modifying and accommodating in areas where accommodation does not violate its core beliefs. (This ability to change and to remain faithful to core beliefs is illustrated by evangelicals' development of progressive dispensationalism.) As a result, these objections do not undermine the proposal of engaging in meaningful dialogue with members of other faith-traditions.

However, other possible objections can be raised to the proposal for greater evangelical involvement in interreligious dialogue, and they may be introduced by the following questions. Do such dialogues produce new converts? How can evangelicals rejoice in religious diversity, which is part of the mission statement for some interreligious dialogue groups?[23]

The first question may assume that the only legitimate way to relate to members of other faith traditions (the only way to obey the Great Commission) is to proselytize. By their very nature, interreligious dialogues should not have proselytizing as their goal; however, interreligious dialogues and evangelism are not incompatible. Frequently, before evangelism can take place, objections to, concerns about, and misunderstandings of religions (whether Christian or non-Christian) must be addressed. Many in our contemporary culture refuse to entertain even elements of a Christian perspective. Dialogue can set the stage for a sort of preevangelism; in this preevangelism a worldview is offered that's conducive to the gospel message. Dialogue may allow a participant to develop an understanding of a gracious, merciful, loving God. Furthermore, any pre-evangelism or evangelistic efforts must rest ultimately on an understanding that it is God who is sovereign, and without God moving upon the heart of an individual, no true salvation will be realized. Our responsibility, from an evangelical perspective, is not to save anyone, but to be faithful and obedient, sharing the good news and allowing God to do with our obedience what God chooses to do. Consequently, evangelicals, in spite of their emphasis on evangelism, must be content to engage in meaningful dialogue and to leave the results of that dialogue to God.

The second question is more problematic; how do evangelicals respond to religious diversity? Can evangelicals rejoice in the faith diversity of our

---

23. For example the mission statement for the Fresno Multifaith Exchange reads: "(1) The context of the program is one of rejoicing in the faith diversity of the Fresno community."

communities? On the one hand, from an evangelical perspective, the contemporary diversity is a result of the fall, and evangelicals do not embrace the notion that all religious persons are necessarily worshiping the same God or traveling up the same mountain. From this perspective, rejoicing in diversity is problematic. However, evangelicals within a fallen world are to be salt and to fulfill the Great Commission. From this perspective, evangelicals may rejoice that God has placed them in their current situations. God has provided a vehicle for fulfilling the mandate, and they can be thankful that, even in a fallen state, some still want to be engaged in God-talk. In a religiously diverse community, they can rejoice in God's sovereign providence. As we saw in the previous essay, Harold Netland suggests that any adequate theology of religions must be capable of giving a theological explanation "for the sheer fact of human religiosity."[24] Evangelicals find that explanation in both the Creator and human nature. On the one hand, we were created in God's image, so it should not be surprising that we are a people who are religious. Second, this fact points to a sovereign God who is still present and active in the creation. If we are to rejoice in diversity, we can do so only in a state of humility. "Humility means reveling in [God's] grace, not our goodness. In pressing us on to all the peoples, God is pressing us further into the humblest and deepest experience of his grace and weaning us more and more from our ingrained pride."[25] The ideal of evangelicals exhibiting humility as they engage followers those of other faith traditions in dialogue illustrates the core of their basic theology. God is actively engaged in drawing the creation back to God, and Jesus provides the model of how we, as persons, can best be part of God's activity.

This type of evangelicals' participation in interreligious dialogue intertwines their understanding of general revelation and their desire to promote the kingdom of God as taught by Jesus. Even a superficial look at the ministry of Jesus as presented by the Gospels will note that Jesus was often engaged with individuals who were outsiders.[26] The ministry of Jesus was a ministry of showing the value of those normally outside the established system of valuation. Anita Silvers and Leslie Pickering Francis offer an interesting version of the social contract theory that we might use to illustrate evangelicals'

---

24. Netland, "Theology of Religions, Missiology, and Evangelicals," 145.

25. Piper, *Let the Nations Be Glad!*, 200.

26. Matt 8:1–5—leper cleansed; 8:28–34—demons cast out; 9:1–8—paralytic healed; 9:27–34—sight to blind and speech to the dumb; 12:9–14—healed withered hand; Mark 5:25–34—woman with the issue of blood; 7:31–37—deaf-mute healed; 10:13–16—blesses little children; Luke 7:11–17—widow's son; 19:1–10—Zacchaeus the tax collector; 23:39–43—penitent thief; John 4:7–38—Samaritan woman; 8:2–11—woman caught in adultery; and 9:1–12—man born blind.

understanding, which connects interreligious dialogues and promoting the kingdom of God.[27] According to Silvers and Francis, recent versions of the social contract theory place individuals with disabilities outside the realm of justice, creating the "outlier problem." For example, they point to a Rawlsian approach. "To make the prospect of reaching agreement plausible, the parties participating in the process are presumed to be roughly equivalent to each other in strength, skills, smartness, sensibilities, and seeking sovereignty over themselves."[28] In this approach, those who have value and are part of the process to determine justice are those who exhibit homogeneity. This homogeneity principle underscores the devaluation of those "outliers" who lack homogeneity and as a result are not significant in the discussion about justice. Silvers and Francis's model attempts to rectify this problem. "Understanding contracting not in terms of people jockeying for position against one another but in terms of people developing bonds of confidence with each other dissipates the challenges made to social contract theory on behalf of disabled 'outliers.'"[29] These bonds of confidence foster trust among the participants in spite of their differences; hence, practices that enhance trust do not exclude those identified as outliers. "The mutual deference elicited by the dynamic of trusting and being trusted should induce contractors to deal respectfully rather than paternalistically with whoever becomes dependent."[30] While Silvers and Francis acknowledge developing trust is "risky and hard," the process promotes a change in attitude. "Thus, when contracting with trust, contractors will not ask what they have to give over to other people to secure advantage. They will instead ask what they must change about themselves ... so that others can be confident in them."[31] As Silvers and Francis conclude, their proposal "is a society that empowers vulnerable people both to trust and to be trusted."[32]

How does Silvers and Francis's proposal of justice through trust apply to evangelicals as they seek to develop a theology of religions? How does it apply to the issue of interreligious dialogue? Furthermore, how does it apply to general revelation for evangelicals? Let us begin with a presupposition held by many evangelicals. God's normative means of engaging and restoring creation today is through the Christian church. Given this position,

---

27. Silvers and Francis, "Justice through Trust," 40–76. For a more complete discussion see Boyd, "Divine Action/Human Replication—Applied Justice," reprinted in *Philosophically Thinking about World Religions* [x-ref].

28. Ibid., 45.

29. Ibid., 59.

30. Ibid., 70.

31. Ibid., 74–75.

32. Ibid., 76.

those engaging in God-talk who are not within the Christian church are "outliers." Given the proposal that interreligious dialogue is essential for evangelicals developing a theology of religions, evangelicals can approach dialogues with an attitude of superiority and either not engage with those outside the faith (so that no interreligious dialogue occurs, which is not really an option given the proposal) or engage in dialogue but demand that all participants keep in mind Christianity's superiority. This approach is as unsatisfactory as a Rawlsian approach is for Silvers and Francis. However, if evangelicals were to engage in dialogues using the model proposed by Silvers and Francis, then evangelicals would strive to develop trust among members participating in interreligious dialogue. It does make evangelicals vulnerable, but such an approach seems closer to the model illustrated by the ministry of Jesus. As trust is developed, defenses go down, and, as a result, evangelicals will be in a better position to evaluate the intentions of those who use different words and pictures to communicate their understanding of spiritual things. This better understanding would inform an evangelical theology of religions.

Furthermore, this approach to interreligious dialogue by evangelicals connects to what we have said about general revelation in two ways. First, Paul, for example, clearly sees a connection between general revelation and justice (Rom 1). As we pointed out earlier, the first Lausanne conference claimed that general revelation provided justice such that no person could claim God to be unfair. However, we objected to the theory of justice assumed by that conference. The trust model provides a different view of justice. Second, the notion of general revelation, as developed above, provides an explanation of why "outliers" may have something to share at the religious round table.

If evangelicals are to develop their own theology of religions, they must acknowledge that the vast majority of persons do not live in an environment that fosters acceptance of the gospel message. This may include individuals born and raised in North America. The Scriptures do teach the end for some will be the lake of fire.[33] Yet, because of the mercy and justice of God, evangelicals remain hopeful for those less fortunate. While no religion saves, not even Christianity, evangelicals remain optimistic that God's glory will be magnified by restoring to community those whom are least expected. In 1976, Dr. Hesselgrave challenged evangelicals to become engaged in interreligious dialogue. He said, "Unless as evangelicals we are willing to risk locking ourselves in a closet of monologue where we speak primarily to one another, the question for us is not, 'Shall we engage in dialogue?' but,

33. Rev 20:9–15.

'In what kind of dialogue shall we engage?'"[34] Unfortunately, today, not only have evangelicals not decided what kind of dialogue in which to participate, but they have not decided whether they want to leave their closet.

In conclusion, it is the position of this project that the notion of general revelation should enable evangelicals to develop their own theology of religions that is both consistent with its special revelation and yet optimistic toward other faith traditions. General and special revelations are God's revelations. They are God-revealing. Furthermore, both require the Spirit of God to illuminate if proper understanding of those revelations is to take place. While one type of revelation may contain fewer details because of the notion of progressive revelation, both are God's revelation, and the Spirit is capable of working with an individual using whatever revelation might be available. In addition, this position does account for the viability of general revelation even in light of the fall. Within evangelical theology, the human race fell, not God. God, the Spirit, is still capable of using the divine means of revelation, which include general revelation. As a result, it is possible that some members of other faith traditions possess knowledge of the same God evangelicals worship. However, an evangelical theology of religions must acknowledge itself agnostic about the details of how God will accomplish the reestablishment of community with the created. In developing an evangelical theology of religions, evangelicals should not feel compelled to tie together all the loose ends. At times, the preservation of tension is preferred. Like other areas of theology, this particular field must be approached with a sense of awe, a sense of reverence, a sense of excitement as we watch God doing God-stuff. For the evangelical, theology is always about God and should lead to God.

---

34. Hesselgrave, "Evangelicals and Interreligious Dialogue," 124. Dr. Hesselgrave identifies five types of dialogue: "1) Dialogue on the nature of interreligious dialogue . . . 2) Interreligious dialogue that promotes freedom of worship and witness . . . 3) Interreligious dialogue concerned with meeting human needs . . . 4) Interreligious dialogue designed to break down barriers of distrust and hatred in the religious world . . . 5) Interreligious dialogue that has as its objective the mutual comprehension of conflicting truth claims" (ibid., 124–25).

Part 3

Application

10

The Great Commission and the Law of Love

The previous essays have established that evangelicals have begun to develop a theology of religions consistent with their core beliefs; however, it is still incomplete, and given the nature of evangelicalism it is unlikely that evangelicals will develop a definitive theology of religions. As a theological community, evangelicals are too diverse to find a single, unified voice on all relevant issues in the theology of religions other than the crucial role of Jesus Christ in God's global mission. Evangelical theology must understand that its strength is not in a monotone presentation but in an understanding of its symphonic nature: different parts, different voices joined together by their core beliefs.[1] Furthermore, it was claimed that evangelicalism not only sees itself as part of the Christian drama, but also as part of the greater drama as God draws the created order back into a relationship. While some within the Christian tradition have suggested that those who are truly seeking God in non-Christian religions are simply anonymous Christians, evangelicals view this position as a disservice to both Christianity and the other religious traditions. The uniqueness of Christianity is Jesus Christ, and an

1. In the second essay above, we defined evangelical theology as a systematic contemplation of orthodox Christian beliefs in light of Scripture, tradition, and the mission of the church, in which Scripture is understood as the norm. Clark Pinnock claims that a theology that reflects evangelicalism must be evangelical, conservative, and contemporary. It must be faithful to the gospel message. It must exhibit "an essential *fidelity* to the doctrinal structure of the biblical and Christian tradition" (Pinnock, "Evangelical Theology," 23; italics original). Furthermore Pinnock pointed out, it must demonstrate a "*responsibility* to the contemporary hearers of the Gospel whereby we seek to communicate the message meaningfully to them and apply it creatively to the modern situation." "For evangelical theology Scripture is both the primary source and the highest norm. However, the primacy of Scripture does not exclude tradition as a secondary source and norm for theology . . . Evangelical theology is also reflection on the sources of the faith and mission of the church in mutual relation. Theology should never be a merely academic enterprise, but rather the search for biblical understanding in the context of the ministry and mission of the church . . . Evangelical theology is properly 'task theology,' i.e., theology hammered out in response to the challenges posed by the Great Commission" (Davis, *Foundations of Evangelical Theology*, 44–45).

evangelical theology of religions must maintain this if it is to play its part in God's drama. We have seen that one avenue to develop such a theology is to make better use of the notion of general revelation. Furthermore, it has been suggested that God may deal with individuals based on their response to the revelation they have available to them.

Now it may be argued that if God deals with an individual based on their response to the revelation available to them, then are they not better left in their ignorance of the gospel? After all, given this position, if they do not know the details of the Christ-event, God will not judge them in the same way as God will one who is raised in a healthy Christian home or one who has the information about Jesus Christ. However, another cornerstone of evangelicalism is its commitment to evangelism, to sharing the good news, the gospel. Should evangelicals give up their missionary-evangelistic efforts and simply adopt a "live and let live" attitude toward the world? The obvious answer is NO! The proposal that this project makes toward developing an evangelical theology of religions does not minimize the importance of continuing the missionary nature of evangelical Christianity, for yet another cornerstone of evangelicalism is its high view of Scripture.

Does Scripture provide reasons for continued evangelistic and missionary outreach in the twenty-first century? Yes! While there may be other reasons for continued outreach, two are easily identified within Scripture. Both, individually, are sufficient conditions for continued outreach. First, Jesus commands that we go. In Matt 28 we find the Great Commission, which we will consider in the first section of this essay. Second, there are advantages of being a Christian in full fellowship with God. Unlike fundamentalist forms of conservative Christianity, which tend to emphasize that salvation is *from* the penalty of sin and that develop modern forms of legalism, evangelicalism emphasizes that salvation is *into* a relationship with God. For example, Christians have a unique relationship with God due to the indwelling of the Spirit of God, which produces the fruit of the Spirit (Gal 5:22–24). There is little question whether evangelicals must do a better job proclaiming what the Scripture says about the benefits of being in full fellowship with God; however, we will only consider one, the first of the fruit (love), in the second section. While there is great diversity among evangelicals on noncore issues, all evangelicals agree that Jesus Christ is the agency by which God brings restoration of fellowship. Evangelicals are also in agreement on the importance of proclaiming the good news. Furthermore, evangelicals strive to make this proclamation in ways that exhibit the love that should characterize their lives. (It is this writer's position that one of the demarcations between evangelicalism and fundamentalism is this issue of love.) In this essay we want to highlight two key passages: Matt 28 and the

Great Commission, and 1 Cor 13 and the "Law of Love." In this third task, we will highlight an interesting problem with Wittgenstein's therapeutical analysis and suggest that possibly some philosophical/theological problems are more important as problems than their solutions.

Great Commission

While the textual unit or *pericope* in which we find the Great Commission or the "final commission" begins with verse 16 of Matthew 28, our focus will consider only the last four verses of the unit. (Verses 16 and 17 provide the historical setting for the section.)

> And Jesus came and said to them, "All authority in heaven and on earth has been given to me. Go therefore and make disciples of all nations, baptizing them in the name of the Father and of the Son and of the Holy Spirit, teaching them to observe all that I have commanded you; and lo, I am with you always to the close of the age." (Matt 28:18–20)

William Hendriksen divides this text into three subsections: The Great Claim, the Great Commission, and the Great Comfort.[2]

According to Henry Alford, the language of the "great claim" references Dan 7:13–14 and is a "fulfillment of the Eternal Covenant, in the Unity of the Holy Spirit."[3] Jesus tells his disciples that all power in heaven and on earth is given to him (cf. Rom 14:9; Eph 1:20–23; Phil 2:9–11; Col 2:10; Heb 1:6; 1 Pet 3:22).

> This power is all-inclusive. It knows no limits, in its nature or its range. Already during his earthly life, Jesus had spoken and acted "with authority" . . . This authority that, although

---

2. Hendriksen, *Gospel according to Matthew*, 996. Davies and Allison, outline several other proposed ways of subdividing this text, including "Hubbard's proposal that our text exhibits the form of OT commissioning narrative: (i) introduction, (ii) confrontation, (iii) reaction, (iv) commission, (v) protest (absent from Matthew), (vi) reassurance, (vii) conclusion. [fn.] Compare Exod 3.1–4.16; Num 22.22–35; Judg 4.4–10; 1 Sam 3.1–4.1; 1 Chron 22.1–16; Ezra 1.1–5; Jer 1.1–10; Ezek 1.1–3:15; etc." (Davies and Allison, *Critical and Exegetical Commentary on the Gospel according to Saint Matthew*, 677).

3. Alford, *Greek Testament*, 1:306. "I saw in the night visions, and behold, with the clouds of heaven / there came one like a son of man, / and he came to the Ancient of Days / and was presented before him. / And to him was given dominion / and glory and kingdom, / that all peoples, nations, and languages / should serve him; / his dominion is an everlasting dominion, / which shall not pass away, / and his kingdom one / that shall not be destroyed" (Dan 7:13–14).

surprising, could not but be limited in time and space, is now made limitless by his resurrection, in which his identity as the Son is manifested and on which his continued activity through his disciples is based.[4]

The purpose of this power, according to Alford, "is to bring men to the knowledge of the truth—to work on and in the hearts, and lift them up to be partakers of the divine Nature . . . [I]t is not [to] "subdue," but make disciples of . . . all nations."[5] Because of this claim—all authority is given to Jesus Christ—the Great Commission follows.

The disciples, and by extension all subsequent believers, are to be going and making disciples of all nations. These verbs (i.e., "going" and "making") are to be understood as imperatives; they are commands. They are not optional. As a result, evangelicals, while developing a theology of religions, are to be doing so as they are going and making disciples. This is part of what it means to claim, as Davis did, that evangelical theology is a "task theology". The Great Commission is not optional but a command based on the fulfillment of Dan 7—all authority in heaven and on earth has been given to Jesus. Thus, any theology of religions that limits the commission must be problematic for evangelicals. As Alford points out, the command to make disciples involves "two parts—the initiatory, admissory rite, and the subsequent teaching . . . the process of ordinary discipleship is from baptism to instruction—i.e. is, admission in infancy to the covenant, and growing up into" the faith.[6]

> We must therefore understand that the present participles give baptizing and teaching as in a general way concomitants of discipling, the ceremony attending it promptly and once for all, the instruction in precepts beginning immediately, and continued without limit, from the nature of the case.[7]

Hendriksen states, "the term 'make disciples' places somewhat more stress on the fact that the mind, as well as the heart and the will must be won for God. A disciple is *a pupil, a learner*."[8] "The prophecy that in Abraham all the families of the earth will be blessed (Gen 12.3) comes to fulfillment in the mission of

---

4. Herrero, "Mission Following the Missionary Mandate of the Risen Christ," 308.
5. Alford, *Greek Testament*, 1:306.
6. Ibid., 1:307.
7. Broadus, *Commentary on the Gospel of Matthew*, 594.
8. Hendriksen, *Gospel according to Matthew*, 999 (italics original).

the church."⁹ While evangelism is an important element, it is not the major and ongoing element in discipleship. According to Warren Carter,

> The scene has significant christological elements. It is the risen Jesus who commissions the disciples. Jesus assumes the role that God plays in the prophetic commissionings. Jesus shares in God's cosmic authority and is able, like God, to be with the disciples forever, even though he is not physically present. It also has ecclesiological elements. The community of disciples, with its imperfections and doubts, is given . . . the task of continuing Jesus' mission and is reassured of Jesus' presence with them. It has ethical dimensions in urging transmission of all Jesus' teaching, which shapes and informs the community of disciples in its alternative existence.[10]

This brings us to the third of Hendriksen's subdivisions of this passage—the Great Comfort.

> Mission means "teaching," passing on what the sole teacher, Jesus, did for his disciples. The substance of the mission is Jesus' commandments. The words "everything I have commanded of you" is a phrase taken from the Bible (Exod 29:35). The "gospel of the commandments" is rooted deep in biblical thought, not only linguistically but also in its very essence. "Everything" is in keeping with the notion of perfection. In other words, the community is meant to distinguish itself from the rest of the world by its works (cf. 5:16). But Matthew goes beyond the commandments and concludes his Gospel with the promise of Jesus' continued presence. Jesus is the Immanuel, the "God with us;" his assistance, his power, his commandments and his teachings are a constant foundation of life.[11]

"Jesus' commandments are the gospel that his disciples owe to the world. They represent the Father's will to redeem his world. But they are not the will of a distant and unreachable God. On the contrary, the 'God with us'

---

9. Davies and Allison, *Commentary on the Gospel according to Saint Matthew*, 3:683. Davies and Allison furthermore state, "28.16–20, which was so important to William Carey and the nineteenth-century Protestant missionary movement, is, from the literary point of view, perfect, in the sense that it satisfyingly completes the Gospel: we could hardly improve upon it. Nothing is superfluous, yet nothing more could be added without spoiling the effect. The grand denouement, so constant with the spirit of the whole Gospel because so full of resonances with earlier passages, is, despite its terseness, almost a compendium of Matthean theology" (ibid., 3:687).

10. Carter, *Matthew and the Margins*, 549.

11. Luz, *Theology of the Gospel of Matthew*, 140.

will remain with his community always, to the end of time, helping it, teaching it, and standing by its side as it faces new challenges."[12] The Great Comfort is that while Christians are to be part of God's drama of bringing all nations into a relationship with God, we are not on our own. God is with us! In addition to the general observation Davies and Allison made, which is included in footnote 9 above, they offer three additional observations worth quoting.

> 28.16–20 expresses the meaning of Jesus' resurrection for Matthew. The resurrection is the exaltation of Jesus as Lord of all so that his cause is now universal: "All authority in heaven and on earth has been given to me; go therefore and make disciples of all nations." The resurrection is the end of an old time and the beginning of a new time: "baptizing them in the name of the Father, the Son, and the Holy Spirit." The resurrection is the vindication of the earthly Jesus, whose words and deeds must be call and command: "Teaching them to observe all that I have commanded you." And the resurrection is the act by which Jesus becomes the ever-present help of his followers: "I am with you always."[13]
>
> 28.16–20 offers a Christological concentration. V. 19 calls Jesus "the Son." The allusion to Dan 7.13–14 confirms Jesus' status as "Son of man". The statement of exaltation and authority suggests the title "Lord." "All that I have commanded you" presents Jesus as teacher. The mission to "all the nations" reminds that Jesus is the Son of Abraham (1.1) and in v. 20 Jesus is "Emmanuel," God with us (1.23).[14]
>
> The climax and crown of Matthew's Gospel is profoundly apt in that it invites the reader to end the story: 28.16–20 is an open-ended ending. Not only does v. 20a underline that the particular man, Jesus, has universal significance, but "I am with you always" reveals that he is always with his people. The result is that the believing audience and the ever-living Son of God become intimate. The Jesus who commands difficult obedience is at the same time the ever-graceful divine presence.[15]

From an evangelical perspective, continuation of the Great Commission is not optional, for it is a command binding upon Christians until the end of

---

12. Ibid., 140–41.

13. Davies and Allison, *Commentary on the Gospel according to Saint Matthew*, 3:688.

14. Ibid.

15. Ibid., 688–89.

this age. Furthermore, it is not a task given without enablement, for the one giving the command has been given all authority and power in heaven and on earth and promises to always be present.

Before we move into the second part of this essay and consider 1 Cor 13, we propose a connection. The Great Commission establishes that the church has not been mandated to *subdue* all nations, but to make *disciples*, followers of Jesus, of all nations. This is significant, for much of church history illustrates an institution attempting to subdue and control the world. Most today would agree that the Crusades of the Middle Ages were more about political attempts to control than about discipleship; though discipleship did occur in many cases, the emphasis was political. Today's crusades are often the same. Today we frequently see churches attempting to legislate Christian morality as a way of subduing rather than discipling all nations. So how do we fulfill the Great Commission without the intent of subduing all nations? First, we teach and bring individuals into a saving relationship with the Master of the Universe. This is accompanied by the initiation act of baptism, in which the individual identifies with God the Father, God the Son, and God the Holy Spirit.[16] It is then followed by a lifetime of learning. But what is to be taught in order to make a disciple of the newly initiated? We are to be teaching them to observe all that Jesus taught. One way of addressing this can be found elsewhere, where the emphasis was on justice;[17] however, an alternative way is to begin with another passage from Matthew. In chapter 22 we find the Pharisees and Sadducees combining forces, attempting to test Jesus. One of them asks, "Teacher, which is the great commandment in the law?" (verse 36). Jesus responds, "You shall love the Lord your God with all your heart, with all your soul, and with all your mind. This is the great and first commandment. And a second is like it. You shall love your neighbor as yourself. On these two commandments depend all the law and the prophets" (verses 37–40). The law of love encompasses all that Jesus taught; however, it is important to notice that Jesus's message was not limited to the topic of love. Love simply captures all that Jesus taught—a life in a vibrant relationship with God.

In Gal 6:2 Paul uses a curious phrase that he uses nowhere else in his writings. He tells us to "bear one another's burdens, and so fulfill the *law of*

---

16. Notice "in the name (singular) of the Father and of the Son and of the Holy Spirit," is a monotheism, not three separate Gods. Also, notice that the nature of baptism is for the individual to identify him- or herself with God, not to identify oneself with a particular local church.

17. Mortimer Arias provides an excellent discussion that shows how justice and the great commandment are connected in Matthew (Arias, "Church in the World," 410–18). (Also see, Boyd, "Divine Action/Human Replication—Applied Justice.")

Christ." Does this phrase, "law of Christ" simply point to love? If not, then how shall we understand the phrase? Michael Winger provides a compelling argument

> that "the law of Christ" is a way of referring to the practice which Paul believes should govern the community of believers, a practice which Paul deliberately refrains from reducing to any verbal formula. He thereby warns us that he neither invokes the old law nor replaces it with a new one, but calls instead on something wholly different in character, which is "law" only in the loose sense that, in the new world brought by Christ, it has a function like that of law in the old world. Paul uses "the law of Christ" as a name for a staple of his thought, implicit in all of his letters and explicit precisely at the end of Gal 5, vv. 13–25. In short, this is a name for living by the Spirit.[18]

Living a life that reflects the fruit of the Spirit is a life dependent upon God; Paul describes it as being filled with the Spirit in Eph 5. To love God with all your heart, with all your soul, and with your entire mind, and to love your neighbor as yourself, requires reliance upon God, the faith-rest of Hebrews. The teaching that Jesus commanded was that we must live our lives in total dependence on God.[19] God enables the believer to live a life that reflects the fruit of the Spirit, but the believer must be dependent and let God produce the fruit. The individual believer does not produce the fruit; it is something the Spirit does. It requires the believer to be a pupil, a learner of God (i.e., a disciple). The law of Christ is a life that reflects the application of the fruit of the Spirit, a life in proper relationship with God. For Paul the first element of the fruit is love. While Paul does delineate additional elements of the fruit in Gal 6, we propose that "love" in Pauline thought is a summary position, following the teaching of Jesus, that points to a life that reflects total reliance on God. That is, "the law of love" is a phrase that points to all the elements

---

18. Winger, "Law of Christ," 538.

19. We must note that the notion of dependency may conjure negative images. We may think, for example, of a relationship in which one party is dependent on another and in which the dependent party exists solely for the good or benefit of the dominant party. The dependent individual has no value apart from the dominant in this sense. However, this image is not the biblical image of dependency. Because we are created in the image of God and have free will, we have value even when we are not in a proper relationship with God. The biblical picture of God is not one of a despotic tyrant, but one who is interested in our well-being. As our Creator, God knows how to maximize our well-being and is willing to produce those characteristics in us that will make us most happy. In this sense, unlike the form, dependency serves the purpose of making us more fulfilled and happy.

of the fruit; it points to a life that is in a vibrant relationship with God—one lived by the Spirit.

The Law of Love

Within Pauline scholarship, 1 Cor 13 is seen as problematic because it appears to be a dramatic shift in the argument being constructed, especially in chapter 12 and then continued in 14.[20] "[First] Corinthians is a long deliberative argument designed to persuade the Corinthians to abandon certain fractious practices and come together as a unified body—the body of Christ."[21] "Some of the Corinthians have placed inordinate emphasis on showy displays of spirituality, especially the gift of speaking in tongues; it seems that some of them are disrupting or dominating the church's meetings by disorderly spirit-inspired utterance that is unintelligible to other members of the community."[22] An examination, such as Patterson does, of the various rhetorical styles used in Pauline literature is important and valuable for the biblical exegete; however, it is not the only way to understanding the role of 1 Cor 13 within the Pauline project. Richard Hays provides the following outline of 12:1—14:40, which he titles Spiritual Manifestation in Worship:

> Complementary Roles of Spiritual Gifts within the one body of Christ 12:1—31a
>
> Preeminence of Love 12:31b—13:13
>
> Specific Directions 14:1-40

Given this outline, verse 31 is divided; the first half of the verse is part of the discussion of spiritual gifts (chs. 12 and 14) and the last half is connected to chapter 13. This interpretation is common. David Ewert reflects this as he states, "As if to prepare us for the discussion of the 'higher gifts' in chapter 14, Paul concludes this paragraph with the exhortation to be zealous for the 'greater' gifts. Among the greater gifts is that of prophecy as will become obvious from chapter 14."[23] F. F. Bruce makes a similar division of 12:31.

> *But earnestly desire the higher gifts:* the "greater" ones (*meizona*), perhaps those which come near the head of the lists in verses 8–10, 28, and 29f. Apostleship, in the nature of the case, was

20. Patterson, "Rhetorical Gem," 87–88.
21. Ibid., 88.
22. Hays, *Interpretation*, 206.
23. Ewert, *Church in a Pagan Society*, 147.

not open to them; but they should cultivate an ambition for the other leading gifts, especially prophecy (14.1).

And I will show you a still more excellent way: this transition to chapter 13 may be rendered: "And yet beyond all this I am showing you a way" (a way to reach the highest goal, to achieve the noblest ambition), or, if we adopt the Western reading (*ei ti*, "if anything," for *eti*, "yet"): "if there is anything beyond all this, I am showing you a (the) way." This Western reading is supported in part by P[apyrus]⁴⁶, but, as P⁴⁶ is mutilated here, its precise wording (which, had it been extant, might have solved the textual problem of this sentence) is inaccessible to us.[24]

While this traditional outline of 1 Cor 12–14 is helpful, it does not adequately address the role of chapter 13, which seems out of place. We propose an alternative reading, which maintains that 12:31, as a whole, is transitional and therefore linked to chapter 13.

Paul opens this section of 1 Corinthians (chs. 12–14) not with an introduction to spiritual gifts, as most English translations present, but by simply stating, "Now concerning spiritual things."[25] In the first three verses of chapter 12, Paul is emphasizing "that those who are inspired by the Holy Spirit will speak and act in ways that glorify the lordship of Jesus."[26] Chapter 12, verses 4–30 then address those gifts that are given to individual believers to help the entire body of Christ.[27] In verse 31 Paul transitions from a discussion of spiritual things that are given to individuals (i.e., spiritual gifts) to spiritual things given to all believers. In verse 31, "Paul promises to show 'a more excellent way' than that of mere gifts. This way is the *way of love* to which the apostle devotes the next chapter in its entirety. Unless gifts are used in a spirit of love, they are of little value. Love is the most important thing of all!"[28]

Before we look at chapter 13, two points must be made explicit. First, if we accept that "the law of Christ" is Paul's shorthand for a life totally

---

24. Bruce, *I & II Corinthians*, 123–24 (italics original).

25. "The translation 'spiritual gifts,' which appears in almost all English renderings of 12:1, is an interpretive paraphrase. The Greek reads simply, 'Now concerning spiritual things'. . . The idea of gifts (*charismata*) is first introduced by Paul in verse 4" (Hays, *First Corinthians*, 207).

26. Ibid., 209.

27. Within the Corinthian church there were those who were using these gifts for self-promotion, claiming that some gifts were more important than others. A discussion of what Paul says is outside the purpose of this project, so we will simply encourage the readers to study Paul's comments.

28. Luck, *First Corinthians*, 101.

dependent upon God (i.e., a life that reflects a vibrant relationship with God), then the love passage, or law of love, in chapter 13 makes complete sense, both in the bigger argument of 1 Corinthians and in its location between chapters 12 and 14, since the law of love summarizes the law of Christ. Following the teachings of Jesus, Paul understands that the law of love highlights the problem of fractious practices and emphasizes the unity of the body. If first we must accept that "the law of Christ" is Paul's shorthand for a life totally dependent on God, then, second, we must recognize a distinction between the fruit of the Spirit (Gal 5) and spiritual gifts (1 Cor 12 and 14). Living the fruit of the Spirit results in a focus for the Christian life: being dependent upon God, one becomes more like God. Spiritual gifts are special enablements given to individuals so that the body of Christ may function in both an orderly and truly edifying way. The higher or greater gifts of 1 Cor 12:31 may be referring not to any of the "spiritual gifts" but rather to the "fruit of the Spirit." This makes the placement of chapter 13 even more consistent with the immediate context within 1 Corinthians, as well as to the overall argument of the book. Even though the Spirit provides enablements to specific individuals to make a stronger body of Christ (the church [chs. 12 and 14]), the Spirit also bestows on all believers the fruit of the Spirit, which should typify a Christ-like life. Given this reading, Paul is using the word "love" to remind the Corinthians of what it means to live a life that reflects unity and dependence on God. That is, the specific spiritual gifts must be utilized in a way that maintains the focus that Jesus taught. With this realignment focus, Paul continues in chapter 14 his exhortation to the Corinthians regarding spiritual gifts.

As we move into chapter 13 and the law of love, we must remember that the love Paul is talking about is impossible to humanly produce. We are not meant to try to produce this love. It is the fruit that the Spirit produces as one is walking in the Spirit, that is, in a vibrant relationship with God. F. F. Bruce, in his introduction to chapter 13, makes the connection with the fruit of the Spirit.

> More important than the gifts of the Spirit is "the fruit of the Spirit" (Gal. 5.23f.), the harmony of the nine graces which make up a mature Christian character and provide conclusive evidence of the Spirit's indwelling presence. First among these graces is love—the divine love which "has been poured into our hearts through the Holy Spirit which has been given to us" (Rom. 5.5), God's love for men displayed in Christ (cf. Rom. 5.8)

and now reproduced in their attitude towards him and towards one another... [T]he love described is divine love.[29]

E. P. Gould says, "Love is shown to be the chief of even the permanent graces."[30] What is that divine love like? Jesus taught and demonstrated it, and Paul expresses it this way:

> If I speak in the tongues of mortals and of angels, but do not have love, I am a noisy gong or a clanging cymbal. And if I have prophetic powers, and understand all mysteries and all knowledge, and if I have all faith, so as to remove mountains, but do not have love, I am nothing. If I give away all my possessions, and if I hand over my body so that I may boast, but do not have love, I gain nothing.
>
> Love is patient; love is kind; love is not envious or boastful or arrogant or rude. It does not insist on its own way; it is not irritable or resentful; it does not rejoice in wrongdoing, but rejoices in the truth. It bears all things, believes all things, hopes all things, endures all things.
>
> Love never ends. But as for prophecies, they will come to an end; as for tongues, they will cease; as for knowledge, it will come to an end. For we know only in part, and we prophesy only in part; but when the complete comes, the partial will come to an end. When I was a child, I spoke like a child, I thought like a child, I reasoned like a child; when I became an adult, I put an end to childish ways. For now we see in a mirror, dimly, but then we will see face to face. Now I know only in part; then I will know fully, even as I have been fully known. And now faith, hope, and love abide, these three; and the greatest of these is love. (NRSV)

"The chapter, as a whole, is not an excursus on love, but has the directest connection with the subject of spiritual gifts that is under discussion, inasmuch as the Corinthians, in their eagerness to possess the best of these, or to make it appear that what they had was the best, had forgotten this greatest gift of love."[31] Whether one has a more visible spiritual gift (wisdom and knowledge, astonishing faith) or exhibits unbelievable altruism, if one lacks love, one have nothing. "This chapter [1 Cor 13] clearly affirms that a real spirit of love for God and for our fellow men is absolutely essential, and

---

29. Bruce, *I & II Corinthians*, 124.
30. Gould, *Commentary on the Epistles to the Corinthians*, 111.
31. Ibid., 112.

without it everything else is valueless."³² Paul then describes the character of this divine love. It is patient and kind. "These two expressions of love are particularly conspicuous in God's dealings with mankind (e.g. Rom 2:4). Long-suffering and kindness are also a fruit of the Spirit (Gal 4:22)."³³ This love produced by the Spirit is not envious or does not brag or is not rude or is not self-centered, nor does it provoke anger or rejoice when wickedness occurs, but it does rejoice in the truth. Furthermore, this love covers or hides all things, "in keeping with 1 Peter 4:8, where we are told that 'love covers a multitude of sins' . . . [L]ove is always eager to believe the best . . . [It is] full of trust . . . It is ready to give an offender a second chance . . . Love remains steadfast under the burdens God asks us to bear—to endure wrongs, losses, disappointments."³⁴ "Love does not make its adherents into foolish Pollyannas. Paul's point is accurately conveyed by the NEB's translation: "there is no limit to its faith, its hope, and its endurance."³⁵

> [Paul] has shown faith, hope, and love to be greater than the charismata, because of their permanence. Now he declares love to be the greatest of these. This supremacy is owing to its comprehensiveness, being, as our Lord says, the great commandment, containing in itself the whole law; and, as Paul says, (Col. iii.14), the bond of perfectness—i.e., it so contains itself all graces, that perfectness is insured.³⁶

As Patterson concludes,

> If we take Paul at face value here, his claim is that no other modality—not even faith—is more central to Christian existence than love . . . We might notice . . . that Paul associates the experience of the Spirit very closely with love. In Romans (5:5), for

32. Luck, *First Corinthians*, 101.
33. Ewert, *Church in a Pagan Society*, 152.
34. Ibid., 153.
35. Hays, *First Corinthians*, 228.
36. Gould, *Commentary on the Epistles to the Corinthians*, 114. "In dispensationalist Christian groups, it is sometimes claimed that 'the complete' (*to teleion*) in v. 10 refers to the completion and closure of the New Testament canon, so that the charismatic gifts were only for the apostolic age and have now ceased to function in the church. This interpretation is simply nonsense. There is nothing in the passage about 'the New Testament' or about a future revocation of revelatory gifts in the church. Paul had no inkling that Israel's Scripture would be supplemented by a new collection of canonical writings. Verse 10 is simply a general maxim stating that the perfect supplants the partial. Paul's references to the abolition of the gifts (v. 8) are to be understood in light of the patently eschatological language of v. 12: the contrast between 'now' and 'then' is the contrast between the present age and the age to come" (Hays, *First Corinthians*, 229).

example, Paul claims that *what* the Holy Spirit actually imparts to those who experience it is nothing other than the love of God. Or again, in 2 Corinthians (5:13–15), Paul claims that whether he speaks rationally or whether he is "beside himself" . . . it is the love of Christ that controls him. To give oneself over to love is what it means to die to oneself and live for Christ . . . To discover Christ, and to be in Christ, is to allow the love of God to control one's whole life (2 Cor 5:14). For Paul there is indeed a way that is higher than all others. It is not faith; it is not hope, or righteousness, or holiness. For Paul, "the highest way" is love.[37]

How does 1 Corinthians 13 relate to Matthew 28 from an evangelical's perspective? In a brief article "The Whole Gospel in One Word: Love," Craig Bubeck poignantly makes the connection.[38] Furthermore, he develops three subpoints: "1. God preemptively loved the world . . . 2. God's wrath is not an exception or counterpart to his love . . . 3. God the Son said that the foundational, preeminent law of the entirety of Scripture is love." What consequence does this have, given the purpose of this essay? As we are going, baptizing and teaching, we must do so in love. We must do so in a way that reflects the fruit of the Spirit. We must do so in total dependence on God. Now what is the significance of this for the development of an evangelical theology of religions?

Summary of Proposal

The question we must consider in this section is, how can we as evangelicals implement the command to proclaim the good news—baptizing and teaching—with love as we encounter those of different faith traditions? The proposal that has been presented in this volume claims that we cannot compromise the foundations of evangelicalism, yet we must view all persons as God views them. (God so loved the world that the Son was willing to die that all may have a relationship with the Master of the Universe.) We must emphasize that the development of an evangelical theology of religions cannot be viewed as a mathematical or logical proof, but rather as a philosophical or dialectical proof. Collingwood makes the following distinction.

> Mathematics and dialectic are so far alike that each begins with an hypothesis: "Let so-and-so be assumed." But in mathematics the hypothesis forms a barrier to all further thought in that direction: the rules of mathematical method do not allow us to ask

---

37. Patterson, "Rhetorical Gem," 93.
38. Bubeck, "Whole Gospel in One Word: Love," 52–55.

"Is this assumption true?" Hence mathematics, although intellectual, is not intellectual *à outrance*; it is a way of thinking, but it is also a way of refusing to think. In dialectic we not only draw the consequences of our hypotheses, but we recollect that they are only hypotheses; that is, we are free to "cancel the hypotheses," or assume the opposite and see what follows from that.[39]

First, we as an evangelical community must consider whether the evidence offered is true and whether other significant pieces of evidence should be brought to the table—evidence that might change our conclusions. Second, whereas some forms of reasoning may be viewed as exclusionary, other forms may be inclusive. For example, consider the reasoning used to answer the following question: Does 5 + 7 equal 12 or 14? One approach to this question may assume a base ten system and, as a result, the "or" would be exclusive because the answer would be 12 and only 12. However, if one does not make the assumption of a base ten, then the answer would be inclusive since 12 would be true in a base ten *and* 14 would be true in a base eight. As we develop our evangelical theology of religions, it seems best to be true to the nature of evangelicalism by being open to alternative positions on issues that are not foundational. That is, while there are positions that we cannot consider as viable because they violate foundational truths of the system, there are positions that are viable that some within the system may reject. For example, evangelicals hold a high view of Scripture. This position is foundational for evangelical Christianity; hence, one wishing to maintain an evangelical position cannot reject it. However, within evangelical thought there are different views regarding eschatology, for example. An evangelical theology of religions will be exclusivistic as it considers the means or agency by which God makes possible the relationship between the One who is holy and those who are sinners. But when considering other aspects of a theology of religions, our theology must be inclusivist; we must realize that Christians are not the only ones with religious truth. Other traditions have spiritual insights that are not inconsistent with scriptural truths, but because of our culture they have not been developed; hence, we can learn from them. For example, what does the psalmist mean when he says to meditate upon the word of God. (Evangelical Christians, for the most part, have avoided the biblical concept of meditation.) Maybe we can learn things about meditation from those who have practiced it for centuries, making appropriate modifications as needed. Evangelicalism is stronger as a theological system because of its inclusivist approach on nonfoundational issues. Furthermore, an evangelical theology of religions

39. Collingwood, *Essay on Philosophical Method*, 13–14 (italics original).

will be pluralistic, embracing all traditions in some aspects of a complete theology of religions. For example, the theology of religions is relevant to social issues such as poverty, crime, unemployment, homelessness, racial tension, or public education. An evangelical theology of religions must inform the evangelical community how we can work together with all parties for the good of the community. As we have seen in previous essays, God is actively drawing individuals into a relationship, and while the agency in all cases is Jesus Christ, some of these individuals may not even know Jesus. Therefore, the development of an evangelical theology of religions, as a task theology will require not agreement but dialogue—a process of listening and sharing that promotes trust. A dialogue that is informed by Scripture, by our tradition, and by the global neighborhoods we now live in, a dialogue worked out as we are fulfilling the Great Commission in love in a way that brings glory to God.

Like Paul, we have hope for all people because of the nature and work of God to provide the means by which a vibrant relationship can exist between the Creator and the created; hence, an evangelical theology must be optimistic. It is God at work. However, because we do not have access to the "rest of the drama," we must be agnostic about the details of the final scene. An evangelical theology of religions must be worked out in a fashion that brings glory to the one who deserves it—God. This will only be possible if we understand that the Great Commission does not call for us to subdue the world, but to baptize and teach all that Jesus taught, making disciples. This requires us as evangelicals to understand what it means to walk in the Spirit and to live lives that reflect a confidence that God will do what God promises, without being dogmatic and claiming that we have more information than we actually have. As Jesus taught, we must learn that God is sovereign. It is God who judges. It is God who decides with whom to establish a relationship. It is God who provides the means. It is God who is directing the drama. We must learn to make love central to our outreach to the world. This is not a love that we produce, but a love that is produced by the Spirit of God, as we are filled with the Spirit, bringing glory to God.

Bibliography

Aleaz, K. P. *Christian Thought through Advaita Vedā*. Delhi: ISPCK, 1960.
———. *The Gospel of Indian Culture*. Calcutta: Punthi Pustak, 1994.
———. *The Role of Pramānas in Hindu Christian Epistemology*. Calcutta: Punthi-Pustak 1991.
Alford, Henry. *The Greek Testament*. 4 vols. Revised by Everett F. Harrison. Chicago: Moody Press, 1968.
Alston, William P. "Response of Hick." *Faith and Philosophy* 14 (1997) 287–88.
Anderson, Bernhard W. *Contours of Old Testament Theology*. Minneapolis: Fortress, 1999.
Anderson, John, and Henry Johnstone Jr. *Natural Deduction: The Logical Basis of Axiom Systems*. Belmont, CA: Wadsworth, 1963.
Anderson, Norman. *Christianity and World Religions: The Challenge of Pluralism*. Downers Grove, IL: InterVarsity, 1971.
Appasamy, A. J. *Temple Bells: Readings from Hindu Religious Literature*. Calcutta: Association, 1930.
Arias, Mortimer. "The Church in the World: Rethinking the Great Commission." *Theology Today* 47 (1991) 10–18.
Armstrong, D. M. *Belief, Truth, and Knowledge*. Cambridge: Cambridge University Press, 1973.
Ash, Carisa. *A Critical Examination of the Doctrine of Revelation in Evangelical Theology*. Eugene, OR: Pickwick Publications, 2015.
Augustine, Saint. *City of God*. An abridged version from the translation by Gerald G. Walsh et al. Edited by Vernon J. Bourke. Garden City, NY: Image, 1958.
———. "On Grace and Freewill." In *Nicene and Post-Nicene Fathers*, vol. 5, *Augustine: Anti-Pelagian Writings*, edited by Philip Schaff. 1st ser. Peabody, MA: Hendrickson, 2004.
Baillie, John. *The Idea of Revelation in Recent Thought*. Bampton Lectures in America 7. New York: Columbia University Press, 1956.
Barnes, Gary. "Why Don't They Listen?" Interview with John Stott. *Christianity Today* 47/9 (2003) 50–52. http://www.christianitytoday.com/ct/2003/september/2.50.html/.
Barth, Karl. *Church Dogmatics* I/1, *The Word of God*. Edited by G. W. Bromiley and T. F. Torrance. London: T. & T. Clark, 2004.
Bauer, Walter. *A Greek-English Lexicon of the New Testament and Other Early Christian Literature*. Translated by William Arndt and Wilbur Gingrich. Chicago: University of Chicago Press, 1974.

Bavinck, Herman. *The Philosophy of Revelation*. Stone Lectures 1908. 1909. Reprint, Eugene, OR: Wipf & Stock, 2003.

Beecher, Willis J. *The Prophets and the Promise*. Grand Rapids: Baker, 1963.

Berkhof, Louis. *The History of Christian Doctrines*. Grand Rapids: Baker, 1937.

Berkhof, Louis. *Systematic Theology*. Grand Rapids: Eerdmans, 1974.

Black, Matthew. *Romans*. 2nd ed. New Century Bible Commentary. Grand Rapids: Eerdmans, 1989.

Blaising, Craig, and Darrell Bock. *Dispensationalism, Israel and the Church: The Search for Definition*. Grand Rapids: Zondervan, 1992.

———. *Progressive Dispensationalism*. Wheaton, IL: BridgePoint, 1993.

Bloesch, Donald G. *Essentials of Evangelical Theology*. Vol. 1, *God, Authority, and Salvation*. 2nd ed. Peabody, MA: Prince, 1998.

———. "The Finality of Christ and Religious Pluralism." *Touchstone: A Journal of Ecumenical Orthodoxy* 4/3 (1991) 5–9.

Blue, J. Ronald. "Untold Billions: Are They Really Lost?" *Bibliotheca Sacra* 138/552 (1981) 338–50.

Bock, Darrell. "The Reign of the Lord Christ." In *Dispensationalism, Israel and the Church: Search for Definition*, edited by Craig Blaising and Darrell Bock, 38–45. Grand Rapids: Zondervan, 1992.

Boettner, Loraine. *The Reformed Doctrine of Predestination*. Philadelphia: Presbyterian & Reformed, 1974.

Boice, James Montgomery. *Romans*. Vol. 3, *God and History: Romans 9–11*. Grand Rapids: Baker, 1993.

Bonevac, Daniel. *Deduction: Introductory Symbolic Logic*. 2nd ed. Malden, MA: Blackwell, 2003.

Bonhoeffer, Dietrich. *Creation and Fall; Temptation: Two Biblical Studies*. Translated by John Fletcher. New York: Macmillan, 1959.

Borland, James A. "A Theologian Looks at the Gospel and World Religions." *Journal of the Evangelical Theological Society* 33 (1990) 3–11.

Boyd, Robert. "The Christian Relationship with the World: Evangelicalism and World Religions." *Direction Journal: A Mennonite Brethren Forum* 39 (2010) 244–54.

———. "Divine Action/Human Replication—Applied Justice." *Evangelical Review of Society and Politics* 6.1/2 (2012) 61–76.

———. "The Nature of Religious Truth." *Perspective in Religious Studies* 41/1 (2014) 31–48.

Breshears, Gerry. "New Directions in Dispensationalism." Unpublished paper presented to the 43rd annual meeting of the Evangelical Theological Society in Kansas City, MO in November 1991.

Bright, John. "The Book of Jeremiah: Its Structure, Its Problems, and Their Significance for the Interpreter." *Interpretation* 9 (1955) 259–76.

———. *Jeremiah*. Anchor Bible 21. Garden City, NY: Doubleday, 1965.

Broadus, John A. *Commentary on the Gospel of Matthew*. American Commentary on the New Testament. Philadelphia: American Baptist Publication Society, 1886.

Bruce, F. F. *The Letter of Paul the Apostle to the Romans: An Introduction and Commentary*. Tyndale New Testament Commentaries 6. Grand Rapids: Eerdmans, 1985.

———. *I & II Corinthians*. New Century Bible Commentary. Grand Rapids: Eerdmans, 1971.

Brueggemann, Walter. *Theology of the Old Testament: Testimony, Dispute, Advocacy.* Minneapolis: Fortress, 1997.
Brunner, Emil. *The Divine Imperative.* Translated by Olive Wyon. Philadelphia: Westminster, 1947.
———. *Revelation and Reason: The Christian Doctrine of Faith and Knowledge.* Translated by Olive Wyon. Philadelphia: Westminster, 1946.
Bubeck, Craig. "The Whole Gospel in One Word: Love." *Christianity Today* (June 28, 2013). http://www.christianitytoday.com/ct/2013/june/whole-gospel-in-one-word.html/.
Burns, J. Lanier. "Israel and the Church of a Progressive Dispensationalist." In *Three Central Issues in Contemporary Dispensationalism: A Comparison of Traditional and Progressive Views,* edited by Hebert W. Bateman IV, 263–91. Grand Rapids: Kregel, 1999.
Calvin, John. *Epistles of Paul the Apostle to the Galatians, Ephesians, Philippians, Colossians.* Translated by T. H. L. Parker. Calvin's Commentaries. Grand Rapids: Eerdmans, 1974.
Carruthers, Gregory H. *The Uniqueness of Jesus Christ in the Theocentric Model of the Christian Theology of World Religions: Elaboration and Evaluation of the Position of John Hick.* Lanham, MD: University Press of America, 1990.
Carter, Warren. *Matthew and the Margins: A Sociopolitical and Religious Reading.* The Bible & Liberation. Maryknoll, NY: Orbis, 2000.
Chafer, Lewis Sperry. *Salvation: A Clear Doctrinal Analysis.* Grand Rapids: Zondervan, 1972.
———. *Systematic Theology.* 8 vols. Dallas: Dallas Seminary Press, 1969.
Chisholm, Robert B. "'To Whom Shall You Compare Me?' Yahweh's Polemic against Baal and the Babylonian Idol-gods in Prophetic Literature." In *Christianity and the Religions: A Biblical Theology of World Religions,* edited by Edward Rommen and Harold Netland, 56–71. Evangelical Missiological Society Series 2. Pasadena, CA: William Carey Library, 1995.
Clark, Kelly James. "Perils of Pluralism." *Faith and Philosophy* 14 (1997) 303–20.
Clement of Alexandria. *Stromata,* book I, chapter I. In *The Ante-Nicene Fathers,* vol. 2, edited by Alexander Roberts and James Donaldson, 299–303. Peabody, MA: Hendrickson, 2004.
Cohn-Sherbok, Dan. "Jewish Religious Pluralism." *Cross Currents* 46 (1996) 316–42.
Cole, Graham A. *He Who Gives Life: The Doctrine of the Holy Spirit.* Foundations of Evangelical Theology. Wheaton, IL: Crossway, 2007.
Collingwood, R. G. *An Essay on Philosophical Method.* Oxford: Clarendon, 1933.
Craig, William Lane. "'No Other Name': A Middle Knowledge Perspective on the Exclusivity of Salvation through Christ." *Faith and Philosophy* 6 (1989) 172–88.
Cranfield, C. E. B. *A Critical and Exegetical Commentary on the Epistle to the Romans.* Vol. 2, *Commentary on Romans IX–XVI and Essays.* International Critical Commentary on the Holy Scriptures of the Old and New Testaments. London: T. & T. Clark, 2004.
Culpepper, Robert H. "The Lordship of Christ and Religious Pluralism: A Review Article." *Perspectives in Religious Studies* 19 (1992) 311–22.
Curtis, Edward M. "The Theological Basis for the Prohibition of Images in the Old Testament." *Journal of the Evangelical Theological Society* 28 (1985) 277–87.

Cutsinger, James S. "The Uniqueness of Jesus Christ and Other Religions." *Greek Orthodox Theological Review* 42 (1997) 427-34.
Davidson, A. B. *Theology of the Old Testament*. International Theological Library. New York: Scribner, 1926.
Davies, W. D. *Paul and Rabbinic Judaism: Some Rabbinic Elements in Pauline Theology*. Harper Torchbooks. New York: Harper, 1967.
Davies, W. D., and Dale C. Allison Jr. *A Critical and Exegetical Commentary on the Gospel according to Saint Matthew*. Vol. 3, *Commentary on Matthew XIX-XXVIII*. International Critical Commentary on the Holy Scriptures of the Old and New Testaments. Edinburgh: T. & T. Clark, 1997.
Davis, John Jefferson. *Foundations of Evangelical Theology*. Grand Rapids: Baker, 1984.
Davis, Stephen T. "Evangelicals and the Religions of the World." *Theological Students Fellowship Bulletin* (1981) 8-11.
D'Costa, Gavin. "Christian Theology and Other Religions: An Evaluation of John Hick and Paul Knitter." *Studia Missionalia* 42 (1993) 161-78.
———. *John Hick's Theology of Religions: A Critical Evaluation*. Lanham, MD: University Press of America, 1987.
De Bary, William Theodore, ed. *The Buddhist Tradition in India, China & Japan*. New York: Vintage, 1972.
Demarest, Bruce A. *The Cross and Salvation: The Doctrine of Salvation*. Foundations of Evangelical Theology 1. Wheaton: Crossway, 1997.
———. *General Revelation: Historical Views and Contemporary Issues*. Grand Rapids: Zondervan, 1982.
Dhavamony, Mariasusai. "The Cosmic Christ and World Religions: Christianity and Other Religions." *Studia Missionalia* 42 (1993) 179-225.
Dinkines, Flora. *Elementary Concepts of Modern Mathematics*. Vol. 1, *Elementary Theory of Sets*. The Appleton-Century Mathematics Series. New York: Appleton Century Crofts, 1964.
Dodd, C. H. *The Epistle of Paul to the Romans*. 1959. Reprint, Fontana Books. London: Collins, 1965.
Doniger, Wendy, trans. *The Rig Veda: An Anthology; One Hundred and Eight Hymns*. Penguin Classics. Harmondsworth, UK: Penguin, 1981.
Dulles, Avery. *Models of Revelation*. 1983. Reprint, with new preface. Maryknoll, NY: Orbis, 1992.
Dummett, Michael A. E. *Elements of Intuitionism*. Oxford Logic Guides 2. Oxford: Clarendon, 1977.
Dunn, James D. G. *Romans 9-16*. Word Biblical Commentary 388. Dallas: Word, 1988.
Eichrodt, Walther. *Theology of the Old Testament*. Translated by J. A. Baker. 2 vols. Old Testament Library. Philadelphia: Westminster, 1961-1967.
Eisen, Arnold. "Covenant." In *Contemporary Jewish Religious Thought*, edited by Arthur A. Cohen and Paul Mendes-Flohr, 107-12. New York: Free Press, 1988.
Erickson, Millard J. *Christian Theology*. 2nd ed. Grand Rapids: Baker Academic, 1998.
———. *How Shall They Be Saved? The Destiny of Those Who Do Not Hear of Jesus*. Grand Rapids: Baker, 1996.
———. "Hope for Those Who Have Never Heard? Yes, But . . ." *Evangelical Missions Quarterly* 11/2 (1975) 122-26.
Ewert, David, et al. *The Church in a Pagan Society: Studies in 1 Corinthians*. Luminaire Studies. Winnipeg: Kindred, 1986.

Fackre, Gabriel. "Claiming Jesus as Savior in a Religiously Plural World." *Journal of Christian Theological Research* 8 (2003) 1-17.
——. *The Doctrine of Revelation: A Narrative Interpretation*. Edinburgh Studies in Constructive Theology. Grand Rapids: Eerdmans, 1997.
Farquhar, J. N. *The Crown of Hinduism*. London: Oxford University Press, 1920.
Feinberg, Paul. "The Hermeneutics of Discontinuity." In *Continuity and Discontinuity: Perspectives on the Relationship between the Old and New Testaments*, edited by John S. Feinberg, 109-28. Wheaton, IL: Crossway, 1988.
Freud, Sigmund. *The Future of an Illusion*. Translated by W. D. Dobson-Robb. New York: Norton, 1961.
——. *Moses and Monotheism*. Translated by Katherine Jones. New York: Vintage, 1939.
Friedman, Richard Elliott. *A Commentary on the Torah: With a New English Translation*. San Francisco: HarperSanFransisco, 2001.
Geisler, Norman L. *Systematic Theology*. Vol. 3, *Sin, Salvation*. 4 vols. Minneapolis: Bethany House, 2004.
Gillis, Chester. "Evangelical Inclusivism: Progress or Betrayal?" *Evangelical Quarterly* (1995) 139-50.
Gillman, Neil. *The Death of Death: Resurrection and Immortality in Jewish Thought*. Woodstock, VT: Jewish Lights, 2000.
Gould, E. P. *A Commentary on the Epistles to the Corinthians*. Philadelphia: American Baptist Publication Society, 1886.
Greeff, Theo de, ed. *To Christ through the Vedânta: The Writings of Reverend P. Johanns, SJ*. 2 vols. Library of Indian Christian Theology. Bangalore: United Theological College, 1996.
Grenz, Stanley J. "Toward an Evangelical Theology of the Religions." *Journal of Ecumenical Studies* 31 (1994) 49-65.
——. *Created for Community: Connecting Christian Belief with Christian Living*. 2nd ed. Grand Rapids: Baker Academic, 1998.
Griffiths, Paul J., and Delmas Lewis. "On Grading Religions, Seeking Truth and Being Nice to People: A Reply to Professor Hick." *Religious Studies* 19 (1983) 75-80.
——. *The Problems of Religious Diversity*. Exploring the Philosophy of Religion 1. Malden, MA: Blackwell, 2001.
Guthrie, Donald. *New Testament Theology*. Downers Grove, IL: InterVarsity, 1981.
Hackett, Stuart C. *The Reconstruction of the Christian Revelation Claim: A Philosophical and Critical Apologetic*. Grand Rapids: Baker, 1984.
The Harper Study Bible: Holy Bible, Revised Standard Version. Edited by Harold Lindsell. Grand Rapids: Zondervan, 1962.
Hawkins, O. S. "A Question for Our Time: Who Do You Say that I Am?" *Southwestern News* 1 (Fall 2003) 12-13.
Hays, Richard. *First Corinthians*. Interpretation. Louisville: John Knox, 1997.
Heick, Otto W. *A History of Christian Thought*, vol. 1. Philadelphia: Fortress, 1965.
Hendriksen, William. *An Exposition of the Gospel according to Matthew*. Grand Rapids: Baker, 1973.
Henry, Carl F. H. *God, Revelation and Authority*. Vol. 1, *The God Who Speaks and Shows*. Waco: Word Books, 1976.
——, ed. *Revelation and the Bible: Contemporary Evangelical Thought*. Grand Rapids: Baker, 1972.

Herrero, Francisco Pérez. "Mission Following the Missionary Mandate of the Risen Christ." *International Review of Mission* 95/378-79 (2006) 306-19.

Hesselgrave, David. "Evangelicals and Interreligious Dialogue." In *Faith Meets Faith*, edited by Gerald H. Anderson and Thomas F. Stransky, 123-27. Mission Trends 5. New York: Paulist, 1981.

Hick, John. *An Interpretation of Religion: Human Responses to the Transcendent*. New Haven: Yale University Press, 1989.

Hodge, Charles. *Systematic Theology*. Vol. 2. 1872. Reprint, Grand Rapids: Eerdmans, 1989.

Holy Bible, English Standard Version (ESV). Wheaton, IL: Crossway Bibles, 2001.

Holy Bible, Revised Standard Version (RSV). Revised Standard Version of the Bible, copyright 1952 [2nd edition, 1971] by the Division of Christian Education of the National Council of the Churches of Christ in the United States of America.

Hooker, Roger Hardham. *Themes in Hinduism and Christianity: A Comparative Study*. Studies in the intercultural History of Christianity 53. Frankfurt: Lang, 1989.

Horne, Charles M. *Salvation*. Chicago: Moody Press, 1971.

House, H. Wayne. *Charts on Systematic Theology*. Vol. 1, *Prolegomena*. Kregel Charts of the Bible and Theology. Grand Rapids: Kregel, 2006.

Iqbal, Allama Muhammad. *The Reconstruction of Religious Thought in Islam*. Lahore: Shaikh Muhammad Sahraf, 1960.

Jacob, Edmond. *Theology of the Old Testament*. Translated by Arthur Heathcote and Philip Allcock. New York: Harper & Row, 1958.

Jacob, Louis. *Jewish Theology*. West Orange, NJ: Behrman House, 1973.

Janzen, J. Gerald. "On the Most Important Word in the Shema (Deuteronomy VI 4-5)." *Vetus Testamentum* 37 (1987) 280-300.

Johnston, Robert K. "Orthodoxy and Heresy: A Problem for Modern Evangelicalism." *Evangelical Quarterly* 69 (1997) 7-38.

Jones, Eli Stanley. *Christ at the Round Table*. New York: Abingdon, 1928.

Kant, Immanuel. *Religion within the Limits of Reason Alone*. Translated by Theodore M. Greene and Hoyt H. Hudson. Harper Torchbooks. New York: Harper, 1960.

Kärkkäinen, Veli-Matti. *Trinity and Religious Pluralism: The Doctrine of the Trinity in Christian Theology of Religions*. Aldershot, UK: Ashgate, 2004.

———. *An Introduction to the Theology of Religions: Biblical, Historical and Contemporary Perspectives*. Downers Grove, IL: InterVarsity, 2003.

———. *One with God: Salvation as Deification and Justification*. Unitas Books. Collegeville, MN: Liturgical, 2004.

———. *Pneumatology: The Holy Spirit in Ecumenical, International and Contextual Perspective*. Grand Rapids: Baker Academic, 2002.

———. "'Surveying the Land and Charting the Territory of the Spirit': A Biographical Footnote to Clark Pinnock's Review of My Pneumatology." *Journal of Pentecostal Theology* 12 (2003) 9-13.

———. "Toward a Pneumatological Theology of Religions: Pentecostal-Charismatic Inquiry." *International Review of Mission* 91/361 (2002) 187-98.

Kaufmann, Yehezkel. *A History of the Religion of Israel*. Vol. 4, *From the Babylonian Captivity to the End of Prophecy*. New York: Ktav, 1977.

Keil, C. F., and F. Delitzsch. *Commentary on the Old Testament*. Vol. 8, *Jeremiah*. Translated by David Patrick. 1873. Reprint, Grand Rapids: Eerdmans, 1973.

———. *Commentary on the Old Testament*. Vol. 1, *The Pentateuch*. Translated by James Martin. 1891. Reprint, Grand Rapids: Eerdmans, 1973.

Kelly, J. N. D. *Early Christian Doctrines*. 5th ed. New York: Harper & Row, 1978.

Kierkegaard, Søren. *The Sickness unto Death*. Edited and translated by Howard V. Hong and Edna H. Hong. Kierkegaard's Writings 19. Princeton: Princeton University Press, 1980.

Kwan, Kai-man. "Is the Critical Trust Approach to Religious Experience Incompatible with Religious Particularism? Reply to Michael Martin and John Hick." *Faith and Philosophy* 20 (2003) 152–69.

"Lausanne Covenant." *Evangelical Missions Quarterly* 10/4 (1974) 313–20.

Lawhead, William, ed. *Philosophical Questions: Classical and Contemporary Readings*. Boston: McGraw-Hill, 2003.

Lightner, Robert P. *The Death Christ Died: A Biblical Case for Unlimited Atonement*. 2nd ed. Grand Rapids: Kregel, 1998.

Lincoln, Andrew T., and A. J. M. Wedderburn. *The Theology of the Later Pauline Letters*. New Testament Theology. Cambridge: Cambridge University Press, 1993.

Lohse, Eduard. *Colossians and Philemon: A Commentary of the Epistles to the Colossians and Philemon*. Translated by William R. Poehlmann and Robert J. Karris. Hermeneia. Philadelphia: Fortress, 1971.

Luck, G. Coleman. *First Corinthians*. Everyman's Bible Commentary. Chicago: Moody Press, 1958.

Luz, Ulrich. *The Theology of the Gospel of Matthew*. Translated by J. Bradford Robinson. New Testament Theology. Cambridge: Cambridge University Press, 1993.

Macquarrie, John. *Principles of Christian Theology*. 2nd ed. New York: Scribner, 1977.

Manahan, Ronald E. "A Theology of Pseudoprophets: A Study in Jeremiah." *Grace Theological Journal* 1 (1980) 77–96.

Martens, Elmer A. *God's Design: A Focus on Old Testament Theology*. 4th ed. Eugene, OR: Wipf & Stock, 2015.

Martin, Ralph. *Colossians: The Church's Lord and the Christian's Liberty*. Grand Rapids: Zondervan, 1973.

Mathews, Ed. "Yahweh and the Gods: A Theology of World Religions from the Pentateuch." In *Christianity and the Religions: A Biblical Theology of World Religions*, edited by Edward Rommen and Harold Netland, 30–44. Evangelical Missiological Society Series 2. Pasadena, CA: William Carey Library, 1995.

Mavrodes, George I. "Response to John Hick." *Faith and Philosophy* 14 (1997) 289–94.

———. *Revelation in Religious Belief*. Philadelphia: Temple University Press, 1988.

McComiskey, Thomas Edward. *The Covenants of Promise: A Theology of the Old Testament Covenants*. Grand Rapids: Baker, 1985.

McCready, Douglas. "The Disintegration of John Hick's Christology." *Journal of the Evangelical Theological Society* 39 (1996) 257–70.

McGiffert, A. C. *Protestant Thought before Kant*. Harper Torchbooks. The Cloister Library. New York: Harper, 1962.

McGrath, Alister E. "The Challenge of Pluralism for the Contemporary Christian Church." *Journal of the Evangelical Theological Society* 35(1992) 361–73.

———. *Christian Theology: An Introduction*. 3rd ed. Malden, MA: Blackwell, 2001.

McLeod, W. H. *The Sikhs: History, Religion, and Society*. Lectures on the History of Religion, n.s. 14. New York: Columbia University Press, 1989.

Menssen, Sandra, and Thomas D. Sullivan. *The Agnostic Inquirer: Revelation from a Philosophical Standpoint*. Grand Rapids: Eerdmans, 2007.

Metzger, Bruce M. *Lexical Aids for Students of New Testament Greek*. Princeton, NJ: Theological Book Agency, 1980.

Meyer, John R. "John Hick's Theology of Religions and Inter-religious Dialogue: A Critique." *Religion & Theology* 8 (2001) 274–97.

Mickelsen, A. Berkeley. *Interpreting the Bible*. 1963. Reprint, Grand Rapids: Eerdmans, 1982.

Moberly, R. W. L. *Old Testament of the Old Testament: Patriarchal Narratives and Mosaic Yahwism*. Overtures to Biblical Theology. Minneapolis: Fortress, 1992.

Monk, Robert C., et al. *Exploring Religious Meaning*. 5th ed. Upper Saddle River, NJ: Prentice-Hall, 1998.

Moreland, J. P. "How Evangelicals Became Over-Committed to the Bible and What Can Be Done about It." Unpublished paper presented at the 59th annual meeting of the Evangelical Theological Society in San Diego in November 2007.

Morris, Leon. *The Epistle to the Romans*. Grand Rapids: Eerdmans, 1988.

———. *New Testament Theology*. Grand Rapids: Zondervan, 1990.

Muck, Terry C. "Evangelicals and Interreligious Dialogue." *Journal of the Evangelical Theological Society* 36 (1993) 517–29.

———. "Is There Common Ground among Religions?" *Journal of the Evangelical Theological Society* 40/1 (1997) 99–112.

Muck, Terry C., et al. "Mission and the Theology of Religions." Special issue. *Missiology: International Review* 33/2 (2005).

Netland, Harold. *Dissonant Voices: Religious Pluralism and the Question of Truth*. Grand Rapids: Eerdmans, 1991.

———. *Encountering Religious Pluralism: The Challenge to Christian Faith & Mission*. Downers Grove, IL: InterVarsity, 2001.

———. "Exclusivism, Tolerance, and Truth." *Missiology* 15 (1987) 77–95.

———. "Professor Hick on Religious Pluralism." *Religious Studies* 22 (1986) 249–61.

———. "Theology of Religions, Missiology, and Evangelicals." *Missiology* 33 (2005) 141–58.

———. "Thinking Christianly about Religious Diversity." Unpublished paper presented at The Christian Worldview: Analysis, Assessment and Development Conference in Madison, Wisconsin, on September 16, 2005.

Nicholls, Bruce. "Compelling Witness to the Uniqueness of Jesus Christ in Our Pluralistic World." *Stimulus* 1/3 (1993) 19–24.

———, ed. *The Unique Christ in Our Pluralist World*. Grand Rapids: Baker, 1994.

Novak, David. *Jewish-Christian Dialogue: A Jewish Justification*. New York: Oxford University Press, 1989.

Nozick, Robert. *The Nature of Rationality*. Princeton: Princeton University Press, 1993.

Nygren, Anders. *Commentary on Romans*. Translated by Carl C. Rasmussen. Philadelphia: Muhlenberg, 1949.

Olson, Roger E. "A Wind That Swirls Everywhere: Pentecostal Scholar Amos Yong Thinks He Sees the Holy Spirit Working in Other Religions, Too." *Christianity Today* 50/30 (March 2006) 52–54. http://www.christianitytoday.com/ct/2006/march/38.52.html/.

Olson, Roger E., et al. "A Forum: The Future of Evangelical Theology." *Christianity Today* 42 (February 9, 1998) 40–48. http://www.christianitytoday.com/ct/1998/february9/8T2040.html/.
Orr, James. *Revelation and Inspiration*. 1910. Reprint, Grand Rapids: Baker, 1969.
Osburn, Evert D. "Those Who Have Never Heard: Have They No Hope?" *Journal of the Evangelical Theological Society* 32 (1989) 367–72.
Otto, Rudolf. *The Idea of the Holy*. A Galaxy Book. New York: Oxford University Press, 1961.
Packer, J. I. *"Fundamentalism" and the Word of God*. Grand Rapids: Eerdmans, 1966.
Pannenberg, Wolfhart. *The Apostles' Creed in the Light of Today's Questions*. Translated by Margaret Kohl. Philadelphia: Westminster, 1972.
Patterson, Stephen J. "A Rhetorical Gem in a Rhetorical Treasure: The Origin and Significance of 1 Corinthians 13:4–7." *Biblical Theology Bulletin* 39 (2009) 87–94.
Paulson, Hank. *Beyond the Wall: The People Communism Can't Conquer*. Ventura, CA: Regal, 1982.
Phillips, W. Gary. "Evangelical Pluralism: A Singular Problem." *Bibliotheca Sacra* 151 (1994) 140–54.
———. "Evangelicals and Pluralism: Current Options." *Evangelical Quarterly* 63 (1992) 229–44.
Pinnock, Clark. *Biblical Revelation: The Foundation of Christian Theology*. Chicago: Moody Press, 1971.
———. "Evangelical Theology: Conservative and Contemporary." *Christianity Today* 23 (January 5, 1979) 23–29.
———, ed. *The Grace of God, the Will of Man: The Case of Arminianism*. Grand Rapids: Zondervan, 1989.
———. "Response to R. Douglas Geivett and W. Gary Phillips." In *Four Views on Salvation in a Pluralistic World*, edited by Dennis Okholm and Timothy Phillips, 256–70. Grand Rapids: Zondervan, 1996.
———. "Toward an Evangelical Theology of Religions." *Journal of the Evangelical Theological Society* 33 (1990) 359–68.
———. "Why Is Jesus the Only Way? No Other Way, Truth or Life Open to God." *Eternity* (December 1976) 12–15, 32, 34.
———. *A Wideness in God's Mercy: The Finality of Jesus Christ in a World of Religions*. Grand Rapids: Zondervan, 1992.
Pinnock, Clark, and Barry Callen. *The Scripture Principle: Reclaiming the Full Authority of the Bible*. 2nd ed. Grand Rapids: Baker Academic, 2006.
Piper, John. *Let the Nations Be Glad! Supremacy of God in Missions*. 2nd ed. Grand Rapids: Baker Academic, 2003.
Plantinga, Alvin. "Ad Hick." *Faith and Philosophy* 14 (1997) 295–98.
Poythress, Vern S. *Understanding Dispensationalists*. 2nd ed. Phillipsburg, NJ: Presbyterian & Reformed, 1994.
Race, Alan. *Christians and Religious Pluralism: Patterns in the Christian Theology of Religions*. Maryknoll, NY: Orbis, 1982.
———. *Christians and Religious Pluralism: Patterns in Christian Theology of Religions*. 2nd ed. London: SCM, 1993.
———. *Interfaith Encounter: The Twin Tracks of Theology and Dialogue*. London: SCM, 2001.

Räisänen, Heikki. *Marcion, Muhammad, and the Mahatma: Exegetical Perspectives on the Encounter of Cultures and Faiths.* London: SCM, 1997.

———. *Paul and the Law.* Wissenschaftliche Untersuchungen zum Neuen Testament 29. Tübingen: Mohr/Siebeck, 1983.

Raitt, Thomas M. *A Theology of Exile: Judgment/Deliverance in Jeremiah and Ezekiel.* Philadelphia: Fortress, 1977.

Ramm, Bernard. *An Evangelical Heritage: A Study in Historical Theology.* Waco: Word Books, 1973.

———. *Protestant Biblical Interpretation: A Textbook of Hermeneutics.* Grand Rapids: Baker, 1973.

———. *Special Revelation and the Word of God.* Grand Rapids: Eerdmans, 1961.

———. "Will All Men Be Finally Saved?" *Eternity* (August 1964) 22–25, 33.

Richard, Ramesh. "Soteriological Inclusivism and Dispensationalism." *Bibliotheca Sacra* 151 (1994) 85–108.

Richardson, Alan. *Introduction to the Theology of the New Testament.* New York: Harper & Row, 1959.

Richardson, Don. *Eternity in Their Hearts.* Ventura, CA: Regal, 1981.

Robinson, Bob. "What Exactly is Meant by the 'Uniqueness of Christ'? Examination of the Phrase and Other Suggested Alternatives in the Context of Religious Pluralism: Part II." *Evangelical Review of Theology* 26 (2002) 76–90.

Ryrie, Charles. *Dispensationalism Today.* Chicago: Moody Press, 1969.

Sanders, E. P. *Paul: A Very Short Introduction.* Very Short Introductions. New York: Oxford University Press, 1991.

Sanders, John. "Evangelical Responses to Salvation Outside the Church." *Christian Scholars Review* (1994) 45–58.

———. "Is Belief in Christ Necessary for Salvation?" *Evangelical Quarterly* 60 (1988) 241–59.

———. *No Other Name: An Investigation into the Destiny of the Unevangelized.* Grand Rapids: Eerdmans, 1992.

———. "A Perennial Debate." *Christianity Today* 34/8 (1990) 20–21.

Saucy, Robert L. *A Case for Progressive Dispensationalism: An Interface between Dispensational & Non-Dispensational Theology.* Grand Rapids: Zondervan, 1993.

Schaeffer, Francis A. *The God Who Is There: Speaking Historic Christianity into the Twentieth Century.* Chicago: InterVarsity, 1968.

Schweizer, Eduard. "Christ in the Letter to the Colossians." *Review and Expositor* 70 (1973) 451–67.

Shedd, William. *Dogmatic Theology.* Vol. 2. Classic Reprints. Grand Rapids: Zondervan, 1969.

Silvers, Anita, and Leslie Pickering Francis. "Justice through Trust: Disability and the 'Outlier Problem' in Social Contract Theory." *Ethics* 116 (2005) 40–76.

Skinner, John. *Prophecy and Religion: Studies in the Life of Jeremiah.* 1922. Reprint, Eugene, OR: Wipf & Stock, 1999.

Smith, Ebbie C. "An Evangelical Approach to the Theology of Religions." *Southwestern Journal of Theology* 44/2 (2002) 6–23.

Smith, Wilfred Cantwell. *Faith and Belief: The Difference between Them.* Oxford: Oneworld, 1998.

———. *Meaning and the End of Religion: A New Approach to the Religious Traditions of Mankind.* Mentor Books. New York: New American Library, 1964.

Stairs, Allen, and Christopher Bernard. *The Thinker's Guide to the Philosophy of Religion.* New York: Pearson Longman, 2007.
Stauffer, Ethelbert. *New Testament Theology.* Translated by John Marsh. New York: Macmillan, 1961.
Steele, David, and Curtis Thomas. *The Five Points of Calvinism: Defined, Defended, Documented.* Philadelphia: Presbyterian & Reformed, 1975.
Stendahl, Krister. "Notes for Three Bible Studies." In *Christ's Lordship and Religious Pluralism*, edited by Gerald H. Anderson and Thomas F. Stransky, 7–18. Maryknoll, NY: Orbis, 1981.
Stott, John, ed. *Making Christ Known: Historic Mission Documents from the Lausanne Movement, 1974–1989.* Grand Rapids: Eerdmans, 1997.
Strawson, P. F. *Analysis and Metaphysics: An Introduction to Philosophy.* Oxford: Oxford University Press, 1992.
Strong, Augustus. *Christ in Creation and Ethical Monism.* Philadelphia: Williams, 1899.
———. *Systematic Theology: A Compendium and Commonplace Book Designed for the Use of Theological Students.* Philadelphia: Judson, 1912.
Swinburne, Richard. *Revelation: From Analogy to Metaphor.* Oxford: Clarendon, 1992.
Talbott, Thomas. "The Love of God and the Heresy of Exclusivism." *Christian Scholar's Review* (1997) 99–112.
Tennant, Agnieszka. "Social Justice Surprise." Interview with Stephen Monsma. *Christianity Today* 50/7 (July 2006) 44–45. http://www.christianitytoday.com/ct/2006/july/9.44.html/.
Tennent, Timothy C. *Christianity at the Religious Roundtable: Evangelicalism in Conversation with Hinduism, Buddhism, and Islam.* Grand Rapids: Baker Academic, 2002.
———. *Theology in the Context of World Christianity.* Grand Rapids: Zondervan, 2007.
Tertullian. "On Prescription Against Heretics." In *The Christian Theology Reader*, edited by Alister E. McGrath, 7–8. 2nd ed. Oxford: Blackwell, 2001.
Thiessen, Henry Clarence. *Introductory Lectures in Systematic Theology.* Grand Rapids: Eerdmans, 1963.
Thomas, Robert L. *Evangelical Hermeneutics: The New versus the Old.* Grand Rapids: Kregel, 2002.
Thomas Aquinas, Saint. *Summa Theologiae.* http://www.newadvent.org/summa/1001.htm/.
Thomas, W. H. Griffith. *Christ Pre-eminent: Studies in the Epistle to the Colossians.* Chicago: Bible Institute Colportage Ass'n., 1923.
Tiessen, Terrance L. "God's Work of Grace in the Context of the Religions." *Evangelical Review of Theology* 27 (2003) 247-67.
———. *Who Can Be Saved? Reassessing Salvation in Christ and World Religions.* Downers Grove, IL: InterVarsity, 2004.
Tillich, Paul. *Biblical Religion and the Search for Ultimate Reality.* The James W. Richard Lectures in the Christian Religion, University of Virginia, 1951–52. Chicago: University of Chicago Press, 1955.
———. *Christianity and the Encounter of World Religions.* Bampton Lectures in America 14. New York: Columbia University Press, 1963.
Van Inwagen, Peter. "A Reply to Professor Hick." *Faith and Philosophy* 14 (1997) 299–302.
Van Til, Cornelius. *A Christian Theory of Knowledge.* Philadelphia: Presbyterian & Reformed, 1969.

Vanhoozer, Kevin J. *The Drama of Doctrine: Canonical–Linguistic Approach to Christian Theology.* Louisville: Westminster John Knox, 2005.

———. *Is There a Meaning In This Text? The Bible, the Reader, and the Morality of Literary Knowledge.* Grand Rapids: Zondervan, 1998.

Vischer, Wilhem. "The Vocation of the Prophet to the Nations." Translated by Suzanne de Dietrich. *Interpretation* 9 (1955) 310–17.

Wang, Mary. *The Chinese Church That Will Not Die.* Wheaton, IL: Tyndale House, 1972.

Warfield, Benjamin B. *The Plan of Salvation.* Grand Rapids: Eerdmans, 1973.

Wieman, Henry Nelson, and Regina Westcott-Wieman. *Normative Psychology of Religion.* New York: Crowell, 1937.

Williams, David T. "Salvation in Non-Christian Religions: A Christocentric Approach." *Journal of Theology for Southern Africa* 97 (March 1997) 68–80.

Winger, Michael. "Law of Christ." *New Testament Studies* 46/4 (2000) 537–46.

Wittgenstein, Ludwig. *Philosophical Investigations.* 3rd ed. Translated by G. E. M. Anscombe. New York: Macmillan, 1968.

Stafford, Tim. "Mere Mission." Interview with N. T. Wright. Interview. *Christianity Today* 51/1 (January 5, 2007) http://www.christianitytoday.com/ct/2007/january/22.38.html/.

Yandell, Keith E. *Christianity and Philosophy.* Studies in a Christian Worldview 2. Grand Rapids: Eerdmans, 1984.

Yao, Xinzhong, and Paul Badham, eds. *Religious Experience in Contemporary China.* Religion, Education, and Culture. Cardiff: University of Wales Press, 2007.

Yong, Amos. *Beyond the Impasse: Toward a Pneumatological Theology of Religions.* Grand Rapids: Baker Academic, 2002.

———. *Discerning the Spirit(s): A Pentecostal-Charismatic Contribution to Christian Theology of Religions.* Journal of Pentecostal Theology Supplement Series 20. Sheffield: Sheffield Academic, 2000.

———. "'Not Knowing Where the Wind Blows . . .': On Envisioning a Pentecostal-Charismatic Theology of Religions." *Journal of Pentecostal Theology* 7 (1999) 81–112.

———. "Turn to Pneumatology in Christian Theology of Religions: Conduit or Detour?" *Journal of Ecumenical Studies* 35 (1998) 437–54.

———. "Whither Theological Inclusivism? The Development and Critique of an Evangelical Theology of Religions." *Evangelical Quarterly* 71 (1999) 327–48.

Yong, Amos, et al. "Christ and Spirit: Dogma, Discernment, and Dialogical Theology in a Religiously Plural World." *Journal of Pentecostal Theology* 12 (2003) 15–83.

Name Index

(**Bold** number indicates volume number)

Adams, George, **1**: 118
Ahmad, Hadhrat, **1**: 92
Al-Basri, Al-Hasan, **1**: 208
Al-Bayhaqu, Imam, **1**: 92
Al-Jabbar, Abd, **1**: 209, 215
Al-Kalābādhī, Abū, **1**: 93
Al-Rummani Ali, **1**: 100n115
Aleaz, K. P., **1**: 128n70
Anderson, Norman, **2**: 92n98
Anselm, **1**: 39
Aquinas, **1**: 42, **2**: 137
Armstrong, D. M., **2**: 174
Aslan, Reza, **1**: 92n86
Augustine, **1**: 194, 197
Austin, John, **1**: 239

Bâdarâyana, **1**: 115
Baillie, John, **1**: 71, 122
Barth, Karl, **1**: 72, 125n62, 265n10, **2**: 160n36
Berdyaev, Nicholas, **1**: 226
Berkhof, Louis, **2**: 52
Bernstein, Ellen, **1**: 146
Blaising, Craig, **2**: 10n6, 180n24, 198n6
Bloesch, Donald, **1**: 121, 265, **2**: 39, 46, 50, 94, 156
Blue, J. Ronald, **2**: 37
Bock, Darrell, **2**: 10n6, 180n24, 198n6
Boettner, Loraine, **1**: 236, **2**: 52, 66
Bonhoeffer, Dietrich, **1**: 170, **2**: 50n42
Borland, James, **2**: 64

Bowker, John, **1**: 21n54, 34, 111n10, 119, 207n31
Boyd, Gregory, **1**: 23n57
Buber, Martin, **1**: 81
Bunner, Emil, **1**: 125n62, 265n10, **2**: 40n14, 44n26, 56n59, 160n36

Camus, Albert, **1**: 218, 235n42, 243
Carnell, Edward, **2**: 78
Carson, D. A., **1**: 53
Chatterji, Jagadîsha, **1**: 174
Chuang Tzu (Zhuangzi), **1**: 148, 150, 154
Clark, Kelly James, **1**: 56, 62
Clement of Alexandria, **2**: 90
Cohn-Sherbok, Daniel, **2**: 44n27
Conze, Edward, **1**: 132n1
Craig, William, **2**: 45
Cranfield, C. E. B., **2**: 26, 125
Culpepper, Robert, **2**: 40, 68

Davis, John, **1**: 47n2, 119, 264, **2**: 29n38, 219n1
Davis, Stephen, **2**: 37
Demarest, Bruce, **2**: 66, 152, 156
Dieterlen, Germaine, **1**: 254n20, 256
Dōgen, **1**: 173, 183, 186
Dooling, D. M., **1**: 251
Dulles, Avery, **1**: 71, 122, **2**: 153
Dupuy, Jean-Pierre, **1**: 169

Eddy, Paul, 1: 51, 62
Erickson, Millard, 1: 126n64, 236, 2: 22, 46n33, 59, 68, 76, 84
Evans-Pritchard, E. E., 1: 43n8

Fackre, Gabriel, 2: 55, 160n37
Farquhar, J. N., 1: 128n70, 2: 190
Feuerbach, Ludwig, 1: 17
Francis, Leslie, 1: 267, 2: 213
Frazer, James, 1: 43n8
Freud, Sigmund, 1: 43n8

Gautama, 1: 173, 183
Geisler, Norman, 2: 47
Gettier, Edmund, 1: 26n61
Ghazālī, 1: 101
Gillis, Chester, 2: 96
Gillman, Neil, 1: 81, 88
Gough, Archibald, 1: 234
Gregory of Naziazus, 1: 121
Grenz, Stanley, 1: 121n49, 235, 237, 2: 40, 74
Griaule, Marcel, 1: 254n20, 256
Griffiths, Paul, 1: 59, 2: 32n49
Gyatso, Tenzin, 1: 139

Hackett, Stuart, 2: 48n38
Haight, Roger, 1: 50n13
Hardy, Paul, 1: 101
Hartshorne, Charles, 1: 35
Hawkins, O. S., 2: 38
Heick, Otto, 2: 42n24
Henry, Carl F. H., 1: 125n63, 266n11, 2: 78, 101n1
Heschel, Abraham, 1: 79, 84, 87
Hesselgrave, David, 1: 270, 274, 2: 209, 215
Hick, John, 1: 49, 55, 247, 2: 19n4, 37, 53
Hodge, A. A., 2: 47n35
Hume, David, 1: 12, 24, 42, 235

Iqbal, Allama, 1: 93n91, 223

Jacob, Edmond, 2: 103
Jacobs, Louis, 1: 80, 200n17
Jahner, Elaine, 1: 251
Jakobsh, Doris, 1: 163

Janzen, J. Gerald, 2: 104, 139
Jasper, Karl, 1: 72
Johanns, P., 1: 128n70
Jones, Stanley, 2: 93n100
Jun, Guo, 1: 182

Kant, Immanuel, 1: 15, 55, 2: 19
Kärkkäinen, Veli-Matti, 2: 31n41, 56, 60, 74, 92, 167
Kempis, Thomas, 1: 75n17
Knitter, Paul, 1: 48n6
Kuhn, Thomas, 1: 9

Lao Tzu, 1: 151
Lawhead, William, 1: 9n4, 2: 28n37
Legge, James, 1: 149
Leibniz, Gottfried, 1: 43
Lessing, Gotthold, 1: 33, 2: 20
Lindsell, Harold, 2: 12
Lui, 1: 31n73, 74n14

Mackie, J. L., 1: 22n55
Marshall, Joseph, 1: 249, 252n18
Martens, Elmer, 1: 240, 2: 193
Martyr, Justin, 1: 128n70, 2: 90, 190
Mavrodes, George, 1: 55
McGrath, Alister, 1: 27, 2: 27n35, 66
Michot, Yahya, 1: 93, 95, 98n108
Molina, Luis, 2: 45
Muck, Terry, 1: 270, 2: 55, 209

Nanak, Guru, 1: 149, 158
Netland, Harold, 1: 49, 53, 62, 274, 2: 31, 41, 60, 182, 213
Nicholls, Bruce, 2: 50
Nietzsche, Friedrich, 1: 18
Nozick, Robert, 2: 174

Ogotemmêli, 1: 258
Olson, Roger, 2: 77

Packer, J. I., 2: 102n2
Paley, William, 1: 43
Pannenberg, Wolfhart, 2: 26
Phillips, W. Gary, 2: 98n114
Pinnock, Clark, 1: 23n57, 120, 264, 2: 21, 24, 30n40, 38, 49, 59, 62, 89n91, 97, 148, 219n1

NAME INDEX

Plantinga, Alvin, **1**: 22, 40, 49, 62, 197
Popper, Karl, **1**: 272
Potter, Karl, **1**: 135, 176
Puligandla, R., **1**: 23

Race, Alan, **1**: 48n4, **2**: 9n3, 18n3, 27, 31, 36, 83, 113
Räisäanen, Heikki, **1**: 66n58, **2**: 126n85, 132
Ramanuja, **1**: 109, 119
Ramm, Bernard, **2**: 21, 34, 78
Ray, Benjamin, **1**: 256
Richardson, Don, **2**: 71, 95
Ricoeur, Paul, **1**: 97, 239
Rowe, William, **1**: 226

Sanders, John, **2**: 69, 89n91, 97
Saucy, Robert, **2**: 10n6, 179n23, 183, 187, 198n6
Schaeffer, Francis, **2**: 55n53
Schmidt-Leukel, Perry, **1**: 50n13
Searle, John, **1**: 239
Shankara, **1**: 75, 109, 111n11, 115, 227, 230
Shapira, Abraham, **1**: 145
Silvers, Anita, **1**: 267, **2**: 213
Singh, Nikki, **1**: 165
Singh, Ram, **1**: 162
Smith, Ebbie, **2**: 64

Smith, Wilfred Cantwell, **1**: 49n7, 160, **2**: 37, 177
Stendahl, Krister, **2**: 9, 197
Strawson, Peter, **1**: 98, 156n21, 196, 226n5, 260, **2**: 175
Strong, Augustus, **2**: 22, 52n46
Suskin, Alana, **1**: 145

Talbott, Thomas, **2**: 84n87
Taymiyya, Ibn, **1**: 102
Tennent, Timothy, **2**: 196
Tertullian, **2**: 170
Theissen, Henry, **2**: 52n46
Thiselton, Anthony, **1**: 238
Thurman, Robert, **1**: 137
Tiessen, Terrance, **1**: 127n65, **2**: 72
Tillich, Paul, **1**: 8, 37, 109, **2**: 18, 27

Vanhoozer, Kevin, **1**: 238n51

Walker, James, **1**: 251
Warfield, Benjamin, **2**: 52n45
Wittgenstein, Ludwig, **1**: 38, **2**: 171, 177

Yandell, Keith, **2**: 28n37
Yong, Amos, **2**: 74, 92, 98, 167

Zhuangzi (Chuang Tzu), **1**: 148, 150, 154
Zwingli, **2**: 90

www.ingramcontent.com/pod-product-compliance
Lightning Source LLC
Chambersburg PA
CBHW031727230426
43669CB00007B/267